CHOOSE
IRELAND
FOR RETIREMENT

Help Us Keep This Guide Up to Date

Every effort has been made by the author and editors to make this guide as accurate and useful as possible. However, many things can change after a guide is published—establishments close, phone numbers change, facilities come under new management, housing costs change, and so on.

We would love to hear from you concerning your experiences with this guide and how you feel it could be made better and be kept up to date. While we may not be able to respond to all comments and suggestions, we'll take them to heart and we'll make certain to share them with the author. Please send your comments and suggestions to the following address:

The Globe Pequot Press
Reader Response/Editorial Department
P.O. Box 480
Guilford, CT 06437

Or you may e-mail us at:

editorial@globe-pequot.com

Thanks for your input, and happy travels!

Choose Retirement Series

CHOOSE IRELAND FOR RETIREMENT

Retirement Discoveries for Every Budget

PATTI CLEARY

The
Globe
Pequot
Press

Guilford, Connecticut

Cover design and text design: Laura Augustine
Cover photos © Stockbyte
Maps: Lisa Reneson

Library of Congress Cataloging-in-Publication Data

Cleary, Patti.
    Choose Ireland for retirement : retirement discoveries for every budget / Patti Cleary.
        p. cm.— (Choose retirement series)
        Includes bibliographical references and index.
        ISBN 0-7627-0394-6
        1. Retirement, Places of—Ireland Guidebooks.   2. Retirees—Ireland Life skills guides.   3. Cost and standard of living—Ireland.
    I. Title.   II. Series.
DA980.C58   1999
646.7'9'09415—dc21   99-37025
                                                  CIP

Manufactured in the United States of America
First Edition/First Printing

DEDICATION

I dedicate this book to my friend Bernie Dignam, who bears considerable responsibility for my enduring love affair with all things Irish. Long ago, Bernie helped me to see beyond the magnificent scenery into the heart of a place poised to become the dynamic, compelling Ireland of today. A fortuitous meeting on the spectacular Dingle Peninsula (she, a hitchhiking teenager exploring her homeland and I, a first-time, guidebook-toting, gawking tourist) launched our nearly twenty-five-year friendship and primed my lifelong bond with this captivating and complex land.

CONTENTS

ACKNOWLEDGMENTS

I wish to express gratitude to the following people, who freely extended their wisdom and support: Bernie Dignam, Kathryn Walsh, Digger, Janet O'Toole, Pam Berry, Maria O'Connor, Bridie and Shane Cashin, Sarah and Aiden Lee, Roisin Healy, Don Merwin, Wendy Flaherty, Siobhan McGrane, Anne and Wally Buell, Denys Bowring, Susan Gallagher, Anne Dugan, Lorie Sumner, Dave Carroll, Anne Farley, Lynda Woodward, Nivea Castro, Wendy Earl, Barbara Kozier, Glen Erb, Brenda Weir, Mark Wales, Carol Hutton, Julie Pickett and the Cleary clan. Special thanks to Shirley Jones for shipping *real* bagels to fortify me, Cari Cagle for well-timed help and unflagging encouragement, Gracie O'Malley for inspiration, Mollie Walsh for scrumptious brown bread scones, and Theresa Dignam for lovely chats and the promise of a knitting lesson one day soon.

WHY CHOOSE IRELAND?

Ireland—land of rugged coastlines, rolling green meadows, picture-postcard villages, and splendid castles. From the low mountains of Wicklow to the misty, craggy shores of Connemara, Ireland beckons to all who admire resplendent vistas and Old World charm. *Céad Mile Fáilte,* a traditional Irish greeting, bestows "a hundred thousand welcomes."

Ireland has a special allure, even magic, that captivates visitors and frequently instills in them a distinct longing to return. For those who are smitten, the desire may emerge for something more substantial than an occasional two-week vacation. Apart from its exquisite beauty and the friendliness of its people, there are many sound reasons to consider Ireland as a retirement destination.

Moderate Climate

Temperatures in Ireland are consistently moderate, influenced by the Gulf Stream's warm waters and breezes moving up from the southwestern Atlantic. Summertime temperatures usually range between 14°C and 18°C (57°F and 65°F), though there may be a few days when they will be higher, especially during July and August, usually the warmest months. May and June are the sunniest time of year, bringing an average of five to seven hours of sunshine per day. The summer brings the added bonus of long days, with sunsets as late as 10:00 P.M. in most places and even later in the west.

January and February are the coldest months in Ireland, with average daily temperatures of 4°C to 7°C (39°F to 45°F). On the rare occasion that snow falls, it tends to melt rapidly, usually well before news programs manage to report the event.

People in Ireland say that their changeable weather often provides four seasons in the space of one day. (Those who claim that this seasonal whirl strikes within the confines of one hour may be exaggerating every so slightly.) If you crave year-round warmth and daily doses of intense sunshine, you may be happier in Florida, Arizona, or Mexico. If, on the other hand, you welcome a temperate climate, without extremes of heat or cold, then Ireland's mild winters and cool summers may suit you, as the Irish say, "down to the ground."

People who have moved to Ireland from places like Florida and Minnesota praise the moderate climate. No one, however, would ever characterize the climate as dry. The exceptionally clean air in Ireland has a high moisture content. Sunlight, emerging after a rain shower and reflecting this moisture, glimmers magically in the air. If you detest rainy weather, this sparkling air will not work its magic on you. The changeable, "soft" climate of Ireland, where showers are common, may instead lower your spirits.

The level of rainfall varies depending on the location in Ireland. Annual rainfall averages a copious 200 centimeters (80 inches) or more in mountainous areas and 150 centimeters (59 inches) in parts of the west, but only 74 centimeters (29 inches) in and around Dublin. The rain, of course, is what creates the many shades of brilliant green that shimmer when the sun does appear (which it will regularly, all year long). There are regions in Ireland that are sunnier and less rainy. Many expatriates settle in the southeast, which is somewhat warmer and drier than other parts of the country.

No Language Barrier

Those who retire in a country where a language other than their native tongue is spoken often must overcome an occasional sense of isolation. In Ireland, however, English is the primary mode of communication in all but a few small areas.

Irish is the national language. It is a Celtic tongue closely related to Scottish, Gaelic, Welsh, and Breton. Irish is the language of choice in government-designated Gaeltacht areas, which lie predominantly along the western seaboard, in Counties Donegal, Mayo, Galway, and Kerry. Small segments of Irish-speaking populations also reside in Counties Cork, Meath, and Waterford.

While many Irish people are able to speak a bit of Irish, few are fluent in it. Attempts to preserve the traditional language are flourishing. Udaras na Gaeltachta, state body, promotes the development of local industry in Gaeltacht regions. Bord na Gaeilge (the Irish Language Board) promotes the use of Irish and its place as a core subject in schools. Radio na Gaeltachta and a television service, Teilifis na Gaeilge, broadcast nationally in Irish. Several periodicals are published in Irish, and government press releases, pamphlets, and official documents are routinely prepared in both English and Irish.

While it is possible to function well in Ireland with no knowledge of Irish, it is sometimes helpful to know a few of the more common terms. (The Resource Guide in the back of this book defines selected Irish terms.) Although a common language certainly aids communication, the absence of a language barrier does not preclude the experience of some symptoms of culture shock. (This condition and other issues relevant to the process of making the transition to living in Ireland are explored in Chapter 12.)

Low Crime Rates

The ability to feel safe from the threat of crime is an important quality-of-life consideration. While crime does exist in Ireland, its highest incidence occurs in urban areas, and even there it consists chiefly of pickpocketing, purse snatching, and car break-ins. The sort of street-smart vigilance that has unfortunately become second nature to most Americans will go a long way toward minimizing risk for these crimes. Home and car security systems are an effective deterrent. Violent assaults are a rare occurrence in Ireland.

In recent years the crime rate has been going down, a result of a tougher stance by law enforcement and judicial bodies. Members of Ireland's unarmed police force, An Garda Siochana, are professional and helpful. Each garda division appoints a crime prevention officer, who serves as a liaison in the community to support various methods of preventing crime. (You'll find additional information about safety and crime prevention in Chapter 8).

The Cost of Living

Ireland offers many economic advantages to retirees. You can live well in Ireland on about the same amount you would need to support yourself in many places in North America. You will need to spend more to live in Ireland if you currently reside in an inexpensive area, but less if the alternative is a much-in-demand retirement community in Florida, Arizona, or Victoria, B.C.

A couple can enjoy a good (but not lavish) standard of living on $30,000 to $35,000 a year. A single person may fare reasonably well on somewhat less.

Tax treaties between Ireland and the United States, Canada, Australia, the United Kingdom, and many other countries serve to prevent people who move between two countries from being taxed twice. In Ireland, there are no state, school, property, or local taxes to pay. The Irish government provides a host of money-saving benefits to pensioners, people with certain illnesses, and creative artists. (See Chapter 3, Financial Matters, for details.) Health care services (discussed in Chapter 4) are more than adequate for most people, and the fees are quite reasonable by U.S. standards, with a doctor visit costing about $30.

Though an economic boom has driven up prices, especially in cities, housing is still cheaper than many places in Europe and North America. (Chapter 5 explores a number of housing options for every budget.)

Except in remote rural areas, public transportation is plentiful and reliable. Those ages 66 and over are eligible for a pass to travel free, within a few manageable restrictions. (See Chapter 7 for additional information.)

The Irish People

From the busy shopkeepers, fresh-faced schoolchildren, and convivial bus drivers to the affable guy on the next stool in the pub, the Irish are a genuine, engaging, and friendly people. They are generally well educated, cordial, and sincere. Many have considerable charm.

Irish people tend to speak in soft, melodious tones. You'll want to listen carefully to the message delivered in their unique and lovely cadence.

There is a long-standing tradition of hospitality in Ireland. A dependence on the tourist trade has encouraged people to welcome those who visit. A "neighbor helping neighbor" approach is common, especially in rural areas. It does, however, take a while to be accepted within the community. Allowing time for relationships to build works best.

The long Irish history of emigration has left its mark. Especially in some areas in the west, emigration reduced the population dramatically and loosened the hold of traditions. Some villages lost all their people during the Great Famine of the mid-nineteenth century. Many of the beautiful cottage ruins that you see today were homes abandoned during that devastating scourge. Massive waves of emigration occurred also in the 1950s and 1980s. Not long ago, a young person with the desire to engage in meaningful and fairly compensated work had little choice but to emigrate, but economic prosperity and the growth in employment opportunities have recently reversed this trend.

Today the Irish population, even in rural areas, is augmented by diverse nationalities, including German, English, Danish, and North American expatriates, as well as Irish people returning home. In many communities, a medley of diverse experience, customs and interests forms a vibrant milieu. To observe or to participate in the dynamic social interchange, you have only to visit the local pub.

Pub Culture

The pub, the center of social life in Ireland, mirrors and fosters a sense of community. The pub provides an informal environment in which to greet friends and neighbors over a relaxing brew and to share local lore and world news. While city pubs tend to acquire a specific kind of crowd, the pubs in small towns and rural areas draw a mix of ages and backgrounds. Parents come in with the kids. Colleagues review the workday over a pint. Couples come to enjoy an inexpensive evening out.

People will often buy you a drink, and it is polite to return the gesture. Pubs serve a wide range of beers, from light ales to dark Guinness stout, with its creamy head. Irish whiskey is usually drunk neat or with water. Wines from Chile, Australia, New Zealand, and South Africa are popular. If you don't drink alcohol, ordering tea or a soft drink is perfectly acceptable.

Whatever you're drinking, you'll receive a warm welcome and experience a level of comfort not found in bars in most other countries. Pam Berry, an American artist living in the west of Ireland, said she'd spent her entire adult life looking for the perfect bar in the States—a place where she could feel genuinely comfortable. She reports that she has found this place, again and again, in many of the pubs in Ireland.

Music is another gift of pub culture. Even in little, remote pubs, you'll find music that is entertaining, and often sublime. Singing along is encouraged. Even those who normally cringe at an invitation to join in may find themselves singing with gusto, their usual discomfort erased by the spirit of companionship and the *craic*. (Pronounced "crack," this expression means good fun that arises when people enjoy themselves, the conversation is lively and flows freely, and laughter abounds.)

Culinary Delights

A food renaissance, which began in the late 1970s in Kinsale, County Cork, and spread across the country, has done a lot to improve Ireland's culinary reputation. Expert chefs from Ireland and around the globe continue to promote the food revival. Their introduction of international cuisine and more innovative use of first-rate local foods have earned the kudos of an Irish palate grown much more sophisticated in recent years.

Economic prosperity has produced a flood of new cafes and restaurants in Ireland and has given many people the means to dine out more often. Though most meals are still taken at home, going out to eat, once reserved for special occasions, has become a more frequent diversion. As families consist more often these days of two wage earners, fast-food establishments are taking hold, take-away (take-out) business is brisk, and supermarkets are devoting more shelf space to ready-made meals for home consumption.

In many restaurants around Ireland, fresh, well-prepared, and interesting dishes have replaced the standard "meat and potatoes" fare of ill repute. The influence of Italian, Spanish, Chinese, Indian, French, Greek, Japanese, and Russian cuisine is evident. There is increasing emphasis on local seafood, meats, produce, and dairy products, known for their superb quality. Health-conscious and even vegetarian forms of cooking are no longer restricted to a few restaurants in major cities, and salads are less likely to consist of iceberg lettuce heaped with mayonnaise. While meat-and-potato dishes are still ubiquitous, alternatives are much more available than in years past.

Product availability has also improved. Baked goods, always wonderful in Ireland, now appear in even greater variety. The range of fruits, vegetables, and herbs has also expanded, even in the smaller markets in outlying areas. Brand names familiar to North Americans are widely available. There are some cross-cultural differences in food tastes, preferences, and packaging (discussed in Chapter 9).

Leisure Activities

Some people contemplate retirement with mixed feelings. On the one hand, they relish the thought of having the freedom to slow down and focus on what truly brings them pleasure, whether it be spending more time with family, fly fishing, painting sunsets, or showing prize Pomeranians. On the other hand, they may worry about how well they'll make the transition to a calendar no longer structured by the day-to-day demands of the workplace. Rather than rested and focused, will they become frustrated and bored? A retirement that offers opportunities for new experiences as well as more time for cherished activities will minimize the risk of personal stagnation.

Walking Through Ireland

Walking is an ideal way to absorb Ireland's beauty. Whether a casual stroll along a tranquil country lane, a vigorous climb known as hill walking, or a serious hike on a long-distance trail, walking is a healthy, cost-free, and invigorating mode of exploration and enjoyment. You may want to join experts in archaeology, folklore, and local flora and fauna who lead guided walks. Walking festivals afford graded walks of varying distance on disused railway lines, trails, hills, and mountains. The Kenmare Whit Walking Festival includes among its walks one on Ireland's highest mountain, Carrantouhill. Annascaul on the Dingle Peninsula hosts a three-day fall festival that provides breathtaking views of seaside and mountains. Two days of organized walks by experienced guides are the focus of the Wicklow Mountains May Walk.

There are a number of long-distance trails or "ways" with signposts in Ireland. The Kerry Way, called the "Walker's Ring of Kerry," covers 216 kilometers (135 miles) and passes through Killarney National Park. The Burren Way traverses the unique, lunarlike landscape of the Burren region and continues to the spectacular Cliffs of Moher. The Dingle Way is a 152-kilometer (95-mile) circular route over mountain passes, old bog roads, and sandy beaches. Extending south for 128 kilometers (80 miles) from the suburbs of Dublin through the Wicklow Mountains, the Wicklow Way passes sites of incomparable beauty, including the Powerscourt waterfall and the ancient monastic settlement and round tower at Glendalough. The Slieve Bloom Way, a 77-kilometer (48-mile) circular route in the geographical center of Ireland, features the striking glens, waterfalls, and summits of the Slieve Bloom Mountains. The 800-kilometer (500-mile) Ulster Way completes a full circuit around Northern Ireland and offers stunning vistas of the country's hills, lakes, mountains, and dramatic coastline.

The Irish are hard-working, but they value a healthy balance between work and play, and opportunities for diversion abound in this tiny land, from golfing to the annual Irish Derby. For a country no bigger than the state of West Virginia, Ireland affords an astonishing diversity of recreational, educational, and pleasurable pursuits. (Chapter 10 explores the wealth of activities to seek on Ireland's waters, racetracks, and playing fields.)

Pleasurable pastimes, often neglected in the tumult of tending to family, home, and career, deserve renewed attention in our retirement years. The time we spend exploring recreational or artistic pursuits has the power to stimulate and renew us. We also gain insight into the unique nature of our adopted community as we do new things and share fun times with the people of Ireland. As we take part, we learn about ourselves as well. Life in Ireland offers much to delight, enlighten, and invigorate the retired newcomer.

Communing with Nature

If your preferred leisure environment is out of doors, those around you will share your interest. Especially in outlying areas, Irish people live "close to the earth." The weather is a constant topic of conversation, as might be someone's recent fish catch, whether the grass is good for the cattle, if conditions are right for turf cutting, or how well your herb garden is doing.

Gardening enthusiasts abound in Ireland, where the moderate climate supports an extended growing season. Formal gardens are featured in stately homes throughout the country. The County Wicklow Gardens Festival, which runs from mid-May to mid-July, showcases heritage properties and gardens in Counties Dublin, Carlow, Wexford, and Wicklow. The Ballymaloe Cookery School Garden, outside of the city of Cork, features fruit trees, herbs, and vegetables, some exotic. The Irish Garden Trade Fair, held in the Royal Dublin Society (RDS) exhibition hall in Ballsbridge, about 3.2 kilometers (2 miles) south of the center of Dublin, provides ample inspiration for the gardening enthusiast.

The close connection that the Irish people feel to the environment makes perfect sense whenever you behold some aspect of its majesty. Ireland is achingly beautiful. Rolling fields parceled by hand-forged stone walls, majestic castles thriving or left in picturesque ruin, ancient churches and cemeteries, imposing cliffs, white sandy beaches, flocks of butterflies, misty mountain passes, and shimmering rainbows deliver this message: Ireland is not a place to hibernate, however cozy your thatched-roof cottage, renovated farmhouse, or city flat. Driving is one way to get out and savor the surroundings. Vacationers have found that it is possible to see a great deal during a fast-paced, two-week tour. But far more rewarding than the blur of the characteristic tourist scramble is exploring at a slower pace on short jaunts from a home base. A good selection of inexpensive B&Bs most anywhere you care to roam will make your getaways affordable and comfortable.

Traveling Ireland's good but often narrow, winding roads initially may present a certain challenge for those who must learn to reverse instinctual right-side habits to drive on the left. The extra vigilance and an occasional nerve-wracking negotiation of a busy roundabout are a small price to pay for easy access to the pristine villages, heather-laden fields, and magnificent vistas along Ireland's roadways. (See Chapter 7 for a discussion of issues related to safe and pleasurable driving in Ireland.)

If you prefer a more intimate link to environmental riches than that afforded by an automobile, Ireland extends a variety of ways to savor a close-up view of its natural treasures. Cycling enthusiasts enjoy minimally traveled roads that showcase an endless variety of scenic wonders, from lowland rural villages to sweeping highland vistas. Horse riding centers offer trail rides and treks over farmland meadows and along riverbanks and beaches. Dolphin-watching cruises along the southern coast of Clare afford close contact with these magnificent marine mammals, which will often follow the boat and leap well out of the water.

Five national parks and seventy-six nature reserves provide another venue for communing with nature. If you enjoy observing birds, you may sight corncrake, cuckoo, or peregrine falcons at more than one hundred special protection areas. You may also encounter many of Ireland's 380 species of wild birds on a casual ramble around your neighborhood.

Festivals

Except for the months of December and January, when time is devoted to preparing for and recovering from a whirl of holiday celebrations, festivals are a key component of leisure time in Ireland. One could attend a different festival nearly every week of the year, and the summer calendar offers a range of choices, which often overlap.

From smaller local fairs to intensely promoted events that draw international attendance, Irish festivals originated as an occasion for a community to mark significant agricultural cycles of planting or harvest. Some, like the Clonbur, County Galway Flying Pig Festival, with its sheepdog trials and traditional crafts displays, revive the fair days of old. Other festivals have a theme or focus, whether traditional, classical, or contemporary music, dance, food, literary, gardening, film, sporting, comedy, agriculture, theater, or visual arts. Many generic festivals embrace all the arts and draw celebrants to cities and towns throughout most of the year. The Resource Guide profiles some of the hundreds of festivals that attract lively throngs from near and far.

Summer Schools

Geared primarily for tourists but not restricted to them, summer schools are educational programs that take place in interesting locations over a few days to several weeks. Programs cover a wide range of interests, from traditional music and dance to archaeology, literature, history, women's studies, language, politics, sociocultural issues, and Celtic culture. Expert speakers offer lectures, and artists discuss their work. Fees charged depend on duration and whether accommodation is required. The Irish Tourist Board (listed in the Resource Guide at the end of this book) provides detailed course information.

Crafts

Ireland is a perfect setting in which to learn or continue to enjoy craftwork. The quiet of winter evenings by the fire inspires many to take up their handiwork, be it quilting, spinning, weaving, knitting, crocheting, or some other creative form. To learn or perhaps just to refresh your skills, you can take formal instruction or ask a neighbor to guide you. Especially in rural areas, a number of people may be able to demonstrate these techniques. Or you might choose to attend the annual Knitting and Stitching Show at the RDS showgrounds in Ballsbridge. Here you may marvel at the work of textile artists, attend seminars on various techniques, and stock up on supplies.

Crafts exhibits, generic or specialized, often provide motivation and inspiration. The Castleconnell Arts and Crafts fair in County Limerick features regional and national exhibitors. You'll also find exhibits in many galleries and craft centers and at various festivals and street fairs, where displays of batik, pottery, wood turning, basket making, jewelry, weaving, and other applied arts afford good browsing. Community centers, art schools, and regional technical colleges (RTCs) offer courses in many craft forms, including bronze casting, fine woodwork, and stained glass.

Glass factories produce exquisite cut glass and crystal in a number of factories, including those in Cavan, Tipperary, and of course, Waterford. Small studios and factories create decorative and functional pottery, the most famous at Belleek Pottery in County Fermanagh. Knitwear often incorporates traditional design features into contemporary styles. A similar blend of old and new emerges in handcrafted jewelry.

The Arts Community

Those who are drawn to the arts will find much in Ireland to gratify an appreciation for artistic vision and expression. Although contemporary approaches are evident in many art forms, much emphasis is given to honoring and preserving traditions. Many artists choose to honor Irish culture by reinterpreting those early influences to create works that blend a respect for heritage with a more contemporary presentation.

Visual Arts

Dramatic landscapes, unique light patterns, and ivy-strewn, old rusted gates offer stimuli for photographers and painters alike. Light reflecting off the moisture-laden air creates a challenge for photographers. The lens does not always do justice to the many subtle variations of vibrant green hues. Sligo, Connemara, and other areas in the west are favored by many painters.

The Achill Island School of Painting and the Irish School of Landscape Painting offer courses in beautiful settings throughout the year. Galleries all over Ireland feature the works of both well-known and emerging artists. In addition to the formal setting of the National Gallery in Dublin, there are impressive university collections; notable galleries in cities like Galway, Kilkenny, Sligo, Limerick, Cork, and Waterford; as well as any number of smaller galleries and working studios in artists' homes.

Dance

Dance is an art form that in recent years has revealed a unique blend of traditional and contemporary influences. Productions like Riverdance and Lord of the Dance served to transform the rather inelastic, arms-rigid form of Irish step dancing into a thrilling, sexy spectacle. While those with purist leanings may protest that a sweaty Yank leaping bare-chested in tight leather pants has little to do with Irish heritage, they cannot deny that the success of these troupes has created intense public interest in Irish dance traditions.

Step dancing, with its characteristic foot percussion, is but one form of Irish dance. Ceili dancing includes balancing on the toes and tends to deemphasize battering (the term for abrupt, foot-hammering movements). In set dancing, four couples form a square, and their movements interpret each segment of a particular tune.

A feis (pronounced "fesh"), or dance competition, showcases the talent of colorfully costumed performers, from children to seasoned adults. The all-world championships are held each spring in Ireland.

Music

Traditional music fills the air everywhere in Ireland. From the solitary street performer, the local community radio station, or an impromptu pub session, to the heavily promoted and sold out "trad" concert, music in Ireland reflects a rich cultural heritage. Ireland also supports a profitable industry of contemporary rock and pop music, whose artists often weave sounds of the traditional within those of the bleeding edge. From the Chieftains to U-2, Mary Black to Sinead O'Connor, Dolores Keane to Brian Kennedy, and Altan to Aslan, the range of styles is diverse and dynamic.

Among the instruments used to create lively or haunting strains of traditional music are the fiddle; the tin whistle; Uillean pipes, a sophisticated member of the bagpipe family, with bellows and keys that create chords; the concertina, a hexagonal accordion with buttons; and the bodhran. Made from goatskin stretched across an open frame, the bodhran ("bow" rhymes with cow, plus "rawn") is played with a double-headed stick called a tipper or beater.

The harp, a national symbol, holds a prominent place in Irish music. Festivals honor the memory of Turlough O'Carolan (1670–1738), Ireland's most famous harpist, composer, and teacher, whose blindness did not prevent him from traveling all around Ireland in bardic tradition. The O'Carolan Harp & Traditional Music Festival in Keadue, County Roscommon, offers classes, lectures, and workshops that culminate in a concert performed by teachers and students. Another festival that focuses on the harp and other traditional instruments takes place in O'Carolan's birthplace in Nobber, County Meath. In County Longford, the Granard Harp Festival features music, competitions, a Queen of the Harp contest, and a parade.

Among the host of traditional music festivals, the All-Ireland Fleadh is the most important. Held at the end of August, it provides music and song competitions for all levels and ages. In recent years, a Winter School session, hosted in Donegal by the traditional group Altan, has become the place to be for the holidays for those devoted to "trad" music.

Singing holds a special place in Irish heritage. Irish people generally love to sing, and nearly everyone seems to have a certain song or two—or twenty—that she or he will readily perform, no coaxing required. Venues for enjoying song include the Cork International Choral Festival, the Clare Festival of Traditional Singing, and the Cavan International Song Contest (which selects a winning original composition from competitors representing many different countries). Artists like Iarla O'Lionaird carry on the traditional form of a cappella singing known as Sean Nos.

Music other than the traditional variety is well represented in Ireland. Festivals that focus on jazz, bluegrass, blues, rock, pop, opera, and classical music are held all over the country throughout the year. Dublin's Temple Bar district hosts an annual summer Blues Festival, where the music and dancing spill onto the surrounding streets. Several large rock or pop concerts are held each summer: one at Slane Castle, County Meath; and others usually at one of the big venues in Dublin, either Lansdowne Road or the RDS showgrounds in Ballsbridge. The "Big Day Out" is a major rock concert held each year in conjunction with the Galway Arts Festival. These outdoor concerts draw huge crowds and feature world-famous performers. The Guinness-sponsored International Jazz Festival, for instance, draws thousands to Cork every October. Opera devotees are entertained each fall at Waterford's Light Opera Festival and Wexford's International Opera Festival. The West Cork Chamber Music Festival is held at Bantry House overlooking Bantry Bay, where events are recorded and rebroadcast in Ireland and across Europe. The National Concert Hall in Dublin holds up to 1,200 people, who come to hear the National Symphony Orchestra of Ireland, the Radio Telefish Eireann (RTE) Concert Orchestra, and the National Youth Orchestra of Ireland. These companies tour Ireland and abroad. RTE FM 3 radio's format is dedicated to classical music.

People in Ireland and around the world tune in faithfully each year to watch the Eurovision song contest. Immensely popular as well as the target of good-humored ribbing, this international competition has launched a number of hit songs and professional careers. Performance quality may range from amateur to sublime as each solo or group contestant vies to win the prize for the country represented. The complex and occasionally bungled process of live voting from each participating nation is a show in itself. This is an international event of great flair and fun.

Theater

Traditional, contemporary, and experimental performances grace the stage of theaters all over Ireland, with an especially varied program presented in major cities. Regional, national and international companies perform at venues like the Abbey, Gaiety, and Olympia Theatres in Dublin; the Belltable Arts Centre in Limerick, the Taibhdhearc and Town Hall Theatres in Galway; the Arts and Lyric Theatres in Belfast; Hawkswell Theatre in Sligo; and Theatre Royal in Waterford and Wexford. Annual drama festivals in Athlone and Dublin showcase a variety of productions. In Tralee the National Folk Theatre of Ireland, Siamsa Tire, portrays the heritage of rural customs through traditional costume, dance, and music. Ireland is generally included on the international itinerary of American and European touring companies, including major musical productions like *Phantom of the Opera* and *Les Miserables.*

Film

The film industry has a highly visible presence in Ireland. Annual film festivals in Dublin, Galway, and Cork screen entrants in various categories. Over the past decade the success of a number of Irish films has further extended their reach among an international audience. *The Field* depicts the passionate sanctification of land; *My Left Foot,* the triumph of spirit. *The Butcher Boy* tells the darkly comic tale of a boy's struggle with madness. *Some Mother's Son, In the Name of the Father, The Crying Game,* and *The Boxer* are films that have explored the emotional toll of political strife. With warmth and humor, films like *The Commitments* and *The Snapper* portray working-class life. Irish whimsy and character are enchantingly portrayed in films like *The Miracle, Into the West, Hear My Song, Waking Ned Devine, Widow's Peak, The Matchmaker, Circle of Friends,* and *The War of the Buttons.*

Multiscreen cineplexes are becoming common in Ireland and are not restricted to cities. At $7.00 to $7.50, the price of a ticket is about the same as in North America. While some foreign-made films will play in

Ireland before the United States and Canada, more often films will appear later on the Irish screen. Local video rental stores do a brisk business in Ireland.

The Literary Arts

Ireland's tradition of literary excellence is well established. There has been a host of Irish Nobel Prize and Booker Award winners. Ireland is often credited with producing a number of literary talents far beyond the country's small size. Early writing was preserved by monks who recorded epics like the *Tain Bo Cuailnge* ("The Cattle Raid of Cooley"), later translated by Thomas Kinsella. Works by James Joyce, C. S. Lewis, Oscar Wilde, Samuel Beckett, William Butler Yeats, John Millington Synge, Lady Gregory, Jonathan Swift, George Bernard Shaw, Bram Stoker, Elizabeth Bowen, Sean O'Casey, Patrick Kavanagh, John B. Keane, James Joyce, Molly Keane, and Brendan Behan have earned international acclaim and influenced generations of writers. The Writer's Museum in Dublin's Parnell Square features a sequential display of photographs, letters, and memorabilia that reveal the evolution of Irish literature from earliest times through the nineteenth-century revival and into recent times.

Festivals like the Cape Clear Island International Storytelling Festival honor the oral tradition. Clifden Arts Week, in County Galway, features literary readings and writing workshops. The Yeats International Summer School in Sligo runs a winter program, too. The leading Irish literary festival takes place annually in County Kerry. The Listowel Writers' Week focuses on poetry, drama, literature, and song. It is popular with beginners and veterans alike, who come to attend workshops and lectures, and to hear well-known authors discuss and read from their work.

Bookstore browsing is a fun pastime in Ireland. Shelves at Eason's or Waterstone's carry the latest publications, though book aficionados may prefer the broader selection and attentive service at shops like Kennys Bookshops & Art Galleries in Galway, Fred Hanna's in Dublin, and O'Mahoney's in Limerick. It is also possible to order from Kennys and Hanna's via their Web sites, as well as from Read Ireland. (The Resource Guide provides Web site URLs.)

A Stabilizing Political Climate

In 1921 the Anglo-Irish Treaty established Ireland as two countries.

Ireland (Eire), commonly referred to as "the Republic," consists of twenty-six counties ruled as a republic by a parliamentary system seated in Dublin. Six counties make up Northern Ireland, which is part of the United Kingdom. Unless indicated otherwise, this book uses the designation Ireland to refer to the Republic.

The extended conflict between nationalists (those who favor reuniting *all* of the above counties under the Republic of Ireland) and unionists (those who want to continue the rule of Northern Ireland within the United Kingdom) has been drawn along religious and political lines. "The Troubles," as the Irish term this long-standing struggle, have been concentrated in the North—in Belfast and smaller towns. Important strides have recently been made toward settling this age-old conflict. Ratified by referendum in the North and South in May 1998, a historic peace agreement marked a renewed effort to end violence and strive for reconciliation.

In recent years an increasingly positive political climate has contributed to economic growth. In turn, fresh optimism and a new prosperity have reinforced the desire for lasting peace.

While there is much history to overcome, the momentum for peace is powerful. In August 1998 a bombing in the northern town of Omagh killed twenty-nine people and injured 220, the deadliest terrorist attack in three decades. This act enraged the conflict-weary public, north and south of the border. It also obliterated any modicum of support that might have existed for several small splinter groups that were attempting to derail the peace agreement. Thus, the Omagh bombing may have actually strengthened the peace process.

Efforts to achieve a lasting peace were strengthened further when the two leaders of the largest Roman Catholic and Protestant political parties in Northern Ireland were awarded the 1998 Nobel Peace Prize. The creation of governmental departments to represent the interests of unionists and nationalists and cross-border bodies to implement policies is seen as moving things further along the road of cooperation and peace.

In the past, vivid reports of disturbances have sometimes led to false impressions about daily life in Ireland. Many mistakenly assumed that political strife in the North had created a dangerous environment all over Ireland. Yet each year thousands of foreigners travel to every part of Ireland, including the North, and encounter nothing more threatening than a runaway sheep. Many signs indicate that peace will hold in the North and usher in greater economic opportunity. Assuming that the conflict ceases, the housing market and health care services in the North may provide reason to consider it as a retirement destination.

The Reign of the Celtic Tiger

A new spirit, boosted by economic growth, flourishes in today's Ireland. Formerly shabby sections in metropolitan Dublin, Limerick, Galway, and Cork now overflow with trendy cafes, bookstores, galleries, and shops. The food revival has encouraged the launch of many good restaurants. Irish music, theater, literature, and film are thriving and finding new devotees worldwide.

The past decade has seen a major turnaround in Ireland's economy as it makes the transition from an agricultural to a technological base. Referred to as the "Celtic Tiger," the economy has in recent years delivered consistent and robust growth. Trade deficits have been transformed into surpluses. Thousands formerly on the dole have become tax-paying earners who are often employed in world-class pharmaceutical, software, and electronics industries. Many more women have entered the paid workforce. Consumer spending is up. Construction, telecommunications, electronics, food services and many other industries are experiencing rapid growth. Job creation has helped to reduce unemployment to the lowest in two decades, though, at 6.7 percent in April 1999, it is still high by North American standards. At the same time a shortage of workers with technological expertise is expected to accelerate.

The government has aggressively courted foreign investors, thereby contributing to growth. Lured by favorable tax rates, a well-educated labor force, and proximity to the European market, many U.S. and Canadian companies have set up branches in Ireland, including high-tech firms like Intel, Hewlett-Packard, Oracle, Nortel, Celestica, Corel, Apple, Sun Microsystems, Motorola, and Dell. The superb job opportunities have encouraged many Irish people living abroad to return home.

Economic growth, however, is not without cost. Some fear that a too-hot economy could plunge, and they worry about the government's ability to curb inflation, which averaged 2.4 percent in 1998. Not all have shared in the new prosperity, and the government has been urged to do more to aid the needy in Ireland. Still, recent years have evidenced visible signs of increased prosperity. Courtesy of billions in funding from the European Union (EU), roads and other infrastructures are much improved. A better class of automobiles now cruises along roads that are flanked by homes that often sport fresh paint and new roofs.

Ireland's membership in the European Union since the early 1970s has encouraged reforms of economic, social welfare, health, and environmental policies required to bring them in line with EU regulations. Ireland's participation in the European Monetary Union (EMU) single currency, known as the "euro" and launched in January 1999, will continue to influence the direction of the economy. Euro notes and coins will become Ireland's official currency on January 1, 2002. By July 2002 national currencies will be withdrawn in those countries that are part of the euro zone.

Although not all economic experts agree, many have projected that the use of a single currency, to be phased in over several years, will unify and strengthen the economies of member countries. No one disputes that the European market represents a powerful force in international commerce. The single currency has brought together nearly 290 million people from eleven EU member countries that qualified for and chose to join the launch of the euro. They are Austria, Belgium, Finland, France, Germany, Ireland, Italy, Luxembourg, Netherlands, Portugal, and Spain. Although the United Kingdom, Denmark, and Sweden qualified for membership, they elected not to participate at launch. Greece is hoping to qualify by 2002.

You Can Go Home Again

Although you may not be able to go Canada or pop back to the States to shop or have your hair trimmed, occasional visits home are not difficult to pull off. Careful comparison shopping well in advance of anticipated travel dates will help to reduce airfare expenditures. Friends and family who wish to visit you will also benefit from fare shopping well before their departure.

When planning an international relocation, it is important to consider the overall implications of the distance you will be placing between your adopted and former homes. If you have strong family ties or depend on easy access to close friends, you may be happier retiring closer to home than in Ireland. And even if you determine after a thorough assessment that relocation to Ireland is a viable plan, it still makes sense to have a backup strategy that allows you to reverse gears should you want to return at some point in the future.

LEGAL ISSUES

The following is an overview of key areas of legal concern for those moving to Ireland. Because laws, policies, and their interpretation can change over time, be sure to consult appropriate authorities and/or professionals for specific details relevant to your situation. The rules and regulations of the Irish government are not always explicit and uniform. Even authoritative documentation will often include phrases like "exceptions may be considered" and "the requirement may be waived." Ireland's mission to comply with a host of European Union policies and regulations means that procedures are shifting and thus may be subject to an even greater degree of interpretation.

Many people in Ireland assert that the issue of whom you know is often at play when policies are interpreted. It is a good practice, therefore, to check first with people in the community and then make a personal inquiry when you need specific information, either by phoning or visiting an Irish consular office in North America or calling the appropriate offices in Ireland.

Residency Status

Taking up residence in Ireland has no effect, in and of itself, on your U.S. or Canadian citizenship. There is no U.S. law requiring you to return to the States periodically to preserve your citizenship.

U.S. and Canadian passport holders do not need a visa to visit Ireland. Those who plan to remain in Ireland for longer than ninety days need to seek permission from the Department of Justice, Equality and Law Reform within the ninety days, and preferably within a few days of arrival. You should register at the Aliens Registration Office, at the An Garda Siochána (Police Department) in Dublin. If you will be staying outside Dublin, you may go to the local police superintendent's office. As long as you are able to demonstrate the ability to support yourself financially without being employed in Ireland, permission is usually granted. To support your intention and your ability to reside in Ireland, you may be requested to provide evidence of either the purchase or rental of property, the transfer of your household goods from abroad, an account in an Irish bank, an order for telephone service, and so forth.

If all is in order, you will receive a Certificate of Registration—also known as a "Green Book"—and you are then considered a nonresident alien. You must renew annually until you have lived in Ireland for five years. At that time you may claim permanent residency and will no longer have to register annually.

Issues related to residency may affect your tax status and eligibility for reliefs and allowances (see the section on taxes in Chapter 3). Your residency status also determines your eligibility for health benefits (discussed in Chapter 4).

Dual Citizenship

"Dual citizenship" means that you are simultaneously a citizen of two countries; you owe allegiance to and must obey the laws of both. For some, the idea of claiming dual Irish/U.S. citizenship holds great appeal. Often the allure is symbolic, a way to officially acknowledge their Irish heritage. There are concrete benefits, too. An Irish passport facilitates obtaining employment and entitlements in Ireland, as well as in all other countries of the European Union. A second passport may also place one in the faster-moving line through customs.

Ireland has historically been more liberal than most countries in its consideration of applications for citizenship. Its less restrictive position has been based to some degree on the belief that many of its citizens have been forced by famine and poverty rather than by free choice to leave Ireland. For these emigrants and their offspring, a claim to Irish citizenship should be regarded as a valid request to restore something that was sacrificed.

This outlook has influenced an immigration policy that at one time extended the rights of citizenship even to great-grandchildren of Irish-born citizens. Many people requested and were granted Irish citizenship based on having descended from Irish ancestors. Although a rationale of heritage is still honored, it is more restrictive now.

Ireland's recent economic prosperity has drawn many to the country. About half are returning citizens; many are from the United Kingdom, the United States, and other developed countries; and a few are political refugees seeking asylum. Concern that continued increases in immigration—a major reversal of the trend of previous decades—could deplete national resources has begun to influence Ireland's policy with regard to granting residency status or citizenship. It is no longer simply a matter of filling out forms, therefore, to obtain an Irish passport. There are a number of conditions that must be satisfied in order to obtain Irish citizenship today.

Those who do manage to meet the requirements, submit an application, and receive an Irish passport will usually not forfeit the citizenship of their home country. The Canadian government has recognized dual citizenship since 1997. The U.S. government recognizes but does not encourage dual citizenship. One step in the process of obtaining Irish citizenship is a required public oath of loyalty to the Irish government. The U.S. government considers this a "routine oath of allegiance" and presumes that those taking it intend to retain their U.S. citizenship. To renounce your U.S. or Canadian citizenship, you must indicate in the presence of a consular or diplomatic officer a clear intention to relinquish it and then sign a statement to that effect. Why would someone want to relinquish citizenship? Until recently, a few creative individuals used this method to avoid paying U.S. taxes, but the U.S. Internal Revenue Service has tightened this loophole.

Obtaining Irish Citizenship

Obviously, people who are born in Ireland are Irish citizens. In addition, anyone with either parent born in Ireland is automatically a citizen. People with these qualifications may obtain an Irish passport by submitting a passport application.

How might others qualify to apply? Under the terms of the Irish Nationality and Citizenship Acts of 1956 and 1986, there are three ways that a non-national can become an Irish Citizen: by descent, through naturalization, and through marriage.

The following section summarizes these avenues. If you meet the current requirements, you might want to consider making an application now, in order to avoid the obstacle of any new restrictions that might be created later on by changes in immigration laws.

Foreign Birth Registration

Anyone with at least one grandparent born in Ireland may claim Irish citizenship through the process of "foreign birth registration." To substantiate a grandparent's citizenship, you will need to unearth a number of documents, such as authenticated birth, marriage, and death certificates. You must present these to an Irish embassy or consular office to support your application to be entered in the Foreign Births Register (FBR). Once registered, you are able to apply for an Irish passport.

This provision no longer applies to great-grandparents. If, however, one of your non-Irish-born parents applied and was entered into the FBR before you were born, you are also entitled to apply to be entered in the Register; once entered, you can apply for a passport. If your parent's registration took place after you were born, however, you are not entitled to apply.

Post-Nuptial Citizenship

The spouse of an Irish citizen may earn citizenship by making a declaration of acceptance of Irish citizenship after three years of marriage. If you have been married for three or more years to a spouse who is entitled to citizenship based on having an Irish-born parent, you may register for citizenship with an Irish embassy or consulate. You can also register three years after your spouse has been entered into the Foreign Births Register.

Naturalization

To qualify for citizenship through naturalization, one must live in Ireland and have done so for five of the nine years preceding the application. The last year of this period must have been one of continuous residence. Applicants must be over eighteen years of age and be of "good character." They must provide a year's notice of their intention to apply and establish that they will reside in Ireland after naturalization. A student cannot apply, but time spent studying may count toward the five-year requirement if the student subsequently finds employment and decides to stay in Ireland.

An application for naturalization must include copies of a number of documents. These may include a passport, Green Book, birth and marriage certificates, recent bank statements, and a statement from the Revenue Commissioners indicating that the applicant has paid all taxes due. The Minister for Justice has discretionary authority to accept or reject an application. It can take as long as two years for naturalization to be granted. Once approved, a fee of $750 is payable, and the applicant must make a formal declaration of loyalty to the state in open court.

Anyone born after, but not before, a parent has become a naturalized

Irish citizen may apply for a passport, once the birth is entered into the FBR. The son or daughter may then obtain a certificate confirming entry in the Register and use it as proof of Irish citizenship when applying for a passport.

Further details and citizenship application forms are available from the Embassy of Ireland in Ottawa, Ontario, and in Washington, D.C., from consular missions in Boston, Chicago, New York, and San Francisco; or from the Department of Justice, Equality and Law Reform in Dublin. (See the Resource Guide for contact information.)

Voting

Any registered resident age 18 or over, regardless of citizenship, may vote in local Irish elections for County Councils, County Borough Corporations, Urban District Councils, and boards of town commissioners. These local authorities provide a range of services including those related to housing and building, road transportation and safety, water supply and sewerage, environmental protection, and recreation. Exercising the right to vote in Ireland will have no effect on your status as a U.S. or Canadian citizen.

U.S. citizens may also vote in U.S. federal elections, including those for congressional representation for the state in which you last resided, whether or not you hold dual citizenship, and even if you haven't been in the United States for years. The U.S. Embassy's American Citizens Service Unit will assist you in registering to obtain an absentee ballot.

Work Permits

Irish nationals and citizens of other European Union countries may work in Ireland without a permit. Unless they can claim citizenship, all others must have a valid work permit before they will be allowed to enter into employment in Ireland. You can obtain a work permit through a prospective employer, who will apply in your behalf to the Department of Enterprise, Trade and Employment. The department will issue a permit only if the employer can make a case that your skills are unique. The employer must also demonstrate that a reasonable attempt to find a suitably qualified person of first Irish, then EU citizenship has failed to produce a candidate.

During the four to six weeks required for approval, you may not work in Ireland. If you succeed in getting approval, you must then apply at a local immigration office for a Certificate of Residence, or Green Book. You are then registered as a legal alien, which allows you to stay and work in Ireland for the specified time. Permits extend for one year. You must renew well in advance of the annual deadline.

If you are married to an Irish national, a work permit will usually be granted upon review of an application submitted with a copy of the marriage certificate and the Irish spouse's birth certificate.

Embassies in Ireland

The United States, Canada, Australia, Spain, Israel, Portugal, Japan, Sweden, and a number of other countries maintain a diplomatic presence in Ireland. Embassies provide information about the country they represent as well as assistance to citizens living abroad. The Resource Guide provides information on how to contact the U.S. and Canadian Embassies in Ireland and the Embassy of Ireland in Canada and the United States.

Assistance from the U.S. Embassy

The U.S. Embassy is located in a circular building in Ballsbridge, an exclusive section of Dublin about 3 kilometers (2 miles) southeast of the city center. The staff is organized into a number of departments; the one relevant for most needs is Consular Services. The Consular Section will

Skilled Labor Shortage

A shortage of skilled workers is a problem for many companies in Ireland today, especially those in the electronics, telecommunications, and software sectors. While there is a great deal of emphasis on developing new educational programs to prepare graduates to assume positions in these sectors, there are indications that the need is immediate and could soon become critical. Service indus- tries in Ireland also have an urgent need for experienced workers, having lost many potential candidates to high-tech industries. The need for part-time workers is also expected to accelerate. In response to the short- age of qualified workers, the govern- ment is reviewing work-permit poli- cies. Reforms that will afford employers greater flexibility in their efforts to recruit are likely.

advise U.S. citizens who experience serious legal problems, including being arrested. When you live in Ireland, you are subject to the laws of Ireland. The laws of the United States will not apply to you in any way, so there is no point in shouting, "But I'm an American citizen!" International agreements entitle you, upon arrest, to get in touch with the U.S. Embassy. While embassy staff cannot get you out of jail or give you legal advice, they will visit you, provide the names of local attorneys, and notify your family and friends.

U.S. Embassy staff suggest that you register, in person or by phone, with the embassy when you arrive at your permanent residence in Ireland. Information about your whereabouts will enable the staff to contact you in an emergency. Embassy staff often help people in the States who need to locate U.S. citizens abroad, but they will not release information about you to others without your consent.

The U.S. Embassy offers assistance with certain other situations, including serious financial or health problems. The embassy will provide names of local physicians, U.S. tax forms, and notary services (at $55, however, the notary service is expensive). It also offers general information about Ireland and how you might get in touch with fellow U.S. citizens residing there. The embassy staff will not provide tourism or commercial services—they can't find you a job, book you a hotel room, or locate your lost luggage. They will help with the issuance of a new passport, however, if you should lose yours or it is stolen. You can facilitate this process by keeping a photocopy of the data page in a safe place, separate from your passport. The Passport and Citizenship Office is open from 8:30 A.M. to noon, Monday through Friday. It is closed for both U.S. and Irish public holidays.

The U.S. State Department has introduced a new passport with high-tech anti-counterfeiting features. Stolen and altered passports command high prices on the illegal market. A digitized photo and data page, however, renders the new, improved passport much more difficult to tamper with and thus less valuable to drug smugglers and other criminals. You may continue to use a traditional passport until it expires, but if it is anywhere near its expiration date, you may want to renew it in the more secure version.

Ireland's Government

Ireland has been a free state since winning independence from the United Kingdom in 1922. The republic's legal system is based on its Constitution (adopted in 1937), legislation, and common law. Its laws that regulate finance and commerce are increasingly subject to revision in order to conform to European Union directives.

Ireland has a parliamentary form of government. The chief of state is the president, elected to a seven-year term. He or she (the latter pronoun applying to the previous and current presidents, Mary Robinson and Mary McAleese) may stand for reelection only once. The official presidential residence is in Phoenix Park, Dublin. While the role is primarily ceremonial, the president can and does influence the course of government.

The real executive power rests with the prime minister, or Taoiseach (pronounced "TEE shuck") and his (to date, the only applicable pronoun) ministers, who are responsible for the leadership of fourteen major departments in areas like agriculture, health, foreign affairs, and education. The president appoints the Taoiseach from the political party that wins the most seats in the Dáil (House of Representatives). The

Census 2000

Since 1993 the advocacy group American Citizens Abroad (ACA) has been raising awareness of the need to include U.S. citizens living outside the country in the year 2000 Census. The group reasons that since federal employees working abroad were included in the 1990 Census and will be included again in 2000, private citizens should be accounted for as well. It has also raised constitutional issues of equitable representation in Congress, apportioned by census results. The group's efforts to advocate for extension of Medicare coverage and other benefits for those living abroad would be strengthened by having access to more data and a better sense of the numbers of American citizens living abroad, now estimated at anywhere from 2.5 million to 5 million. The U.S. Bureau of Census has acknowledged that constitutional issues are a consideration but has also claimed that logistics and funding limitation could prevent the inclusion of those living abroad. The ACA has asked expatriates to be sure to register with the U.S. Embassy and inform it of any relocations, as well as request to be counted, which will have no effect on a person's tax or voting status. (See the Resource Guide for how to contact ACA for additional information.)

Taoiseach nominates members to the cabinet who must then win approval by the Dáil. The Dáil has 166 members, each elected to a maximum five-year term. The other branch of Parliament, the Seanad (Senate), is composed of sixty members, eleven nominated by the prime minister and the rest elected.

Each house may introduce proposals for new legislation, except for those dealing with taxation and expenditure (Money Bills) or amendments to the 1937 Constitution. Only the Dail may initiate financial legislation or bills to amend the Constitution. An amendment becomes law in Ireland only through referendum.

A number of city and county councils or corporations handle administrative duties on the local level. Each administrative body has a manager, a chairperson, and a group of councillors.

Political parties in Ireland are dynamic and visible. They command copious media coverage, and the antics of political personalities are a source of lively common interest. The major political parties are Fianna Fail, Fine Gael, Labor, Progressive Democrats, Democratic Left, Sinn Fein, and Green Alliance.

The Irish Legal System

Based broadly on English common law, the Irish legal system originated from Brehon law, a Celtic tradition uprooted by English authorities several centuries ago. The judicial branch of government comprises a system of civil and criminal courts and the ultimate authority, the Irish Supreme Court, with its chief justice and five other justices. Disputes involving European law raised in Irish courts may be appealed to the European Union court system.

Ireland's criminal courts deal with prosecutions of offenses ranging from petty theft to murder. Minor offenses are dealt with in the District Court without a jury. The Circuit Court sits with judge and jury to consider more serious offenses. For crimes of rape, murder, or terrorism, the Central Criminal Court conducts jury trials. The Court of Criminal Appeals entertains appeals from the criminal courts. The Supreme Court is the court of final appeal for both civil and criminal cases.

A greater awareness of the rights of consumers has emerged in recent times, and the Office of Consumer Affairs enforces legislation designed to protect consumers. A government ombudsman agency reviews complaints and issues rulings in the event of individual disputes with local authorities; health boards; life insurance companies; banks; and enterprises that provide services such as phone, electricity, and mail.

Small claims courts, administered within the civil district court system, provide a means to redress consumer claims in relation to goods or services. The amount of a claim must not exceed $900. The fee for filing such a claim is $9.00. If the respondent accepts liability, the court will request and enforce payment. If the respondent disputes the claim, the small claims registrar will call both parties to an informal, private meeting and attempt to resolve the matter. If the attempt fails, the parties will attend a hearing before a judge of the district court.

FINANCIAL MATTERS

Financial well-being is a key consideration at any stage of life. Projecting what you'll need in retirement, even for those who do not relocate, requires prudent deliberation. Those who plan early and carefully usually come out ahead. Financial considerations become more complex in the context of an international move. Effective strategy requires not only a proper assessment of your current resources but also sound projections of how you will manage them within the parameters of a new financial environment. Over time, consulting a financial advisor could save you a lot of money. Some financial consultants specialize in advising clients who are considering an international relocation. (For information on locating them, see the Resource Guide.)

This chapter presents an overview of key financial issues relevant to living in Ireland and includes general information about housing and food costs—typically the leading expenditures in a household budget. (Detailed information about the costs and process of acquiring housing in Ireland is presented in Chapter 5.) The cost-of-living comparisons offered below may help provide a general sense of how much your dollar will buy in Ireland. The relative decrease or increase in your budget depends, of course, on how much things cost where you live now. In the last few years, Ireland's economic boom has brought new prosperity to many of its people—along with higher costs, particularly in housing. However, tax decreases, deregulation of utility companies, and increased competition across the euro zone are reducing other expenses.

Comparisons can be very helpful, so by all means weigh the charge for, say, a dozen eggs in Ireland against what you pay for them now. Factor in the gain from a number of perks you may be entitled to receive in Ireland, like free transport on public conveyances, discounts on utilities, and relief for rent and certain medical expenses. Project your costs for housing and medical coverage (discussed in Chapter 4). As you look at all of the financial factors, remember to view them also within the broader context of quality of life.

Quality of life is what draws many people to Ireland. And it is what they continue to praise after living there, even after many years. How do you place a value on feeling relatively safe from violent crime? So what if butter is a bit more expensive—you'll never taste better. How important is it, after all, to be able to choose from twenty-five different makes and models of washing machines? How simpler your life is when you are spared this dizzying range of choices! How much is it worth to breathe clean air, to live among decent people close to their land, their art, their kin, and their history? To greet cows on your daily walk? To enter a pub as a stranger and instantly feel welcomed and at ease? Veteran expatriates recommend that you include these intangibles in your thoughtful assessment of the financial implications of a move to Ireland.

Currency

Ireland is in the process of converting to the euro (€), the European single currency. Until the year 2002, the unit of currency in Ireland will continue to be the Irish pound (£ or IR£), also called the "punt." One pound equals one hundred pence (p). The Irish pound fluctuates in value against the U.S. dollar. In recent years it has traded generally between U.S. $1.35 and U.S. $1.61. U.S. dollar values are listed throughout this book using an exchange rate of U.S. $1.50, to give an idea of costs.

During the intervening transition period, people will exchange euros only in cashless transactions. These noncash uses include checks, credit cards, credit transfers, and direct debit payments of utility bills and taxes.

On January 1, 2002, bank accounts in Ireland will automatically convert to use of the euro. U.S. credit and ATM cards will convert charges into euros and apply foreign exchange rates as before with Irish pounds.

The euro will have seven notes, worth 5, 10, 20, 50, 100, 200, and 500 euro. Coins worth 1 and 2 euro; and six others, worth 1, 2, 5, 10, 20, and 50 cents, will be issued. Eleven designs, each representing an EMU member country, will appear on one side of the euro. While some confusion is anticipated during the transition, Irish and worldwide businesses and institutions have long been preparing for the changeover to the new currency.

Banking

There is no restriction on the amount of funds you may bring into or take out of Ireland. You may hold bank accounts in either or both Ireland and the United States or another country. Irish banks with the greatest number of branches are AIB, Bank of Ireland, Ulster Bank, and

Irish Permanent. Banking hours generally are from 9:30 A.M. to 4:00 P.M., with extended hours one day per week, usually Thursday. Many maintain Web sites that provide information on financial products and will soon provide online banking. In the more remote rural areas, mobile vans sometimes provide bank services.

Building societies and credit unions also offer financial services, including loans and savings accounts. You are eligible to join the local credit union based on your residency within a geographical area, regardless of your employment status. Credit unions also provide discounts on home, automobile, and travel insurance. Some now offer insurance against serious illness as well. In addition to selling stamps, the postal service, An Post, offers a number of savings and investment vehicles; it also administers social welfare payments.

Many people living abroad find it advantageous to set up an account in the adopted country while maintaining banking and investment accounts back home, transferring funds as needed into the local account. You'll find automated teller machines (ATMs) at all banks in Ireland as well as in many shopping malls and grocery stores. Whether or not you elect to carry a credit card from an Irish lender, continuing a credit card account from your home country is a good idea. (Credit limits on charge cards issued in Ireland rarely exceed $1,500. Should you need to access credit quickly in an emergency, the maximum on credit cards issued in the United States is generally much higher.) MasterCard and Visa are widely accepted throughout Ireland, American Express and Diners Club less so.

Most U.S. and Canadian credit-card companies will accommodate a change to a foreign address. Their systems, however, are not always sufficiently sophisticated to manage accounts based outside the United States For example, issues related to timely receipt of a statement and payment of the bill could arise. Whether or not you receive your statement on time, you are obligated to pay by the due date. Payments need to be made in the currency of your native country. The amount due may be different from what appears on your statement, since the exchange rate that will be applied will be the one in effect on the day the transaction is processed between the merchant and the lender, not when you made the purchase. If you rarely use the credit card, you run the risk of cancellation; lenders are not likely to want to continue an account on which there is little activity. These issues may be viewed differently, however, if you deal with a local bank where you maintain other accounts and have had some sort of relationship over the years.

However much they have boosted consumer spending and the overall economy, low interest rates have reduced returns on savings vehicles. Rates of return are lowest on demand deposit accounts, which permit instant access to funds. Typical rates of return of between 2.0 to 2.5 percent per year have encouraged people to consider more productive alternatives. Credit unions often pay higher rates and also allow depositors to borrow a portion of their savings. Banks pay higher rates on notice savings accounts, with notice periods of anywhere from seven to ninety days. Still higher rates will be earned in accounts that hold deposits for one or more years. Special investment accounts (SIAs) and special savings accounts (SSAs) carry lower rates of deposit interest retention tax (DIRT) and often pay higher returns. An Post offers SSAs, demand accounts, and tax-free, state-guaranteed savings certificates and savings bonds of varying maturities. It also sells prize bonds; if you win the tax-free weekly or monthly prize (currently $22,500 and $150,000, respectively), you'll realize a generous return. Otherwise there is no gain, though your original investment is safe.

U.S. Social Security Checks

U.S. Social Security recipients residing in Ireland can receive their checks through the American Embassy. It usually takes longer to deliver checks outside the United States because of the distance and extra handling needed. To avoid delays or the risk of a lost or stolen check, you may have your payment deposited directly into an account at a financial institution in Ireland or in the United States. You can sign up for direct deposit at the U.S. Embassy.

Cost of Living

It is important to do your best to gauge what you will need to live to the standard you desire in Ireland. Be sure to allow a cushion when calculating your resources. The Irish economy is dynamic, in the midst of being absorbed into the wider arena of the European Monetary Union. The result will be a reduction of some costs, but the transition will unfold gradually. There is much speculation about the effects of Ireland's move to a single currency but no way to predict them with certainty. For the most current information, consult the resources in the appendix that provide regular updates. The following are general guidelines only.

Comparing Costs

Expatriates find that costs diminish as they settle into their new environment and learn more about where to find good bargains locally. Generally, things do cost a bit more in Ireland than in North America. Buying and fueling an automobile is undoubtedly much more expensive, though repairs are cheaper. Home-produced goods such as dairy products and bread are generally cheaper and of higher quality, while other foods usually cost somewhat more. There are seasonal fluctuations as well as special offers in the supermarket chains.

Dining Out

Breakfast is usually an inexpensive meal in Ireland, even in nicer restaurants. The typical Irish breakfast is a full complement of rashers (bacon) and sausages, eggs, tomatoes, mushrooms, brown bread or toast, and coffee or tea. It can cost as little as $3.00, somewhat more in fancier places.

Cafes serve tea or coffee with a delicious scone, butter, and jam for just $1.95 to $2.25. Comfortable places to enjoy a soup-and-sandwich lunch or a supper of traditional Irish stew, pubs offer good fare at reasonable prices. Excluding alcohol, lunch at a pub typically costs $3.00 to $5.00, dinner $8.00 to $12.00. A bonus—splendid traditional music—may well follow your evening meal.

Expect to spend $25 to $40 per person for dinner (with wine) at better restaurants in metropolitan areas or in the finer country hotels, although there are many more moderately priced establishments that serve good food. A meal in a nice restaurant away from the city will generally run $20 to $25.

The service charge is usually included with the bill. Thus, tipping is unnecessary except if you wish to acknowledge superior service. If no service charge is included, a 10 percent tip is considered adequate.

Some typical menu items and prices: crab pâté starter, $6.00; chowder, $4.50; salmon entree, $12.00; seafood combo, $13.00; coffee/tea, $1.20; and various desserts, $3.75.

Typical Costs for Prepared Meals and Groceries

Pub	
Soup	$1.95
Sandwich	$2.70
Meat and vegetables	$9.00
Guinness	
glass	$1.88
pint	$3.38
Mixed drink	$3.75
Fruit juice	$1.75
Heineken, pint	$3.75
Wine, glass	$2.93
Cafe	
Sandwich and salad	$5.60
Coffee and pastry	$2.15
Restaurant (moderate)	
Salad and lasagna	$9.75
Salad and steak	$14.00
Restaurant (trendy)	
Side salad	$3.50
Cannelloni	$9.75
Gourmet pizza	$11.00
Sea bass entrée	$18.00
Tiramisu/cheesecake	$4.00
Coffee/tea/cola	$1.50
Cappuccino	$2.00
Hotel lobby	
Toasted ham and cheese sandwich	$2.50
Crab salad	$5.25
Cappuccino	$1.80
Tea, scones, cream, jam	$3.75
Hotel dining room	
Soup	$3.30
Garlic mushrooms	$5.75
One-half roast duck	$14.50
Garlic prawns	$17.25
Pear tart	$3.75

Burger King	
Whopper Jr. meal	$4.04
McDonald's	
Big Mac with cheese, fries, drink	$4.50
Chinese take-away	$4.20
Fish and chips take-away	$4.80
Grocery items	
Bread, regular loaf	$1.19
Garlic bread	$1.64
Milk, 1 liter (.908 quart)	$ .96
Flour, 1.35 kilograms (3 pounds)	$1.28
Sugar, .45 kilograms (1 pound)	$ .60
Bread (baking) soda	$ .66
Butter, .45 kilograms (1 pound)	$2.39
Eggs, dozen	$2.25
Cheese, cheddar, .23 kilograms (½ pound)	$2.10
Coffee, .23 kilogram (½ pound)	$4.94
Tea bags, 80	$2.66
Coke, 1.5 liters (.40 gallons)	$1.43
Iceberg lettuce	$ .74
Tomatoes, .45 kilogram (1 pound)	$1.19
Onions, .45 kilogram (1 pound)	$ .59
Broccoli, bunch	$1.52
Celery, bunch	$1.34
Carrots, .45 kilogram (1 pound)	$ .44
Bananas, .45 kilogram (1 pound)	$ .81
Orange	$ .24
Apple	$ .30
Cucumber	$ .74
Avocado	$ .74
Garlic	$ .29
Olive oil, 500 milliliters (.13 gallon/.53 quart)	$8.84
Ketchup	$1.58
Mayonnaise	$2.39
Tomatoes, canned	$ .74
Spaghetti, .45 kilogram (1 pound)	$1.34
Frozen pizza	$2.99

Rashers (bacon), .45 kilogram (1 pound)	$4.49
Chicken, whole, 1.36 kilograms (3 pounds)	$5.99
Chicken breast fillets, 4	$7.74
Pork chops, .45 kilogram (1 pound)	$3.44
Minced (ground) beef	$4.49
Sirloin steak, .45 kilogram (1 pound)	$4.49
Lamp chops, .45 kilogram (1 pound)	$4.49
Fresh cod fillets, .45 kilogram (1 pound)	$2.84
Kellogg's Corn Flakes	$2.60
Kellogg's Bran Flakes	$3.11
Ice cream	
Vanilla, 1 liter (.227 gallon/.908 quart)	$3.29
Ben & Jerry's, 500 milliliters (.114 gallon/.455 quart)	$5.69
Gingernut cookies	$1.32
Chocolate-chip cookies, 400 grams (14.108 ounces)	$2.24
California red wine, 750 milliliters (.19 gallon, .79 quart)	$10.03
South African Sauvignon Blanc, 750 milliliters (.19 gallon/.79 quart)	$7.49

Household items

Dish detergent	$2.45
Laundry detergent	$2.99
Toilet paper, 4 rolls	$2.84
Paper towels, 2 rolls	$1.79
Toothpaste	$1.49
Shampoo	$3.44

Appliances/electronics

Oven	$899
Microwave	$179
Washing machine	$419
Clothes dryer	$299
Refrigerator, basic	$419
Refrigerator, top of line, side by side with icemaker	$2,249

Dishwasher	$449
Toaster	$24
Electric Kettle	$27
Television, 140 portable	$4,239
Television, 250	$569
VCR	$344
Desktop computer	$1,048–$2,699

Monthly utilities/services (3-bedroom home)

Electricity	$60
Natural gas	$81
Oil	$74
Telephone-line rental	$15
Internet service per month, including VAT	$25
Gasoline, per liter (4.4 liters per gallon)	$.83

Sample Budgets

The following sample monthly budgets project costs for basic expenditures for two adults sharing a household in Ireland. Obviously, there is some degree of variation depending on how warm you keep your dwelling, how often and how far you drive your car, how nice a car it is, and whether you are addicted to Ben & Jerry's Ice Cream, like some expatriates I know.

There are two versions: one a no-frills, frugal monthly budget; the other a budget that will accommodate a more comfortable lifestyle. Note that Internet service, which many consider a necessity rather than a luxury, is included in both sample budgets.

Some expatriates report that they do well in Ireland on $18,000 to $20,000 per year, but their housing costs are lower than what would be the norm in the current economic climate. There are many ways, of course, to trim or expand either of these monthly budgets.

No-frills Budget

Housing	$1,069
Rent	$850
Utilities	$140
Phone	$45
Internet	$25
TV license	$9

Food	$450
Automobile	$175
	(plus car payments)
Road tax	$25
Insurance	$50
Gasoline, oil	$70
Maintenance	$30
Health care	$150
Entertainment, travel, gifts	$80
Clothing	$30
Miscellaneous	$40
Total per month	$ 1,994
Total per year	$23,928

Comfortable (not lavish) Budget

Housing	$1,499
Mortgage plus insurance, or rent	$1,225
Utilities	$180
Phone	$60
Internet	$25
TV license	$9
Food	$600
Automobile	$300
	(plus car payments)
Road tax	$50
Insurance	$75
Gasoline, oil	$120
Maintenance	$55
Health care	$280
Entertainment, travel, gifts	$120
Clothing	$50
Miscellaneous	$60
Total per month	$ 2,909
Total per year	$34,908

Tax Treaties

Ireland has entered into tax treaties with a number of countries, including the United States and Canada. These double-taxation agreements ensure that tax paid in one country is allowed as a credit against tax payable in another.

The Ireland–U.S. agreement, originally approved in 1951, was revised and renewed in 1997. You may obtain a copy directly from the Irish Revenue Commissioners or the Internal Revenue Service as well as on the Internet. (See the Resource Guide for contact information.)

U.S. citizens living in Ireland are held to the same IRS filing requirements that apply to those living in the United States. They are also allowed the same exemptions, deductions and credits, but they are granted an automatic extension to the usual April 15 filing date, to June 15 to file the return and pay any tax due. U.S. citizens must pay interest on any unpaid tax from April 15 to the date they pay the tax. They may claim on their U.S. returns a tax credit or an itemized deduction for any foreign income taxes paid. There are benefits that may apply to those who have a tax home and receive income in Ireland. Because taxation, especially across national boundaries, is complex and subject to interpretation and legislative modification, it is wise to consult a specialist.

The foreign earned income exclusion allows U.S. citizens living overseas to treat some income as not taxable by the IRS. They must meet one of two tests of residency: They are a bona fide resident of a foreign country and reside in the foreign country for an uninterrupted period that includes an entire tax year, or they are physically present in a foreign country for at least 330 full days during a period of twelve consecutive months. The maximum amount they can exclude is $74,000 in 1999, $76,000 in 2000, $78,000 in 2001, and $80,000 in 2002 and thereafter. To claim the exclusion, they must file a tax return and attach Form 2555, "Foreign Earned Income." For more information contact the IRS or, in Ireland, the U.S. Embassy.

Taxes in Ireland

In general, the levying of tax in Ireland is considered relatively straightforward and fair, without many loopholes. Still, it is possible to plan your financial affairs in such a way as to minimize your tax bill. Unless your situation is uncomplicated, you should seek professional advice for specific tax-planning strategies in advance of a move to Ireland.

Although there has been some discussion of changing to a calendar year, the tax year in Ireland extends from April 6 to April 5 in the following year, with the tax return to be filed by January 31 after the end of the tax year. Thus, for the 1999/2000 tax year (April 6, 1999–April 5, 2000), one would need to file on or before January 31, 2001. Tax forms are available from the Revenue Commissioners. See the Resource Guide for contact information. Aided by a significant investment in technology, the Revenue Authorities have stepped up enforcement efforts in recent years, with a resulting increase in timely returns and income reported by the self-employed.

Tax Residency

Your liability for Irish tax depends on your status within three categories, as discussed in this section.

Resident versus Nonresident

There are two tests for tax residence in Ireland, both based on length of time spent in the country. You are a "tax resident" in Ireland if you spend 183 or more days there during the tax year (April 6 to April 5) or if you spend a total of 280 days or more in that year and the preceding year. Sometimes residency is advantageous, since it may entitle you to certain tax reliefs and allowances.

If you do not meet the length-of-time tests, you may elect to be considered a resident by submitting a written request to the Revenue Commissioners. You must indicate your intention to meet either the 183- or 280-day test for the following year.

A tax resident may be liable for tax on income less business expenses from a trade or profession carried on outside Ireland.

Ordinarily versus Not Ordinarily Resident

Ordinary residence is a separate concept, used to describe an individual's customary pattern of life. Someone who has resided in Ireland for three consecutive tax years becomes "ordinarily resident" at the start of the fourth tax year and, after leaving the country, continues to be ordinarily resident until the end of the third tax year of nonresidency. Thus, for up to three years after leaving Ireland, your worldwide income could be subject to Irish tax. It is, however, unlikely that any tax will be due once exemptions are applied for provisions of the double taxation agreement, remittance basis, income from business carried on outside Ireland, and non-Irish investment income. You technically must still file a return, however, for three years after you leave. As with a number of requirements in Ireland, this one is sometimes waived upon request.

Domiciled versus Not Domiciled

Another concept of Irish general law is "domicile," defined as permanent home. Your "domicile of origin" is fixed at birth. "Domicile of choice" is a country you chose to move to, reside in, and where you determine to stay permanently or indefinitely (not for a limited time or specific purpose). While you could be considered a tax resident in more than one country in a given tax year, you can be domiciled in one only. If you establish domicile in Ireland, you are subject to Irish income tax on worldwide income. If you maintain your permanent home in the United States or Canada, you will be liable for Irish tax on income that you earn in Ireland and income remitted to you in Ireland. Once the annual exemption is subtracted, capital gains tax (CGT) on assets held outside Ireland arises for the "not domiciled" only if gains are remitted to Ireland.

Your status in these three categories will have an impact on capital gains, capital acquisitions (gifts/inheritance), and property taxes and the reliefs that you may claim from these taxes. Your tax residence status also affects your eligibility for health coverage (discussed in Chapter 4).

Income Taxes

Compared to U.S. federal rates, income tax rates in Ireland seem high. It is well to remember, however, that Ireland has nothing comparable to the U.S. individual state income tax; nor does it levy any local, county, or city taxes. The Irish system for withholding tax from wages is called "pay as you earn" (PAYE). The self-employed and those employed and paid outside Ireland and the United Kingdom pay tax via the self-assessment system. A preliminary payment is due by November 1 in a given tax year, final payment by April 30. Refunds of overpayments include interest.

In Ireland, people ages sixty-five and over whose income falls beneath a specified threshold are exempt from paying any income tax. Marginal relief is available if total income is slightly over the limits, which change periodically. For the 1999/2000 tax year, a single person (age 65 or over) earning less than $9,750 or a married couple earning less than $19,500 escape income tax. Individuals under 65 pay no tax if their income is less than $6,150.

For all others, a personal allowance of the first $6,300 of income for a single individual ($12,600 for a married couple) is not taxed. Above that amount, and after allowances, the first $21,000 ($42,000 for a married couple) is taxed at a standard rate of 24 percent, while income above $21,000 (married, $42,000) is taxed at 46 percent.

People in Ireland perceive themselves as overtaxed and continue to clamor for rate decreases. The government has reduced tax levels in recent years and has indicated a goal of eventually reducing the standard rate to 20 percent.

Pay-Related Social Insurance

Pay-related social insurance (PRSI) pays for the costs of state-provided social welfare, disability, and pensions. Most employees pay 6.5 percent of first $38,100 earned and 2.0 percent of income above that for the health levy. The first $150 per week is exempt from PRSI but not from the levy. Employer rates and ceilings are higher than those of employees.

U.S. citizens who are resident in Ireland are liable for income tax only on the amount of earnings remitted to them in Ireland. For PRSI, however, the payment is calculated on gross earnings within the ceiling of $38,100. Those coming to Ireland on assignment for less than five years may remain in the U.S. Social Security payment system and thus not will have to pay PRSI. Those ages sixty-six and over do not pay PRSI, but they do pay the levy. Self-employed people pay PRSI on income, less capital allowances, up to $38,100, with the first $1,560 of income exempt, but subject to the levy.

Value Added Tax (VAT)

Value added tax (VAT) is a sales tax included in the price of many Irish goods and services. Unless it is exempt, each business or service provider charges VAT. The standard rate of VAT is 21 percent. A reduced rate of 12.5 percent applies to certain goods or services, including newspapers and periodicals, building services, fuels and electricity, food services, and hotel accommodations. A special rate of 4.0 percent applies to livestock, greyhounds, and the rental of horses. Some items, including food, stocks and other securities, educational supplies, passenger transportation, and funeral services, are exempt from VAT.

Capital Gains and Acquisitions

Capital gains tax (CGT) is due on gains realized from the disposal of certain assets at a rate of 20 percent, less a personal exclusion in 1999/2000 of $1,500. If you are resident or ordinarily resident, you may be liable to CGT on gains that you realize from the disposal of worldwide assets. If you are not domiciled in Ireland, your liability for gains on disposal of assets held outside of Ireland will be limited to what is remitted or actually paid to you in Ireland. Gains from the sale of a primary residence are exempt. There is also relief for those over age fifty-five when assets are transferred to certain relatives or gains do not exceed $375,000.

Capital acquisitions is a gift/inheritance tax with a number of provisions for relief, including inheriting a house from siblings or other close relatives if you have lived in it for a specified number of years. Gifts or inheritances from a spouse or parent are generally exempt.

DIRT Tax

Banks and building societies deduct deposit interest retention tax (DIRT) at the standard rate (24 percent for 1999/2000). Credit unions do not deduct DIRT; thus interest earned is fully taxable. The 2 percent health levy is also payable on interest earned. You may claim a refund of DIRT if you satisfy certain income and age criteria. Nonresidents who complete a declaration form may receive interest without deduction of DIRT.

Vehicle Registration Tax

Due when a vehicle is registered in Ireland, the Vehicle Registration Office calculates the vehicle registration tax as a percentage of the expected retail price or open market selling price (OMSP). You are exempt from this tax if you are transferring residence and can prove ownership and personal use of the vehicle for at least six months before your move. You must lodge your application at the Customs Office as soon as your vehicle arrives, and you may not sell the vehicle during the twelve months following registration. Unregistered vehicles may be confiscated.

Road Tax

You are liable for road tax the first time you use your car in a public place. You must show your vehicle registration certificate and proof of insurance. The tax is assessed based on engine size. For the 2.20-

liter engine of a Toyota Camry, for example, the annual tax is about $645. For smaller cars, which are easier to maneuver on narrow Irish roads, the tax is less. For instance, the annual road tax for engines between 1.2 and 1.8 liters ranges from $240 to $432. (Other automobile-related expenses and issues related to safe driving in Ireland are discussed in Chapter 7.)

Tax Breaks

The Irish government provides a variety of tax breaks, reliefs, and allowances. The status of your residency in Ireland as well as your income level determine your eligibility for many of them. The following is intended as a general guide only. Consult the Revenue Commissioners for the latest information.

Duty-Free Import of Personal Goods

You may import your personal belongings free of tax or duty provided that you can prove that you have owned them for at least six months and are moving them to Ireland in order to set up a primary or secondary residence. You should consider carefully, however, which items are worth transporting. (Chapter 8 presents guidelines for what to bring and what to leave behind.)

Allowances/Reliefs for Pensioners

Ireland has concluded a number of bilateral Social Security agreements with other countries. Expatriates who are recipients of Social Security and are legally resident in Ireland may be entitled to receive certain in-kind benefits received by Irish pensioners. Various allowances are available for those who meet certain criteria. These include:

- age allowance that applies in the tax year you or your spouse turns sixty-five.
- credits against your electricity or gas bill.
- free television license.
- reduction in telephone service and call charges.
- winter fuel allowance.
- rent relief for those ages fifty-five and over of $1,500 (single), $2,250 (widowed), or $3,000 (married) for rent paid for private accommodations.

- medical-expenses relief for most unreimbursed nonroutine medical and dental expenses (cost of doctor visits, maintenance or treatment in a hospital or approved nursing home, transport by ambulance, and specialized dental treatment).
- dental, optical, contact-lens, and hearing-aid benefits.
- an allowance for living alone.
- allowance for costs to employ a carer (someone who provides daily personal assistance).
- dependent-relative allowance for maintaining at your expense a son or daughter who lives with you and on whom you depend because of age or infirmity, or a relative incapable of self-care due to age or infirmity.
- allowance for the blind.
- vouchers to purchase butter.

Free Travel

A terrific perk in Ireland is free travel on public transport and some private bus and ferry services during all but certain hours. You qualify if you are permanently resident and age sixty-six or over, regardless of income. A spouse, regardless of age, may travel free when accompanying you. People under age sixty-six with certain disabilities also qualify; if they are not able to travel alone, they may be eligible for a free pass for anyone over age sixteen to accompany them.

Free travel for people meeting these criteria is available on all road and rail services of Ireland. These include Dublin Bus (Bus Atha Cliath), which serves the city and surrounding suburbs; the countrywide bus service, Bus Éirann; the rail service, Iarnród Éireann (including Mainline, Outer Suburban, and DART services); and some private bus and ferry services. Iarnród Éireann has a free travel anytime policy. Other services prohibit free travel in or near major cities on weekdays during hours of peak commute time. Organized group travel is also not included. Applications for a travel pass and a list of qualifying private services are available from the Pensions Services Office in Sligo.

Service Charges

Some local authorities levy charges for water and refuse-collection services. Tax reliefs are available to those who bear these costs—usually property owners rather than those who rent.

Artist's Exemption

Writers, visual artists, composers, and sculptors who reside in Ireland may claim exemption from tax on income they earn from the sale of their works if they are able to meet specific criteria. The work (for example, a book or other writing, play, painting, musical composition, or sculpture) or a body of work must be both creative and original and have either artistic or cultural merit. The Revenue Authorities determine eligibility on a case-by-case basis. They may consult with appropriate experts to evaluate the work, and they will confirm the income from the work as tax-free if the criteria are satisfied. Revenue Authorities will also provide advance opinions regarding eligibility for the exemption to those considering a move to Ireland and a formal determination when residency is established. They define "original and creative" as "any unique work which is brought into existence for the first time as an independent entity by the exercise of its creator's imagination."

Written works include the following nonfiction categories, as long as the essence of the work is original and the author casts new light on the subject: arts/literary criticism, arts/literary history, arts/literary diaries, essays, autobiographies, biographies, cultural dictionaries, literary translation, archaeology, and publications on topics of significant heritage value.

Works that do not meet the "original and creative" requirement are textbooks, newspaper and magazine articles, plays and music created for promotional purposes, utilitarian photographs and drawings, functional objects produced by processes rather than by hand, and functional objects produced by hand but by those not actively engaged as bona fide artists in the field of visual arts.

Financial Trade-Offs in Retirement

The transition to retirement affords a host of opportunities for embracing positive external and internal change. Approaching this life phase, we may decide we need and/or want to alter our approach to finances. These opportunities exist also for those who exchange the pressures of the workaday world for a life based more on personal enrichment.

Generally, financial needs decrease when official employment ceases. Working for a living can be an expensive pursuit. Expenses that attend employment often drain a substantial portion of our resources. Costs of commuting, maintaining an extra car, updating a business wardrobe, paying union dues or association membership fees, buying gifts for coworkers, and a variety of other expenses diminish our resources. Until they cease, we may not fully grasp the extent to which they deplete our spending power. Many people find that they realize considerable savings when they hang up their briefcase, toolbox, or uniform.

The transition to a new life also offers opportunities to try new things. Naturally, these sometimes cost money. Taking up golf or resolving to play more often, for example, will add to expenses, though in Ireland, except for the most exclusive clubs, greens fees are reasonable. A new interest in gardening, painting, or sailing may require an outlay for equipment, supplies, or class fees.

When retirement signals the end to a salary with regular increases and bonuses, a new sensibility may arise. Often we become less cavalier about spending. We learn or reaffirm the merits of being more mindful about where our money goes. We have a chance to consider more carefully what we truly need in our lives and how much we do—and don't—wish to spend for it.

The idea of trade-offs—giving up something to get something—becomes more evident in our retired lives. Often what we give up is an unhealthy, fast-paced lifestyle driven by obligation, habit, and wasteful ways. What we get is a chance to reconsider the value of our true resources, including one we tend to value more as we age—time. Many find that when there is time to enjoy life, the simpler pleasures yield greater enjoyment.

A shift to a slower pace, commonly found in Ireland, offers many opportunities to conserve resources without any sense of deprivation. When you have time to go to the library or explore second-hand book-stores, you may find it easy to pass up the $25.95 hardcover recently released in mainstream stores. When there is time to cook and perhaps even to grow vegetables, you can prepare a delicious, healthy, and economical feast rather than race to a take-out counter for a less-than-gratifying meal. When there is time to exercise, it is more pleasing to go outdoors than to squeeze in a quick workout at an expensive health club. Some people resolve to teach themselves basic auto maintenance and proceed to do their own oil changes and minor tune-ups, taking great satisfaction at learning a new skill that allows them to avoid an unnecessary expense.

Projecting financial needs, especially when contemplating an international relocation, requires you to gather information and examine the facts about costs. This process may help you gain a new sense of what you need—to have comfort, to be stimulated, and to maintain your health and well-being. Retirement confers the chance to reexamine your values, reinvent yourself, and refashion the role that money plays in your life.

HEALTH CARE

Ireland's health care policy is evolving in response to rising costs and an increase in the elderly population, which will escalate over the next decade. Recent years have brought major reforms to health care delivery in Ireland, and it is likely that others will follow. An effective strategy for addressing health needs and expenditures is to explore all options and select the one that corresponds best to your individual needs. Your general state of health and your need for medications, specialists, or alternative services are key considerations, as is your ability to pay to improve your coverage.

The Irish Health Care System

The health care system in Ireland is composed of both private and public hospitals and clinics. Ireland's Department of Public Health develops health policy and oversees eight regional health boards, located around the country. These health boards implement policy and administer health services for those who reside within their assigned geographical area. Inquiries about coverage, services, and benefits should be directed to the health board in your particular geographical area. (See the Resource Guide for locations.)

Irish health care is relatively progressive, and the country's health services are much less expensive than those in the United States. General practitioners (GPs) are routinely praised by expatriates in Ireland and physicians in North America as proficient professionals who provide excellent care. Nurses in Ireland consistently earn high marks as well.

Generally, health services are considered to be of higher quality in or near Dublin, Cork, Galway, and Limerick than in less populated areas of

Global Health Insurance

*S*ome U.S. citizens, especially those who frequently travel abroad, purchase supplemental medical insurance that covers overseas health care services, including medical air evacuation. Premiums are expensive, age-related, and subject to a range of deductibles. (For carriers that provide global health and travel insurance, see the Resource Guide.)

Your Medicare Coverage

*A*nyone who has struggled to decipher the complex system of Medicare—the U.S. health insurance program for people ages 65 and over or disabled—will find the Irish system a bit easier to understand. Though they have contributed throughout their working lives to U.S. Social Security, American citizens living abroad are not entitled to Medicare benefits, except for special situations requiring care in Mexico or Canada.

Thus, if you permanently leave the United States, Medicare will discontinue your eligibility. "Permanent" means an uninterrupted absence of more than ninety days from your defined geographic service area. If you visit Ireland to explore making a permanent move, continue to have your Medicare Plan B premium withheld, and then return to the United States after several months, your eligibility for coverage under Plan B may not be compromised. It may not be to your advantage to pay Plan B premiums, however, if you will be out of the United States for a longer period of time. You should be aware, though, that when you do sign up, your premium will be 10 percent higher for each twelve-month period that you could have been enrolled but elected not to be.

You may elect to continue to have Plan B premiums withheld while you are living outside the United States, even though you are not entitled to benefits. Then, if and when you return to the United States, you will not be penalized with a higher premium when you again become eligible

for Plan B. The value of this strategy will depend on your length of time out of the country and the extent of your cash resources. If you decide after careful consideration to discontinue your Medicare coverage, you will need to notify Medicare. Your eligibility to receive hospital insurance benefits under Plan A resumes whenever you return to the United States. Even if you have lived in Ireland for many years, if you visit the United States and require health care services that are normally provided under Plan A, you will be entitled to receive them.

Urgent and Emergency Care

For those absent only temporarily from the United States, many Medicare supplemental plans will cover medically necessary emergency care anywhere in the world at the nearest medical facility, usually at 80 percent coverage after you pay a deductible. You pay directly for the medical services, and the plans will reimburse you, usually within thirty days. Plans define "emergency care" as a medical emergency that includes severe pain or an injury, a sudden illness, or a suddenly worsening illness that you believe may cause serious danger to your health if you do not seek immediate medical care. "Urgently needed care" is an unexpected illness or injury that needs immediate medical attention and is not life-threatening. It is generally supposed to be provided by your primary care physician, unless you are temporarily out of the service area and cannot wait until you return home. Routine medical care will not be covered while you are away.

Ireland. Cardiology care is provided at many hospitals throughout Ireland, but bypass surgery is performed only in Dublin, at Blackrock Clinic and Mater Private Hospital; and in Cork, at University Hospital. Cardiac catheterization is now available in Dublin, Cork, Galway, and Limerick.

In Ireland, the small general practice, managed by one doctor, is increasingly being replaced by health clinics staffed by a variety of professionals, including doctors, nurses, physiotherapists, dietitians, and mental health counselors. Most every community, even in rural areas, has a health center that provides routine care. Yet amidst the move to more modern practice structures, Irish doctors still regularly make house calls! (Understandably, house calls are provided only for those who would have great difficulty traveling to the health center or doctor's office.)

While the public health care system is good by most standards, it does have drawbacks. The primary disadvantage is delayed access to care for certain nonemergency surgical procedures. Those who depend on the public health care system must often contend with long waiting lists. For example, it can take many months for a bed to open up for hip replacement or cardiac surgery. Quality of life can be compromised during these long waits. Emergency cases are moved to the top of the list, which is good for those needing immediate attention. It does, however, serve to make the wait grow longer for the rest.

There is much public disapproval of long waiting times, and Ireland's 1999/2000 budget included an allocation of $30 million to reduce them. Those who carry private health insurance have access to private hospitals and receive attention much sooner than those without this coverage. More than 30 percent of the population carry private health insurance.

Other criticisms of health care in Ireland include the crowded conditions at some hospitals and a level of neurologic care that does not compare well with European Union standards. The government is being urged to simplify the many layers of bureaucracy and to focus more attention on patient care. The Irish Patients' Association, a volunteer group, has been lobbying for the creation of a structured process for issuing complaints. The process for monitoring the competency of health care professionals is under scrutiny, as is ambulance response time. In heavily populated areas, an ambulance usually arrives within twenty minutes, but narrower roadways and wider population distribution may lengthen response time in outlying areas.

Comparing Costs

The following table provides a general comparison of customary charges for various health care services in the United States and Ireland. Actual costs depend on the type and level of health care coverage as well as the severity and complexity of the health need, medical complaint, or illness.

COMPARISON OF HEALTH CARE COSTS

Service	United States	Ireland
Office visit	$10*–$70	$27–$45
House call	not available	$45–$75
Hospital stay, per day	$0*–$2,000	$0–$260**
Emergency room	$35*–$800	$0–$30
Nursing home, per week	$646–$1,038	$525
Dentist		
Filling	$65	$30–$45
Extraction	$100	$55
Cleaning	$80–$100	$50
Crown	$600–$1,000	$300–$500

*Heath maintenance organization (HMO) co-pay
** Private patient

Entitlements to Health Care

All people who reside in Ireland, regardless of nationality, are entitled to free inpatient and outpatient public hospital care. The Department of Health defines "residency" as an intention to remain in Ireland for a minimum of one year. Evidence to support a claim of residency includes bank statements showing transfer of funds, a Green Book, work permits, and proof of rental or purchase of property.

EU citizens receive the same medical benefits as Irish citizens. Canadian and U.S. citizens who are nonresident, however, must pay for all care, though the rates will be less than those charged at home.

Category One

The free public hospital system is organized into two categories. Category One entitles those who qualify at a low income level to carry a medical card. Medical cardholders receive a number of benefits free of charge. These include general practitioner services, prescribed drugs and medications, and all inpatient services in public wards. Cardholders also receive outpatient hospital services; maternity and infant care; dental, ophthalmic and hearing services; and appliances (eyeglasses, hearing aids, wheelchairs, and walkers) free of charge.

About 30 percent of the population holds a medical card. The Department of Health revises qualifying guidelines every January, basing them on age and weekly gross income less amounts deducted for pay-related social insurance (PRSI) and allowances. The following were in effect for 1999:

MEDICAL CARD QUALIFICATIONS

Status	Under Age 66	Ages 66–69	Ages 70–79	Ages 80 and up
Single				
Living alone	$138.00	$150.00	$199.50	$209.48
Living with family	$122.25	$129.75	$172.57	$179.55
Married	$199.50	$223.50	$297.26	$312.23
Allowances				
Each child under 16				$24.00
Other dependents				$26.25
Rent, mortgage in excess of				$24.00
Cost of weekly travel to work in excess of				$21.75

Applying for a Medical Card

To apply for a medical card, contact the local health board for an application form and advice on how to complete the application. The medical card normally covers the cardholder, spouse, and any children under age sixteen. It also covers persons over age sixteen if they are financially dependent on the cardholder.

Those whose incomes exceed the requirement slightly and/or who have a considerable amount of medical expenses may in some cases still receive a card. The health board gives special consideration if you are unable to provide medical care for yourself or your family. Health boards may provide services free of charge in cases of hardship to people who are not normally eligible for these services.

Category Two

If you are resident in Ireland but do not meet the qualifications for a medical card, you automatically have Category Two eligibility. This entitles you to inpatient public hospital services subject to a maximum annual charge of $375 (ten days in any consecutive twelve-month period at the daily rate of $37.50). You need to keep receipts as evidence of payment. Once you exceed the daily charge limit, you are exempt from further inpatient charges. In hardship cases, health boards may waive the initial charges.

If you want to avoid the public wards, you may choose to be a private patient. You'll pay the charges for a semiprivate or private room (from $150 to $260 per day). You may select your doctor, but you will have to pay doctor and specialist (radiologist, pathologist, anesthetist) fees for this privilege.

Category Two status also covers all outpatient public hospital services, but not general practitioner visits, medications, and routine dental, eye, and hearing care. Accident and emergency care is subject to a charge of $18 if you arrive without a referral note from a doctor. Though Category Two does not cover equipment, the Health Board may be able to provide a loan of equipment or may pay part of the cost.

Prescription Drug Benefits

There are several programs that refund expenses for prescribed drugs and medications to those who do not qualify for the free prescription drugs that are provided to medical cardholders.

Drug Refund Scheme

Under the drug refund scheme (DRS), you may claim back costs in excess of a specific amount ($135 in 1999) in three consecutive calendar months (January to March, April to June, July to September, and October to December). Get receipts from the chemist (druggist) for any drug expenses you incur, and then apply for a refund from the local health board.

Drug Cost Subsidization Scheme

You qualify for the drug cost stabilization scheme (DCSS) if, in the opinion of your doctor, you have a long-term medical condition with an ongoing need for prescribed medicines. Obtain a form from the chemist, have your doctor fill it out, and then take it to the health board. You are then not charged for medicines costing more than $48 per month.

Long-Term Illness Scheme

People with specific illnesses or conditions receive free medications for their treatment. These illnesses or conditions include acute leukemia, cerebral palsy, cystic fibrosis, diabetes mellitus, diabetes insipidus, epilepsy, hemophilia, hydrocephalus, mental illness, multiple sclerosis, muscular dystrophy, Parkinson's disease, phenlyketonuria, and spina bifida.

Private Health Insurance

The Voluntary Health Insurance Board (VHI) is a semi-state organization, established in 1957 and, until recent years, the only alternative to the public system. With more than 1.4 million members, it continues to dominate the private insurance market.

Community Rating

Required by a European Union directive to open the way for competition, Ireland passed the Health Insurance Act of 1994. This act mandates several important provisions. Insurers must adhere to a policy of community rating, charging the same premium without regard to age, sex, or health status, except for a separate category for those under age eighteen. (An aside note: Community rating has all but disappeared in the United States. United Healthcare/AARP is the only carrier selling community-rated policies in most states, and only six states require insurers to offer them. In Ireland, however, there has been a solid commitment to maintaining a community-rated system.) Insurers must allow open enrollment, providing coverage for all who want to enroll. An insurer must offer lifetime coverage and thus cannot refuse coverage after someone is enrolled.

Competition for Market Share

Two companies are now authorized to sell private health insurance in Ireland. The Health Act of 1994 paved the way for British United Provident Association (BUPA) Ireland to enter the Irish market. It was launched in 1996 and now claims more than 50,000 members. VHI and BUPA Ireland offer an array of plans and rates.

With each of these insurers, you must join by age sixty-five. There are no rate changes over age eighteen. Premiums will not increase as a result of making a claim or increased age; when these insurers raise premiums, they do so across the board for all insured. Premiums may be paid monthly or annually. Age is a factor in determining the length of waiting periods before coverage begins. And while premiums are very low by U.S. standards, the waiting periods are much, much longer. Benefits are immediately available, however, for any treatment resulting from an accident.

In 1998 BUPA Ireland's annual rates for individual coverage ranged from $308 for the "Essential" program, to $425 for its mid-range "Essential Plus," to $1,526 for "Essential Gold" coverage. VHI rates are comparable. Generally, BUPA is a bit cheaper at the lower end of market, while VHI charges less for its higher-end policy. BUPA includes some forms of preventive screening and alternative therapies, such as acupuncture, chiropractic, and homeopathy, but VHI offers a somewhat wider choice of health care practitioners and hospitals.

Group rates offer a discount and apply to professional organizations of six or more people. Many companies and credit unions run group programs.

Tax Reliefs

Those who opt for private insurance may claim a refund at the standard tax rate for premiums and for any expenses they incur above a deductible minus payments received from the health board or insurance companies. They must provide receipts and complete tax form MED-1.

Health Promotion in Ireland

Within the Department of Health, a health promotion unit coordinates various campaigns to influence health maintenance behaviors among the Irish. One area of emphasis is a reduction in the number of people who smoke, an effort supported by ASH, an antismoking lobby group. The percentage of smokers among the Irish population has fallen from 40 percent in the late 1970s to 28 percent currently. Smoking among teenagers remains a major concern.

The leading cause of death in Ireland is coronary heart disease. The Irish Heart Foundation supports campaigns to encourage smoking cessation, better diet, and regular exercise. Similar campaigns urge moderation in drink and emphasize the health toll of alcohol-related illness, accidents, and absenteeism. Suicide among young men is another health concern that receives widespread attention. One focus of health promotion in Ireland relates to people's risk for skin cancer from overexposure to sun. Although the tanning index in Ireland will never rival that of Arizona, skin cancer is the most commonly diagnosed cancer in Ireland. The Irish Cancer Society coordinates campaigns to raise public awareness about the dangers of excessive exposure to the sun's rays.

Special Health Services

Respite Care

Respite care for people with disabilities seeks to relieve their isolation by providing temporary health and social services, which also offer relief to family members who serve as their primary caregivers. Respite care facilities are found within each of the regional health boards. Some provide assistance across the board, while others specialize in services for learning, mental health, or specific physical disabilities; or for children or adults. Some, like the Irish Wheelchair Association and Muscular Dystrophy Ireland, provide services in the home. The Alzheimer's Society of Ireland offers respite care at the Rosemary Centre facility in Tralee, County Kerry. Individual health boards can advise on services within their region. The National Rehabilitation Board provides a guide to respite care facilities in all health board regions.

Irish Cancer Society

In addition to funding research and sponsoring educational and health promotion programs, the Irish Cancer society provides a confidential telephone "Helpline," staffed by nurses, and offers support and guidance for patients and families. It provides in-home nursing care and family support. The Society also operates a night nursing service, providing care for cancer patients who are unable to afford it.

Cairde

Established in 1985, Cairde is Ireland's largest voluntary provider of support services for individuals and families affected by HIV and AIDS.

Volunteers provide one-on-one practical and emotional support, including help with household tasks.

National Disability Resource Center

A division of the National Rehabilitation Board, the National Disability Resource Center (NDRC) is an information clearinghouse for all issues related to diabilities. The Resource Center's Dublin office also displays equipment designed or adapted for people with disabilities, and provides ordering information.

Patient Support Groups

There are a number of grassroots support groups for people coping with any of a variety of diseases and conditions, including asthma, diabetes, lupus, arthritis, cancer, glaucoma, osteoporosis, and stroke. These groups provide a valuable network for those seeking support. (See the Resource Guide for contact information.)

Before You Move

Regardless of which strategy you employ to ensure adequate health coverage, there are several things you should attend to before undertaking an international relocation:

- Have a thorough physical and schedule dental, eye, and hearing exams.
- Allow time to schedule and complete health care procedures within your current health coverage. Have your teeth cleaned, fillings replaced, eyewear prescriptions filled, and any labwork or screening or surgical procedures performed that you may require.
- Organize all of your medical records, including forms from previous health insurance claims.
- Bring an extra pair of eyeglasses and/or contact lenses and your current prescriptions for vision correction.
- Be sure that you know the generic name of any medications you require, and plan to transport an ample supply. Keep your medications in their original containers rather than in unmarked pillboxes. Bring copies of your prescriptions and a letter from your doctor confirming your need for specific medications.

- Check with an Irish embassy or consulate to verify the availability of a medication in Ireland.
- If you have allergies or other unique health problems, consider wearing a medical alert bracelet or carrying a letter from your doctor explaining the desired treatment should you become ill.
- Verify the status of your current coverage for emergency medical services outside your home country, including any provided with gold credit cards. Check with each carrier for specific provisions and restrictions. Always carry policy numbers and proof of insurance.
- Carry the address and phone number of the U.S. or Canadian embassy in Dublin. Remember that should you be injured or become ill in Ireland, embassy staff will provide a list of local doctors, dentists, and specialists and inform your family or friends.
- For additional information and guidance about insurance matters, contact your state insurance commission, insurance department, or advisory program.

COUNTRY COTTAGE, VILLAGE HABITAT, CITY FLAT: FINDING YOUR HOME

Owning a home is considered nearly a birthright in Ireland. Nearly 80 percent of the population are homeowners, a level far above that in North America and continental Europe. And in Ireland, people often live in the same home for most of their adult lives, rather than moving frequently.

Economic and social change, evident in so many aspects of Irish life, has also influenced housing trends. Younger people might no longer live in the home of their parents until they marry. Instead, encouraged by better job opportunities and higher incomes, many are opting to buy property. Members of the burgeoning middle class are now more likely to trade up for increased space, additional bedrooms, a larger garden (yard), and "mod cons" (modern conveniences like dishwashers, microwaves, laundry facilities, and superior heating and plumbing systems). Those who are well off may buy a second home in the country. Urban pioneers buy houses in less than fashionable areas of one of Ireland's major cities and transform these fixer-uppers into lovely homes, renovating structures and systems while retaining their character.

Changing social dynamics, rapid income growth, and readily available financing at historically low mortgage rates have fueled an unprecedented demand for housing. Returning emigrants and home buyers from abroad are also contributing to this demand. There are no restrictions on the purchase or rent of residential property in Ireland. Anyone who is not a European Union national and wishes to purchase agricultural land over five acres, however, will need to seek approval from the Irish Department of Agriculture.

Targeting an Area

The budget-conscious will want to avoid areas with the strongest demand, which command the highest prices. Unless you have a compelling reason to locate within a 1,000-kilometer (60-mile) radius of

Dublin, it would be best to avoid this region's rapid growth, high demand, skyward spiral in prices, and traffic jams. While Dublin has much to recommend it, it might be wise to reserve the "Fair City" for an occasional outing and seek housing in a less expensive area. Galway is also a wonderful city, with Old World charm and an arts scene that appeals to many. Its price tag, however, has been steadily increasing over the past few years. If city life is highly desirable, you might consider Cork or Limerick, where housing will cost a bit less.

In addition to the calmer pace they offer, smaller towns and rural areas are generally more economical than Ireland's cities. However, locations that are popular with tourists (such as the town of Kinsale, the area in and around Killarney, the Dingle Peninsula, and the entire Connemara region), are more expensive than average. Coastal areas are much more expensive than the area in the center of Ireland known as the Midlands. Some of the lesser-known counties offer the best bargains. While they may lack the drama of a rugged coastline, counties like Roscommon, Longford, Laois, Offaly, Cavan, and Leitrim yield better buys, captivating vistas, and a quieter pace.

In Northern Ireland, demand has not exceeded supply to the extent that it has in the Republic. Thus, an investment here will buy more house than in many places south of the border. While concerns about political strife have some merit, the momentum continues for creating a lasting peace and is further fueled by economic progress. Many areas in the North are exquisitely beautiful. Thus, if the goal is to find good value at an affordable price, all but the most nervous may want at least to consider the North. (This area and all regions of Ireland are profiled in Chapter 6.)

Housing in Ireland versus North America

Referred to as "semidetached" or a "duplex," two houses that share a common wall are common in Ireland's cities and towns, as are row homes, also called townhouses. Houses and apartments in Ireland will generally be smaller than those in North America. A home of 125 square meters (1,346 square feet) is fairly standard in Ireland, though newer houses often are somewhat roomier. Rooms and yards tend not be as large as those in North America. An apartment with 80 square meters (861 square feet), for example, will often be advertised in Ireland as "spacious." While newer and more expensive homes may feature large, walk-in closets, closet space typically is not overgenerous. The space in living areas and bedrooms can be cramped, though one bedroom in most homes will usually accommodate a bed that is larger than a double.

Kitchens may also be smaller than North Americans are used to. In typical apartments and houses, shelf space and overall storage capacity may be limited. Although colossal side-by-side refrigerator-freezer units are now more available for sale in Ireland, most people are happy with a "fridge" that is comparable to what would be considered apartment size in the United States. The freezer section of these appliances will be fairly small, too. Cookers (stoves) are smaller as well. They are fueled by electricity or gas, though in rural areas older stoves that use turf, coal, or wood are not uncommon. These ranges may also provide primary or supplementary heat for the home.

Less ample living spaces do offer certain advantages. Smaller homes and apartments are easier to clean and maintain. They discourage the tendency to accumulate too much "stuff." A smaller lot means that yard work is less demanding, leaving more time and energy for other pursuits. If smaller spaces feel too confining, however, there are approaches to decorating that help to create a more open feeling in them. The use of light, neutral, or pastel colors on walls and ceilings will serve to expand rooms visually. Other elements that create a sensation of spaciousness include the use of mirrors, the choice of simpler lines and lighter woods in furniture, and sticking to plain patterns in area rugs, upholstery, and draperies. Multi-use furniture, like an ottoman that doubles as a storage center for linens or a sleeper sofa to accommodate guests, helps to make limited space more efficient.

If a bathroom has been updated, it may feature a separate heating element and a power shower. These electric devices produce a stronger stream than the paltry dribble that issues from many showers of older plumbing systems. Still, water pressure overall is never forceful, and some toilet tanks seem to take forever to refill. Even a power shower rarely approaches the intensity of most North America showers. I often ask my Irish friends if when they visit the United States and take a shower, they don't feel as though someone has turned a fire hose on them!

Modern comforts, including double-paned windows and central heating systems, are now found in many dwellings in Ireland. Older properties lacking these amenities still have considerable charm. It is hard to resist the romantic appeal of a thatched-roof cottage or even a medieval castle. But beware winter winds, which may dispatch gusty drafts through old, poorly sealed windows.

Rent Before You Buy

Regardless of how enthralled you are with Ireland, it makes good sense to rent for a while before purchasing property. Ireland's power to seduce is renowned. It is important to give yourself a chance to discover if the infatuation will evolve into enduring devotion. If you've spent time in Ireland as a tourist, that experience will not necessarily serve you well. Before investing in property you need to experience Irish life from the perspective of a dweller rather than a vacationer.

Purchasing property abroad requires careful consideration of your "must have" versus "nice to have" needs, thorough planning, and careful comparisons—all of which take time. Thus, unless a property falls into your lap through the good fortune of an inheritance, renting for at least six months up to a couple of years before purchasing is strongly advised. There are indeed bold (some might say rash) people who on their first visit to Ireland spot a bargain property, fall in love, and snap it up. This was not uncommon in years past, when prices were quite low. Adjusting to life in another country is best, however, when you retain the ability to reverse plans if you are not content.

The ideal approach to housing is first to secure suitable rental accommodations central to areas that hold appeal. As a renter, you will be able to establish a base from which to investigate those areas where you might like to live. Living for a while in or near a potential locale will allow you to begin to build a network in the community. Among many other benefits, such a network may provide advance information about desirable houses or sites that may come onto the market.

Costs to Rent

Monthly rents can range from a modest $225 to $300 for a "bedsit" (efficiency apartment) to an obscene $7,000 for a three-bedroom luxury penthouse apartment in Ballsbridge, a posh Dublin location. Rents are much steeper in urban centers than rural areas. Most expensive of all is Dublin, where two-bedroom apartments below $975 per month are rare. Rents are lower in Galway, Limerick, and Cork Cities, where a similar apartment would run between $600 and $900. Rents are much cheaper overall in small towns or rural areas, where a two-bedroom apartment would range between $375 and $600. One-bedroom apartments are in high demand and thus more scarce.

Most rental apartments and houses come furnished, and landlords will sometimes discount the rent if you agree to sign a long-term (two- or three-year) lease. Rent qualifies for tax relief subject to certain limits. Current with the 1999 budget, those under age fifty-five can claim relief of $750 per year as a tax credit at the standard income tax rate. Those ages fifty-five and over are entitled to relief of $1,500 per year at their top rate of tax.

Locating Rentals

To find suitable accommodations, network among friends and relatives. Check ads in local and national papers. Several firms assist people to find accommodation. One of the largest is Home Locators in Dublin and Galway. Others include Celtic Accommodation and Apartmentfinders. (See the Resource Guide for details.)

Examples of recent ads for apartment and house rentals:

- Garrettstown, near Kinsale, County Cork: "New 4-bedroom house near Garrettstown beach, great ocean views. Pine floors and doors, master bedroom with ensuite shower room, fully fitted kitchen, dining room, sliding door to patio, utility washer/dryer, dishwasher. Sitting room with stone fireplace, TV, video, garden. Central heat. $825 per month."

- Kinsale, County Cork: "Three bedrooms, living room, kitchen/dining room, tastefully furnished. Small enclosed garden with shed. $975 per month."

"Period-style house on 3.5 acres of orchards, lawns and paddocks including croquet lawn and dog runs. Five large bedrooms, 3 bathrooms, 3 reception rooms, kitchen, utility, playroom and study/office, garages, stables, kennels. $1,350 per month."

"Viking Wharf townhouse overlooking marina, estuary and outer harbor. Fully fitted kitchen, 2 baths, garage, balcony. $1,050 per month."

"Two-bedroom ground floor apartment on quiet, residential tree-lined avenue, five-minute walk from town center. Off-street secure parking. Small patio. $600 per month."

- Sandycove, near Kinsale, County Cork: "Lovely bungalow with superb views, garden, patio, 3 large bedrooms, one ensuite, fully fitted kitchen and utility. $1,200 per month."
- Dame St., Dublin City, County Dublin: "One bedroom, stylish, fully equipped first floor apartment, living room with galley kitchen, washer/dryer, double bedroom with fitted wardrobe, tiled bath with shower. $900 per month, higher rent for shorter-term lease."
- Salthill, County Galway: "Luxury one-bedroom apartment. $525 per month."
  "Person to share house, own room. $45 per week."
  "Exceptional three-bedroom semi-detached house. $900 per month."
- Galway City, County Galway: "Three-bed house, all mod cons, close to university. $225 per week."
  "Two-bedroom apartment, private parking. $720 per month."
  "New two-bedroom apartment, fully furnished, all mod cons, private access. $863 per month."
  "New three-bedroom penthouse apartment, panoramic views over Galway Bay, secure parking. $1,275 per month."
- Mount Juliet, Thomastown, County Kilkenny: "Home on country estate with golf course. 2/3 bedrooms, all ensuite, walk-in closets, lounge, dining area, w/c, kitchen. $2,250 per month."
- Dunboyne, County Meath: "Three-bed duplex townhouse, close to shops and village. 1,200-sq. ft. (111.5 square meters), fully furnished. Bathroom upstairs and shower room downstairs. Kitchen has all appliances. Alarm system, gas central heat. Close to IBM, Intel, and Hewlett Packard. $1,050 per month."
- Dunshaughlin, County Meath: "New, fully furnished, semi-detached 3-bedroom house, ten minutes walk to village, master bedroom ensuite, guest WC, rear garden. $975 per month."
- Navan, County Meath: "250-acre estate on Blackwater River, 30 miles north of Dublin. Completely renovated castle, central heat and all mod cons. Golf nearby. $9,000 per month."
- Castlerea, County Roscommon: "Imposing period residence on 2 acres of beautiful grounds and orchards. Entrance hall, drawing room with marble fireplace and bay window, study, sitting

room also with marble fireplace and bay window, cloak room, kitchen with modern built-in units and full range of appliances, utility room, 6 bedrooms (2 ensuite), main bathroom. Furnished, oil-fired central heat. Two hours' drive from Dublin, one hour from Galway. $1,800 per month."

- County Waterford: "Three-bedroom house, Waterford City center, gas central heating, fully furnished. $135 per week."

  "Three bedroom apartment, kitchen, living room, 2 baths, fully self-contained, all mod cons, on beach front in Tramore. $150 per week."

- Brittas Bay, County Wicklow: "Five-bed family house on superb acre site beside beach and golf club. 3 baths, 2 ensuite, 2 large reception rooms with open fireplaces, fully fitted kitchen, fully equipped office, lighted tennis court, basketball court. Tastefully furnished. $2,250 per month."

Buying Property

Once you've lived in Ireland for a time, you'll have a better sense of the kind of locale you prefer, whether city, town, small village, or a rural setting.

Consider also which location will best meet your needs. How close do you want to be to shops and banks, hospitals and clinics, entertainment and recreation, educational facilities, and public transportation? Before you begin your property search, determine how much you can afford. Lenders will be happy to meet with you and offer advice on various mortgage programs and to assist you in the purchase process. Then determine what type of property you want to buy. A convenient apartment, modest bungalow, traditional cottage, new townhouse, or old farmhouse each affords advantages and disadvantages. What features can you live without, and which are essential to your sense of well-being? Although it is helpful to be able to articulate your ideal purchase in order to focus your search, keeping flexible will ease the process. You may have to settle for your second choice in property style in order to secure your first choice in location, or vice versa.

Leasehold versus Freehold

Property in Ireland may be held either in freehold or under a lease.

"Freehold" is ownership of the property and the land it stands on, and may continue in perpetuity. "Leasehold" is a form of property ownership wherein the owner leases to a leaseholder or tenant for a fixed number of years. The tenant or leaseholder may pay "ground rent," usually a modest amount.

High Demand Expected to Ease

Over the past decade, the explosive demand for housing in Ireland has driven prices up dramatically. In some areas, older homes (which may be better built and offer more character) are more expensive than new homes of comparable size and in similar locations. Homes are much more expensive in major urban areas, especially in and within commuting distance of the Dublin area. As of September 1998, new homes in Dublin averaged $190,607; secondhand homes, $221,423. Communities within a 1,000-kilometer (60-mile) radius of Dublin are booming, too, and have spawned a throng of rail and motorway commuters. Galway is Ireland's fastest-growing city; the average price of a new home is $136,830, and for a secondhand home, $148,491. Waterford City's average secondhand home price compares favorably at $109,535, while the price for new homes, $142,134, is higher than Galway's. Homes in Cork and Limerick Cities are not quite so expensive. Cork's average price for a new home is $130,785, and secondhand home prices average $130,092. In Limerick the range is $118,170 for new and $116,186 for secondhand.

New construction is under way everywhere in Ireland, in response to rising need. Department of Environment statistics indicate that more than 40,000 new housing units were completed in 1998, the highest rate of new homes construction in Europe. The availability of a greater number of new homes has begun to stabilize rising costs. Higher inventories should also ease the situation for those people who have found it difficult to enter the market.

Despite the meteoric rise in prices, housing in Ireland is still less expensive than many places in North America and Europe. A patient search will uncover properties at good value. The days of capturing a quaint cottage for $20,000 are no more, but it is still possible to find bargain properties, especially if one avoids high-demand areas.

Economists and real estate experts express a range of opinions about the long-term direction of housing prices in Ireland. As mentioned above, the pace of price increases has slowed as the rate of new-home building has begun to meet demand, though prices for more expensive Dublin homes continue to appreciate. Some experts have predicted a crash in home values, similar to what occurred in Britain and Boston in the 1980s. Others feel that such a bust is not likely ever to hit the Irish property market. With interest rates at the lowest levels in forty years, some predict that demand—and prices—will continue to increase.

Whatever direction prices follow, careful evaluation of a range of issues before you buy should be mandatory. As many financial experts suggest, the primary purpose of a home is a place to live. Investment goals should generally be a secondary consideration.

The Irish government has taken steps to alleviate pressures on the housing market. Legislation spurred by the release in 1998 of the Bacon Report made real estate a less attractive vehicle for investors. Since one third of all properties in Dublin in 1997 were bought by investors, the government sought to remove some incentives in order to improve access to the market for owner-occupiers, especially first-time buyers. While some inventory was freed up, investors continued to buy rental properties, putting the rental market under enormous strain. Corporations seeking apartments for employees, and renters, have contributed to high demand.

The government is being pressured to enact other changes that will ease housing pressures. A second Bacon Report in 1999 urged the government to consider additional reforms, including an increase in the tax relief for renters. It is likely that over the next several years the government will increase housing-density levels, Ireland's being among the lowest in Europe. Changes to enable the rezoning of land for building are likely, as are reforms of a planning system that often is felt to obstruct rather than control new construction and renovation.

Finding a Property

There are many ways to find properties to buy in Ireland. Check national and local papers. Ask neighbors and folks in the local pub or supermarket. Drive or walk around and look for signs that say FOR SALE. Visit the offices of estate agents (realtors), or hop on the Internet, where you can often view photos and data and also contact the appropriate estate agent. Estate agents routinely provide listings of available properties (mostly of secondhand houses). Register with several, inform them of your requirements, and ask to be notified when properties that fit your criteria come onto the market.

When you view a property that interests you, be sure to visit more than once, at different times of day, and in various kinds of weather. Note the condition of the structure, walls, and floors; and the heating, electrical, and plumbing systems. Determine which appliances are included. Be sure of your entitlement to water and access to the property. Walk around the area, and ask people you see about the property and the neighborhood. You should also check with the local office of An Bord Pleanala to find out if any developments are planned nearby that could affect the value of the property.

If you are bargain hunting in a less-than-fashionable area, you might check with local police to alleviate any worries about crime rates or to eliminate your choice of this area if crime might be a problem. Beyond the minimal inspection required by a lender, you should engage an architect, surveyor, engineer, or estate agent to provide a detailed evaluation of a secondhand property in order to uncover any major problems that may exist. There are no full-disclosure provisions; in the Irish secondhand real estate market, what you buy is what you get.

Here are some typical properties from recent ads:

- Carlow Town, County Carlow: "New apartment development, prime waterfront site, short distance from town center. One, two, three bedroom apartments and penthouses. Parking included. First time buyer's grant. Close to golf courses, angling, horse riding. $101,925–$146,925."
- Dowra, County Cavan: "Three-bedroom cottage, completely remodeled, magnificent views of mountains, close to River Shannon and Lough Allen, two miles from village. Open plan ground floor, double-glazing and central heat. Complete privacy. Includes 13 acres of surrounding land. Offers in the $90,000s."
- Broadford, County Clare: "Thatched house with sitting room, kitchen, bathroom, dining room, 2 bedrooms, 2 baths. Kennels and sheds on elevated site with excellent views. Gas fired heating. Within walking distance of village. $104,250."
- Clonlara, County Clare: "Cottage in need of repair, 3 bedrooms, kitchen, utility room. Hay barn, old sheds, ⅓ acre. No heating. $58,500."
- Kilkee, County Clare: "New 2-bedroom townhouses. $112,500–$127,500."

- Scarriff, County Clare: "4 bedroom bungalow, living room with loft, kitchen. Garage. ¾ acre, fronts onto Lough Derg, own harbor. Adjoining site can also be purchased. $277,500."
- Kinsale, County Cork: "New, spacious duplex apartment with garage. Panoramic view of inner harbor. Well-fitted kitchen, spacious living room with balcony, 3 bedrooms, 2 full baths. Walk to town center. Close to yacht club and marina. $300,000."
- Mitchelstown, County Cork: "Detached, 6 bedrooms, lounge, dining room, kitchen, bath, dual heating, beautiful surroundings on 1.5 acres. $270,000."
- Skibbereen, County Cork: "Two-bedroom cottage on 1 acre, fine rural views, open fireplace, tiled roof, electricity, phone, water and sewage, good condition but could be modernized. Two miles to town. $52,500."
- Killiney, County Dublin: "Ground floor, 2 bedroom apartment, 820 sq. ft., south facing patio, close to beach and transportation. $187,500."
- Enniskillen, County Fermanagh: "New waterfront apartments and townhouses. $108,277–$173,243."
- Galway City, County Galway: "Two-bedroom first floor apartment overlooking canal. Two balconies facing east and south. $190,500."
- Castle Island, County Kerry: "Spacious bungalow on 33 acres. Accommodation for 40 greyhounds. Sitting room, kitchen, dining room, 5 bedrooms, bath. $225,000."
- Listowel, County Kerry: "Picturesque cottage in rolling countryside on ½ acre sheltered site, five minutes to town. Well maintained, two bedrooms, high ceilings, small rear lawn. Offers over $63,000."
- Tarbert, County Kerry: "Detached house with sitting room, dining room, kitchen, utility room, garage converted to bedroom, shower and 2 toilets, 3 bedrooms, bath upstairs. Built 1935. Large south facing back garden, 2 sheds. $112,500."
- Naas, County Kildare: "Two-bedroom, 100-year-old cottage on ⅓ acre of sheltered gardens a few miles from town in quiet country setting. $135,000."
- Tullogher, County Kilkenny: "Two-bedroom cottage on ¼ acre of mature gardens. Excellent condition, double glazed windows, central heat, large shed, carport with cobbled driveway. $100,500."

- Carrigaholt, County Limerick: "Lovely old style cottage, 3 bedrooms, new windows and roof, acre. $45,000."
- Limerick, County Limerick: "Terraced 3-story house with basement, converted to 2 flats, each with living room, kitchen, shower room and 3 bedrooms. Income of approximately $232.50 per week. $123,000."
  "New development of 2- and 3-bedroom townhouses. $99,000–$126,375."
- Murroe, County Limerick: "Extended cottage with sitting room, kitchen/dining area, bathroom, 3 bedrooms, old garage, 2 acre. New roof in 1995. $93,750."
- Rathkeale, County Limerick: "17TH century Gate Lodge with stone extension, entrance hallway, living room, 2 bedrooms, bath, kitchen with 2 rooms overhead. Double glazed windows, electric heat, drylined walls, recently rewired, 1.1 acres with planning permission for 2 houses. $142,500."
- Drogheda, County Louth: "Three-bedroom, two-story house, modern kitchen, central heat, front garden, rear patio, off street parking. Mahogany and marble surround fireplace. $112,500."
- Termonfeckin, County Louth: "Two-bedroom apartment, bright and spacious, wood floors, antique open fireplace. One mile to beach and golf club. Intercom security system, double glazed windows, walled communal gardens. Annual service charge of $450. $120,000."
- Castlebar Town, County Mayo: "3-bedroom bungalow on large site close to town. Excellent condition throughout. $105,000."
- Boyle, County Roscommon: "Three-bedroom extended cottage on ¾ acre, central heat, garage. Quiet location with views of Lough Arrow. $60,000."
- Ballina, County Tipperary: "1 bedroom bungalow, kitchen with fireplace, living room with fireplace, bath, oil central heat, front and rear gardens. $97,500."
- Cullen, County Tipperary: "Detached house on 8 acres, built 1895. Sitting room, dining room, kitchen, 4 bedrooms, bath. Solid fuel heating, double glazed windows, garage, 2 sheds, large old stone cow house, elevated site with excellent views, $187,500."
- Monard, County Tipperary: "Thatched cottage, 1.2 acres, 2 double bedrooms, bath, hall, living room, kitchen. $67,500."

- Tipperary, County Tipperary: "New development of 16 3- and 4-bedroom homes, 3-bedroom semi-detached and 4-bedroom detached. $94,500–$112,500."
- Barntown, County Wexford: "Large family home, ¾ acre. Views, stone entrance, 4 bedrooms, studio, landscaped, patio. $121,500."
- Ashford, County Wicklow: "Retirement bungalows in Clonnmannon Active Retirement Village. Set on 21 acres. Brick, central heat, fitted kitchen/breakfast nook, sitting room with open fire, fitted wardrobes in bedrooms. Buyers must be over age 50 and satisfy certain health and financial criteria. 45-year leasehold, can be resold. Annual service fee for window cleaning, exterior paint, grounds maintenance. Country club with dining room, games room and bar. $105,000–$135,000 plus $5,445 entry fee."

Mortgages

Mortgages are obtained through banks and building societies. A down payment of at least 10 percent is customary. Rates for variable loans in 1999 ranged between 4.85 and 5.5 percent, the lowest level in forty years. It may pay to compare charges for various mortgage services among several lenders. Most will lend up to 90 percent of a property's value, provided that this amount does not exceed 2.5 times the annual income of the primary buyer plus 1 time the income of a partner. Many lenders offer a discount on the interest rate in the first year, and some will waive the application fee.

Lenders require copies of recent bank and other financial statements. In the seller's market of recent times, getting pre-approved for a mortgage provides an edge.

Most people in Ireland take out twenty-year mortgages, but other terms, from ten to thirty-five years, are available. There are fixed, variable, split, and capped rate loans. With a fixed rate the interest rate is fixed for a predetermined term, usually from one to ten years, after which you either agree to another fixed rate for a set term or change to the prevailing variable rate. Some lenders offer a split rate, in which you repay part of your mortgage at a fixed rate and the rest at a variable rate. With a capped loan, the interest rate is guaranteed not to rise above the cap but can be lowered if rates fall. Most fixed mortgages charge early repayment penalties, but typically there are no such penalties with variable and capped mortgages. Lenders routinely give better rates to new customers.

Most people select an annuity as opposed to an endowment loan. With an annuity loan you repay interest and principal each month, paying more interest in the early years of loan and more on the principal as the loan matures. Lenders require a separate life insurance policy to pay off the mortgage in the event of death.

There are a number of lenders in the mortgage business as well as mortgage brokers who will shop for best deals. Examples of current offers on twenty-year annuity mortgages of $75,000:

AIB:

Variable: 5.5%, monthly payment: $514.50
1-year fixed: 4.4%, $469.50
5-year fixed: 5.0%, $494.25

EBS Building Society:

Variable: 4.85%, $489.00, year one; 5.1%, $498.75 thereafter
1-year fixed: 4.4%, $470.25
5-year fixed: 5.1%, $498.75

ICS Building Society

Variable: 4.99%, $494.25, year one; 5.49%, $515.25 thereafter
1-year fixed: 4.4%, $470.25
5-year fixed: 5.1%, $498.75

With an endowment loan, the borrower takes out an insurance policy that repays the loan either upon death or after a number of years (usually twenty). Only interest is paid on the loan. Each monthly payment consists of the premium on the insurance policy and interest on the loan. Nothing is paid on the principal until the insurance policy matures. You get no automatic life insurance with an annuity loan, but again, lenders usually require you to take out a separate policy.

Other Costs

Carefully reviewing all fees with the lender well before a purchase is good practice. Various fees are discussed in this section.

Solicitor's Fees

It is customary to engage a solicitor (lawyer) to handle the sale. Legal fees are negotiable; thus it may be possible to do better than the standard rate of 1.5 percent of the purchase price. Establish the solicitor's fee in advance of a purchase.

Inspection, Title Search, Insurance

Required by the lender to establish market value of the property, an inspection will cost around $150. A more comprehensive evaluation, recommended in order to identify any defects in secondhand houses and to estimate the cost to repair them, will run approximately $450. The title search and registration range between $225 and $525, and miscellaneous fees may add another $250.

Insurance coverage for your mortgage, generally $12 to $18 per month, may be expanded to include critical illness. You will also have to take out homeowner insurance, often discounted for those who are over age fifty, belong to community-alert programs, and install burglar and smoke alarms and special door and window locks. Discounted premiums range between $25 and $35 per month (higher in city locations).

Stamp Duty

While there is no longer a residential-property tax in Ireland, a so-called stamp duty is payable on the purchase of all secondhand houses. It is charged at the following rates:

$0–$90,000	0%
$90,001–$150,000	3%
$150,001–$255,000	4%
$255,001–$375,000	5%
$375,001–$750,000	7%
Over $750,000	9%

The purchase of a new house smaller than 125 square meters (1,346 square feet) is exempt from stamp duty. Everyone pays a stamp duty on the mortgage deed itself of $1.50 per $1,500 borrowed on loans over $30,000, up to a maximum of $750.

Tax Relief and Grants

First-Time Buyers Grant

First-time buyers of new homes that meet square-meter requirements are also eligible for a grant of $4,500, provided that they occupy the dwelling for five years. The Irish Home Builder Association has urged the government to expand this grant to $9,000 and extend it to secondhand homes as well. While this did not happen within the 1999 Budget, it may yet come to pass.

Mortgage Interest Relief

Restricted to mortgages on property in Ireland, this relief is calculated as a tax credit at the standard rate, currently 24 percent. The maximum relief that you can claim depends on your marital status and whether you are a first-time buyer. First-time buyers are entitled to extra relief during the initial five years of the mortgage term. Annual interest ceilings for calculation purposes are $7,500 for a married couple, $5,400 for a widowed person, and $3,750 for single taxpayers.

To calculate tax relief, multiply annual interest up to the ceiling by 80 percent (100 percent if a first-time buyer). Subtract $150 (single/widowed), $300 (married), or $0 (first-time buyer). Multiply the result by 24 percent to get the value of the relief. The maximum annual relief allowed is as follows:

	First-Time Buyer	Non-First-Time Buyer
Married	$ 1,800	$ 1,368
Widowed	$ 1,296	$ 1,000
Single	$ 900	$ 684

Capital-Gains Tax

The sale of property that is considered a principal residence is free of capital-gains tax.

Dynamics of the Sale

There are two associations in Ireland for estate agents; the Institute of Professional Auctioneers and Valuers (IPAV), and the 1,300-member Irish Auctioneers & Valuers Institute (IAVI). Many estate agent firms maintain active Web sites. While smaller, local firms may not offer Internet access, they are excellent sources for properties that receive less visible promotion and may therefore be somewhat less costly. The seller pays the estate agent's fee for representing the property, usually between 2.5 and 3.5 percent of the cost of the property.

Private Treaty Sales

Most sales are conducted by private treaty, in which negotiations take place between the seller and/or the seller's estate agent and any number of interested parties. In an environment of low interest rates and high demand, multiple offers are common. Thus, you may have to meet or exceed asking price. In a less dynamic market, it is fine to bargain over price.

Normally, a deposit of 10 percent of the asking price is required. Once you sign a contract, you must insure the property.

It is important to recognize that paying a deposit often will not constitute a binding contract on the seller. "Gazumping," wherein the seller accepts an offer and later rejects it for a better one, is a practice that, understandably, is unpopular with prospective buyers. Consumer pressure for governmental intervention may yield legislative protection from this occasional practice.

Auctions

A smaller portion of sales is conducted by way of auction. In order to bid, you must have the property title approved by your solicitor; have a structural survey of the house done by a qualified architect, surveyor, or engineer; and have secured written loan approval. You must also be able to pay a 10 percent deposit on the day of the auction if your bid wins the property and pay the balance within one to two months after the sale.

Properties carry "guide prices," which tend to be conservative. A recent auction of a Wexford cottage had a guide price of $150,000; it sold at auction for $240,000. It made headlines because of the unusually wide gap. While the IAVI recommends that guide prices should ideally not exceed 10 percent of the reserve price (the price below which the property would not be sold at auction), the dynamics of a seller's market have often driven up bids.

Building a Home

Key to the process of building a home in Ireland is engaging the services of an architect, who will advise on sites, design, building contractors, regulations, and costs. The architect also will get competitive bids and monitor the quality of the work. Architects provide invaluable assistance in coping with the process of securing permission from the planning board, An Bord Pleanala. The Royal Institute of Architects will make referrals. Also check within your community for recommendations.

Construction loans can be set up from which to draw funds as you need them for each phase of the project and can often be converted to a mortgage loan when construction is complete. If cost is an important concern, consider building a basic home and adding on later. It takes up to a year to build a traditional brick-and-mortar home. Timber frame homes, currently gaining popularity in Ireland, can be built in much less time. They also cost less to build than traditional structures, and they are more energy-efficient.

Finding a Site

Building sites are advertised in the same way as properties. Beyond checking local and national newspapers and consulting estate agents, the "drive around" method is effective once you've targeted a locale. Networking never hurts, either. You never know: A neighbor or a friend of a friend may have a site to sell at the right price. Evaluate potential sites for access to sewage, gas, electric, phone, and cable services as well as for convenience to local shops, public transport, and other services.

Determine the best way to situate the house in order to shelter it from winds and to take full advantage of sunlight. A solicitor will assist with title conveyance; fees for this service are negotiable.

Typical sites available from recent ads

- Kinsale, County Cork: "Level, ¾ acre site in pleasant rural surroundings west of Kinsale. $52,500."
- Claregalway, County Galway: "One-half acre with outline planning permission. $52,500."
- Headford, County Galway: "Secluded, undulating site of ⅔ acre, lovely rural views of countryside and lake, surrounded by high stone walls. Outline planning permission, mains water and electric. $37,500."
- Oughterard, County Galway: "One-acre superb site, good views over Lough Corrib and Connemara hills. $60,000."
- Rosscahill, County Galway: "One-half acre with outline planning permission, $37,500."
- Spiddal, County Galway: "One acre, 150 ft. road frontage, beautiful views of Galway Bay. Short walk to sandy beach, ¾ mile from village. Full planning permission for single story dwelling of 1700 sq. ft. $57,750."
- South Connemara, County Galway: "One-half acre in scenic location on shore of Rossaveal Bay. Filled and prepared, full planning for bungalow. Large mobile home on site with services. $39,000."
- Leckaun, County Leitrim: "Approximately 13 acres elevated on side of mountain, panoramic views. $45,000."
- Cross, County Mayo: "One-half acre, good road frontage, in village center, full planning granted, well sunk for water. $33,750."

- Athlone, County Westmeath: "Parcel of 9 acres of grazing land with full planning permission for 2-story house. $37,500."
- Barntown, County Wexford: "Elevated, ¾ acre site, available subject to planning permission. Close to village with superb panoramic views over surrounding countryside. $60,000."

Planning Permission

If you want to buy land on which to build or if you want to renovate or extend a house, you will likely need to obtain planning permission from An Bord Pleanala. You will need to have drawings prepared and then submit an application. This process requires some patience, since it can take up to four months to get approval.

There are approximately ninety planning authorities in Ireland governed by the Irish Planning Acts, which provide for the development of cities, towns, and countryside. The planning process is controlled by these local authorities, which range from small district councils to the large Dublin Corporation, which deals with a population of over half a million. Each planning authority administers a set of development guidelines, and any proposed construction must fall within them. Consideration is given to the effect on the environment and the local community. (In 1998, for example, An Bord Pleanala refused to grant planning permission to Costco, the US retail-shopping club, for a large store in west Dublin. Planning officials weighed Costco's intention to provide 250 new jobs against the potential harm to local merchants and ruled to deny permission.)

Renovations that are internal and do not materially change the outside of a building may not require planning permission. The bigger challenge with regard to home improvement is finding skilled workers. With construction in high gear, workers are in great demand. Networking in the community can prove valuable for securing a reliable work crew.

The planning board may grant "outline permission," which indicates that the planning authorities agree in principle to the outlined development. You must then submit detailed plans for full permission, or you can submit a full proposal and skip the outline step. There are penalties for breaches of building regulations. Usually your architect or professional advisor will make the application for you. The planning board may request additional information. Should permission be refused, you are entitled to appeal.

Building in scenic or conservation areas is generally more tightly controlled. While efforts to retain the beauty of the countryside are laudable, the process of securing permission is sometimes perceived as an obstacle to meeting housing demand. There are perceptions of bias favoring those with deep pockets over those struggling to enter the housing market. The government is under pressure to make significant reforms to the planning process.

WHERE IN IRELAND?

If you are moving to Ireland to accept or seek employment, your search for a place to call home will focus on the vicinity of your workplace. For those who are less restricted, because they are retiring or perhaps planning a home-based business, factors other than commuting distance will be at play.

Criteria for the perfect locale are highly individualistic and may include proximity to superior health care services or a desire to be near (or to escape) other expatriates. For some the key factor may be the wish to be close to a university, to be able to fly to London with relative ease, to avoid areas of heaviest rainfall, or to live amidst the beauty of a more remote and natural landscape. A clear preference for the tranquillity of rural life over the bustle of a market town or the dynamic milieu of the city will help focus your search.

Unless your funds are unlimited, the need to stretch retirement dollars may be a major consideration. Lesser-known counties in Ireland generally yield better value for that budget-hogging expenditure, housing. Often ignored in tourist itineraries, these lower-profile counties deserve serious consideration. When you investigate areas in an "undiscovered" county, you are likely to uncover a cohesive community of friendly, generous, involved, and loyal people. The Irish can be fiercely loyal to their community, whether they perceive it as the immediate neighborhood within a sprawling city or the entire county in which they reside. With media attention riveted on Dublin and surrounding areas where so many work and live, those in lower-profile counties are often unified by a sense that the attributes of their community may be ignored or unappreciated. Sometimes the less glamorous and not quite so trendy locations are the butt of jokes for their "culchie" (countrified) ways. Many people, however, do not require a fashionable, sophisticated, expensive, and high-profile address to achieve a good quality of life.

When considering potential locales, weigh carefully those factors that are important to you. Take time to learn all you can about locations that interest you. Resist the temptation to buy property until you've actually lived in and become familiar with the characteristics of a given community. Recognize that the qualities that attract people to a location sometimes have less to do with logic than with romance. For example, a remote Irish village that has been mentioned over the years in family conversations may beckon, but it may not be your best choice. A place where relatives once lived or still reside may hold special appeal but not necessarily the particular amenities that will support your needs.

Some are drawn to a specific locale for reasons that have little to do with concrete advantages it may offer. At times the pull may be irresistible. One American who settled on the west coast in Clifden, County Galway, told me that she wandered into this charming town early one morning, suitcase in hand, and knew at first glance this would become her home. "Somehow, I knew every step of the way," she said, "though I had never been here before." Some fifteen years later she has no regrets. Honoring a gut instinct has served her very well. But to increase the likelihood of achieving a favorable result, your search should incorporate logical considerations as well as feelings.

To choose a suitable locale, have a clear idea of what you will need, what you would prefer, and what you can reasonably settle for in terms of surroundings. Prioritizing your criteria is helpful, as is keeping an open mind as you weigh the relative merits of various locations in Ireland. However you order your priorities, you'll have a number of options. For a small country, Ireland offers an incredible range of terrific places to call home.

Tips on Locale

- If better weather is a priority, areas in Counties Waterford or Wexford will provide the most sun. Many North Americans settle here.
- To avoid areas inundated with tourists, steer clear of Killarney, Tralee, the Ring of Kerry, the Dingle Peninsula, and County Galway's Connemara region.
- If a remote location is not off-putting, consider the wild beauty and sparse population of County Donegal.
- To find more reasonable housing prices, try the less dramatic yet still lovely vistas of Counties Cavan, Laois, Leitrim, Monaghan, Offaly, Longford, and Roscommon, or, if the peace process continues to solidify, consider Northern Ireland.
- If health care is a primary consideration, locate near the superior health services in Galway, Limerick, Cork, or Dublin. Cardiology

services are offered at many hospitals, but only those in Dublin and Cork perform bypass surgery. Cardiac catheterization is available in Dublin, Cork, Galway, and Limerick. (See the Resource Guide for guidelines on how to access information about hospitals and other health care services in each county.)

- If roads jammed with commuters are not your style, avoid not only Dublin, but also the surrounding commuter belt in Counties Carlow, Meath, Westmeath, Kildare, Louth, and Wicklow.

Big Pond versus Little Pond

Forty percent of Ireland's population of approximately 3.75 million live within a 100-kilometer (60-mile) radius of Dublin. Nearly a million people inhabit the city of Dublin, the place to be if you want to dwell among a large, diverse population. The urban centers of Galway, Cork, and Limerick are smaller in scale but experiencing rapid growth.

City life in Ireland has much to offer. In addition to a lively pace, there are a variety of theaters, shops, galleries, museums, cafes, and restaurants. Nightlife abounds. Services are good, from medical centers with staff of considerable expertise to easily accessible transportation. The possibility of foregoing a car and its attendant expense is much more feasible in a city. Offsetting these advantages are traffic problems, higher costs, and crowded queues at the bank and post office. Crime, though much less of a problem everywhere in Ireland, occurs more frequently in urban areas.

Rural life in Ireland appeals to many prospective expatriates. As the Irish economy has continued to rely less on agriculture, there has been flight from the countryside to urban areas, leaving many rural areas sparsely populated. In 1990 a small but visible program called Rural Resettlement was initiated to help boost population in certain rural areas. The government continues to assist urban families willing to try a new life in the countryside. Many who have participated praise the quieter pace and less expensive cost of living. Beautiful scenery, more living space, a greater sense of community, and a simpler way of life are reasons some are drawn to the country. They accept that they may not have so many choices for shopping, entertainment, and other services. Access to public transport and health care is more limited. One may need to go to a different health board to see a specialist, which could mean a drive of some distance for a doctor's appointment. A rural setting can feel isolating, in winter especially.

If you are not keen on either a lively city *or* a remote rural environment, a small or mid-size town (or a village nearby) may be more suitable. Ireland offers a cornucopia of villages and small towns, each with its own distinct character and charm. Taking time to explore a number of them can be enlightening as well as enjoyable.

As you select places to investigate, you may want to consider those that have received special recognition for appearance and community spirit. For more than forty years, competitions in the Republic ("Tidy Towns") and in Northern Ireland ("Best Kept Towns") have encouraged volunteers within local communities to spruce up their towns and villages. Originating as a public-relations effort to boost tourism, these programs have served to improve the local environment and foster community spirit. In recent years the inclusion of an All Ireland category has also inspired cross-border cooperation.

More than 700 towns compete each year on criteria that include litter control, landscaping, condition of roads, and conservation of natural amenities and wildlife. Categories include Best Overall, Best Village (population up to 1,000), Best Small Town (population 1,001–5,000), and Best Large Town (population 5,001 and over). Past winners include Adare, County Limerick; Ardagh, County Longford; Ardmore, County Waterford; Carlingford, County Louth; Clonakilty and Kinsale, County Cork; Ennis, County Clare; Enniskillen, County Fermanagh; Glenties, County Donegal; Keadue, County Roscommon; Kilkenny City, County Kilkenny; Loughgall, County Armagh; Malahide, County Dublin; Malin, County Donegal; Sneem, County Kerry; Terryglass, County Tipperary; and Waringstown, County Down.

Regional Overview

Slightly larger than the state of West Virginia, the island of Ireland extends about 480 kilometers (300 miles) from north to south and 270 kilometers (170 miles) east to west. Ireland's terrain is often described as a bowl, with a rolling interior plain surrounded by rugged hills and low mountains. Imposing cliffs grace parts of the West Coast. Surrounded by the waters of the Atlantic, the North Channel, and the Irish Sea, Ireland also features within its interior numerous lakes and rivers, the Shannon being the largest.

More than 70 percent of the land is composed of meadows and pastures. A significant portion of Ireland's forests was cleared ages ago; thus, trees are not abundant, and only 5 percent of the land is wooded. Bog lands consisting of thick layers of poorly drained, moss-covered soil called peat turf have provided an energy source for many generations of Irish people. Today some still cut, stack, and dry turf for heat and cooking fuel.

Ireland is divided into four provinces that contain the twenty-six counties of Ireland and six counties of Northern Ireland. Approximately 3.75 million people inhabit the Republic, and 1.6 million reside in Northern Ireland. The following section provides a brief description of each province and county in the Republic and of Northern Ireland. Mostly main towns are indicated, but numerous small towns and villages are found in every county.

Connacht (Counties Galway, Leitrim, Mayo, Roscommon, Sligo)

The five counties of Connaught, situated in the west of Ireland, claim a population of 432,551, the least of any province. This region, known for its natural beauty, offers rugged coasts, mountains rising dramatically from the sea, rocky moorlands, green landscapes, grazing pastures, and glittering lakes. There is more rain here than average. Irish culture and language thrive in Gaeltacht areas, where road signs may appear in Irish only.

County Galway

The second-largest county in Ireland, Galway is divided by Ireland's second-largest lake, Lough Corrib. East of this lake lie low pastures and farmlands. To the west are the jagged coasts, wild landscapes, and ever-changing light of Connemara, revered by painters, photographers, and all who admire natural beauty. Just beyond Galway Bay are the Aran Islands of Inishmore, Inishmaan, and Inisheer. Here much of traditional culture is preserved, and though English is used, it is Irish that is more commonly spoken. Tourists visit the islands by air or sea, and summer finds the narrow roads congested with visitors. Many make their way to Dun Aenghus, an ancient stone fort that provides sweeping views of the mainland from its clifftop perch on Inishmore.

Within this province of nearly 190,000 people, the largest town is

CONNACHT

Donegal Bay

Manorhamilton •
Coney Island   *Rosses Point*
Easkey •   Sligo
Ballycastle •   Strandhill •   **Leitrim**
• Enniscrone
Ballina •   **Sligo**   *Lough Allen*
Achill Island   Keadue •
Lough Conn   Ballymote   Drumshanbo •
Boyle •   Ballinamo
Charlestown •   Carrick o
Mayo   Shannon
Clare Island   *Clew Bay*
Westport •   Knock •   **Roscommon**
△ Croagh Patrick   Castlerea •   Strokestown •
Inishbofin   *Lough Mask*   Roscommon •
• Cleggan   Cong •
Connemara   △ Knockmaa Hill   • Tuam
• Clifden   Oughterard •
Lough Corrib   Ballinasloe •
Inishmore   • Galway   **Galway**
Galway Bay
Inishmaan   • Loughrea
Inisheer

Clare

Tippera

Limerick

Galway, with a population of 57,095. Located on Galway Bay, with its world-famous oyster beds, Galway is one of the fastest-growing cities in all Europe. This spirited city is loaded with good bookstores and other retail shops, shopping centers, restaurants, and cafes. Galway supports a vibrant community of painters, writers, and musicians. A popular tourist destination, its medieval walls and quays contribute to its charm. Though not as expensive as Dublin, housing costs rise above the national average. Students who attend University College create a strong demand for rentals.

The area is well served by public transportation, including a regional airport 8 kilometers (5 miles) from the city center that is being expanded to enable direct flights to the United Kingdom and continental Europe. Health care services are especially good in Galway City, where there are a number of hospitals, Merlin Park and University College chief among them.

Several miles inland from Galway is the busy market town of Loughrea. Ballinasloe, an old market town, plays host each October to a traditional horse fair, where thousands of horses change hands in lively transactions conducted in the crowded streets. Tuam is an active market town, with a twelfth-century High Cross in the town square and an operating corn mill and museum. Nearby Knockmaa hill, surrounded by scattered ruins, is reputed to be the final resting place of Maeve, the legendary Queen of Connacht. (Maeve's tomb is also claimed to be located at Knocknarea, a mountain near Strandhill, County Sligo.) Oughterard is a small and lovely town near Lough Corrib's western shore, known for good fishing. Pretty cottages and stately homes with colorful flower gardens flank the main roadway.

Connemara is the rocky, hilly, and wildly beautiful area along County Galway's western seaboard. You would be forgiven if you were to ignore advice to avoid elevated prices in this high-demand area by deciding to settle here. The area is incredibly beautiful. Connemara's unique and rocky terrain, windy roads, placid lakes, glittering ocean views from the often deserted beaches, and brilliant sunsets are extremely compelling. The imposing Gothic Revival structure of Kylemore Abbey, now a girls' boarding school, enhances the natural beauty of the surrounding blanket bogs and moorlands.

Connemara is somewhat isolated, and the drive to Galway City takes nearly an hour. Roads become fairly congested close to the city center.

Many services are available in local Connemara towns, especially Clifden, where some are fortunate enough to live on the Sky Road, one of the most scenic spots in Ireland. Many small and charming villages are found throughout this region. The fishing village, Cleggan, provides ferry service to the tiny island of Inishbofin.

County Leitrim

One of the lower-profile counties, Leitrim is often skipped by tourists. Known as the "Cinderella County," Leitrim lost a significant portion of its population to emigration during the Great Famine, and there has been no marked population increase in recent years like that experienced by many other counties. Still, levels seem in recent years to have stabilized at approximately 25,000, with the lowest density of any county. Winters in this area can be wet and windy, yet those who live in Leitrim praise the tranquil beauty, unhurried pace, and better housing values. The county is situated mostly inland, though a small area hugs the coast near the resort town of Bundoran in County Donegal. Leitrim is a quiet, scenic area of hills and valleys. The Shannon flows along its western border, and many lakes grace its interior.

Leitrim's largest town, Carrick-on-Shannon, is a boating and fishing center and host to numerous international fishing festivals and competitions. An annual regatta is popular, and the local rowing club often trains on the river. In the center of town is Ireland's smallest church, the Costello Memorial Chapel, built in the nineteenth century by a wealthy merchant to memorialize his wife. Ballinamore is a lively town, surrounded by lakes and waterways and the location of the Leitrim Heritage Center, the first of many such centers in Ireland where people come to examine birth registers and other records in order to trace their Irish roots. A lovely village located near the southern tip of Lough Allen, Drumshanbo is the setting for An Tostal, a summer festival of traditional song and dance. Manorhamilton, originally a Scottish settlement, is surrounded by mountain peaks that afford beautiful views of lush countryside. The town hosts the annual Wild Rose Festival.

County Mayo

North of County Galway, Mayo is the third-largest county in Ireland. It features a mountainous coastline along the west and, to the east, lakes and rolling pastures. Like other counties in this province, Mayo lost much of its population to emigration during the famine. Its density, at a current population of 111,395, is quite low. While tourism is important here, Mayo's northwestern location makes it somewhat less accessible than other areas. It does, therefore, offer better housing value for those who do not need to be close to a major city. Ballina, an angling center on the River Moy, is Mayo's largest town. It offers services typical of a mid-size town, but with 7,000 people, it is small compared to Galway or Limerick. Castlebar is another small town bustling with commerce and surrounded by lakes known for great fishing.

Mayo is graced by a stunning coastline and the imposing Croagh Patrick, a mountain of 765 meters (2,510 feet) that towers over Clew Bay and is the site of an important pilgrimage. Each year as many as 100,000 people, some barefoot, ascend Croagh Patrick on the last Sunday of July in memory of the venerable St. Patrick. The village of Knock, the site in 1879 of an apparition of the Blessed Virgin Mary, is another pilgrimage center and the location of Ireland's largest church, Our Lady's Basilica, capable of accommodating 20,000 people. Nearby, the Knock airport provides limited service, including daily flights to England. The village of Cong, near the Galway border, is best known as the location for scenes from John Ford's 1952 film, *The Quiet Man*.

On Clew Bay lies the attractive and cosmopolitan town of Westport. Upscale restaurants and shops, friendly pubs, and good music make this a popular tourist destination. A tree-lined mall adds to the town's charm, as does Westport House, an elegant Georgian mansion open to the public. Beyond Clew Bay is Clare Island, inhabited today by several hundred people. It once sheltered the infamous Grace O'Malley, referred to as the Pirate Queen and also by her Irish name, Granvaile. Born around 1530, this wild, beautiful woman earned her living as a sea captain, commanding a loyal crew whom she occasionally led to plunder cargo ships. She would escape authorities by hiding among the numerous coves and inlets along the West Coast. A momentous meeting in 1593 between Granvaile and Queen Elizabeth I resulted in each earning the admiration of the other.

Achill Island, largest of Ireland's offshore islands, is connected by bridge to the mainland. Fine beaches, ancient ruins, pretty seaside villages, and imposing cliffs contribute to Achill Island's beauty. Along the sparsely populated northern Mayo coast near Ballycastle village is Ceide

Fields, an interpretive center detailing an archaeological excavation of a 5,000-year-old Stone Age field preserved by blanket bog. The views afforded by the cliffs opposite the center are equally compelling.

County Roscommon

An inland county with 51,881 residents, Roscommon is another low-profile area that may yield better housing bargains and a more relaxed pace. It is a quiet and rural county with splendid scenery. Roscommon is world-renowned for superior fishing in Loughs Key, Gara, and Ree, and Rivers Boyle, Suck, and Shannon. It is also a county steeped in ancient history, where ruins dot the rolling countryside and excavations uncover a multitude of treasures from previous centuries.

Boyle, one of Roscommon's main towns, is on the main N4 route, which runs between Dublin and Sligo. It is known for its summer arts festival of exhibitions, drama, and music performances as well as a twelfth-century Cistercian monastery, Boyle Abbey, its original grandeur now in picturesque ruin.

Castlerea is a small market town and leisure center for golf, fishing, and tennis. Just outside the town is Clonalis House, a mansion and ancestral seat of the O'Conor Clan. A number of O'Conors served as high kings. On display in the lavishly appointed estate is the harp of Turlough O'Carolan, a blind harpist and composer who traveled around Ireland teaching and performing songs that survive to the present day. The O'Carolan Harp & Traditional Music Festival in Keadue, County Roscommon, celebrates his legacy.

The village of Strokestown, a center for crafts, is known also for its museum presenting the tragic history of the Great Famine. Roscommon, a charming market town, is the location of the thirteenth-century Roscommon Castle. Northwest of town is Rathcroghan, the coronation site and graveyard of ancient Connacht's high kings.

County Sligo

Known for beautiful seaside resorts, May fly fishing on Lough Arrow, and Ben Bulben, the table mountain, County Sligo also features championship golf at Rosses Point and Carrowmore, Ireland's largest cemetery of megalithic tombs. A population of approximately 56,000 resides in this county, where the poet W. B. Yeats and his brother, Jack, the painter, lived for a time. The bustling market town of Sligo, population 19,000, marks the end of the rail line from Dublin. One can fly to Dublin or London from Sligo's regional airport at Strandhill. Popular with tourists who enjoy the arts, Sligo supports an active artists' community and hosts a number of festivals. Sligo's Institute of Technology offers a wide range of part-time evening courses.

From the pier at Rosses Point, you can hop a boat to the original Coney Island, after which the island off New York was named. The Irish version is small and lost nearly all of its inhabitants decades ago. Known for the historical significance of its fourteenth-century castle ruins, Ballymote is a favorite of those who love to fish. Situated 32 kilometers (20 miles) south of Sligo Town, Tubbercurry maintains a rich heritage of Irish music and dance. The South Sligo Summer School is held here, providing instruction for students all over Ireland and around the world in traditional Irish music. Enniscrone on Killala Bay is a seaside resort favored by families for its sandy beaches. Easky, another seaside resort, is popular with surfers.

Leinster (Counties Carlow, Dublin, Kildare, Kilkenny, Laois, Longford, Louth, Meath, Offaly, Westmeath, Wexford, Wicklow)

The twelve counties of Leinster are situated in the east and the midlands of Ireland. With a population of 1,921,835, Leinster is home to more people than any other province. This region encompasses a coastal area of promenades and sandy beaches; an interior of rolling pastures, numerous parks, historical buildings and settlements; and Ireland's capital, Dublin. There is less rain here than average.

County Carlow

Often overlooked by tourists making their way to nearby Kilkenny, Wexford, and Waterford, Carlow is Ireland's smallest inland county. Its population numbers 41,616. The rolling farmland of this county is bordered by the Blackstairs Mountains and Mount Leinster and is divided by the Barrow and Slaney Rivers. It is near enough to Dublin to draw homebuyers looking for good value. There are good roads and train service to Dublin and Waterford.

Carlow boasts many historical monuments, great fishing, boating, and golf. Mount Leinster is a well-known center for hang gliding. Carlow Town, population 15,000, hosts an annual arts festival called Eigse.

Approximately 2,500 students attend the Carlow Institute of Technology, which offers degree courses and part-time adult education classes. Other main towns are Muinebeag or Bagenalstown and Tullow. The little town of Leighlinbridge is the location of the Black Castle, built in the twelfth-century and rebuilt in the sixteenth-century before falling to Cromwell in 1650. The nine-arched structure that crosses the River Barrow was built in 1320 and is considered the oldest functioning bridge in Ireland.

Dublin City/County

Founded in A.D. 840 by the Vikings, Dublin City has become one of Europe's finest capitals. For those who prefer city living and have few budget constraints, Dublin provides many services and amenities, including superior health care facilities; worthy shops and restaurants; a variety of performance arts; numerous museums, galleries, and bookstores; and superior public transportation, including a busy international airport. With an average annual rainfall of 76 centimeters (30 inches), Dublin offers the driest climate. The high cost of housing has driven many to outlying areas, which have in turn experienced their own boom in property and services.

Fueled by improved roads and employment opportunities at companies like IBM and Intel, communities north, west, and south of Dublin are experiencing rapid growth. Coastal communities above and below Dublin, from Drogheda in County Louth to Arklow in County Wicklow are rife with commuters and have soaring home prices. There are, however, many lovely towns along this corridor. If you can afford the inflated housing prices of places like Howth, Dalkey, Killiney, or Bray, you'll benefit from convenient DART service into Dublin.

County Kildare

Home of the National Stud, dedicated to breeding Ireland's renowned first-class stallions, County Kildare is known as horse country. The 5,000-acre Curragh is the site of world-famous horseracing. Kildare is rich in history, favored with lovely scenery, and offers a number of highly rated golf courses. Approximately 135,000 inhabit this county. Kildare Town's Derby Festival in June and its ancient cathedral, St. Brigid's, are popular with tourists.

Other main towns are Athy, Maynooth, and Naas. Their proximity to

Dublin on the M7 motorway and the presence in Leixslip of Hewlett-Packard and Intel have contributed to this county's rapid growth and higher-than-average housing prices. The National University of Ireland at Maynooth offers a number of degree and continuing education programs.

County Kilkenny

County Kilkenny's flowing pastures, limestone caves, green forests, and medieval towns make it a leading tourist destination. Some 75,336 people call this county home. A blend of ancient and modern influences, Kilkenny City boasts a restored twelfth-century castle, an inviting craft center, Old and New World shops, and good restaurants. Other main towns are Callan and Castlecomer.

County Laois

One of the lesser-known, Midland counties, Laois (pronounced "leash") is a landscape of lush pastures bordered in the northwest by the Slieve Bloom mountains. Residents number approximately 53,000, and housing is less expensive here. Abbeyleix, Mountmellick, Portlaoise, and Portarlington are the main towns. The Rock of Dunamase, near Portlaoise, served as a military stronghold as early as the Iron Age. Remains of an ancient ring fort are still present.

County Longford

Stellar scenery and better value in the housing market recommend Longford, a rural, inland county of pristine lakes, rivers, and wooded hills, with a population of just over 30,000. The principal town is Longford, a busy center of commerce. Many areas of Ireland are easily accessed from Longford's central location, and public transportation here is good. Granard, Lainesborough, Edgeworthstown, and Ballymahon, a prime fishing center, are the other main towns.

County Louth

The smallest county in Ireland, Louth's coastal setting provides sandy beaches, panoramic views, and rugged beauty. Just one hour from both Belfast and Dublin, this is a prime location for outlying commuters, and some 92,000 people reside here. Main towns are Ardee; Drogheda, on the Boyne River; and Dundalk, a busy port town.

County Meath

Known as the Royal County, Meath was the seat of the High Kings of Ireland. On the northwest border of County Dublin, Meath at one time afforded bargain-housing prices amidst a lovely area known for antiquities, fishing, boating, and golf. Then home buyers fleeing rocketing Dublin prices began to move into the area. Meath has just over 109,000 residents. Navan, in the center of the county, is its principal town.

County Offaly

Another county often overlooked in favor of those with more dramatic vistas, Offaly offers lush forests, blanket bogs, the waters of the Grand Canal and the nearby Shannon, and the mountains of Slieve Bloom. Just over 59,000 reside here. Main towns are Tullamore and Birr, noted for Birr Castle and its ornamental gardens. Clonmacnoise, located in the northwest corner of the county, is an internationally renowned monastic settlement.

County Westmeath

Westmeath is close enough to Dublin to have become a bedroom community of sorts. Thus, while house prices are much less than those in Dublin, other undiscovered counties farther from Dublin may offer better value. Still, Westmeath's lush farmland is lovely, its superb lakes are an angler's dream, and its villages are picturesque. The population of the county is 63,236, and the main towns are Athlone and Mullingar, which features a new Integrated Arts Center and Theater.

County Wexford

Situated in the sunny southeast corner of Ireland, Wexford's rolling countryside, orchards, mountains, wildlife, forests, coastal beaches, and inlets are popular, but not overrun, with tourists. Just over 104,000 people live in this county. The Old World town of Wexford, home to 16,000 people, is best known for its annual International Opera Festival. Other main towns are Enniscorthy, Gorey, and New Ross, a busy port town with narrow, winding streets. Dunganstown is the site of the cottage where John F. Kennedy's grandfather was born; at Slieve Coilte, a memorial arboretum and park pay tribute to this U.S. president. Rosslare is a seaside resort and a ferry port, with service to Wales and France.

County Wicklow

Proximity to Dublin makes County Wicklow a convenient, but more expensive location. Called the "Garden of Ireland," Wicklow offers woods, valleys, lakes, rivers, coastal beaches, seaside resorts popular with Dubliners, and the Wicklow Mountains. Glendalough, a monastic site founded in the sixth century by St. Kevin, is known for its beauty and tranquillity. The county has 102,417 residents, and its principal towns are Arklow, Baltinglass, Bray, and Wicklow.

Munster (Counties Clare, Cork, Kerry, Limerick, Tipperary, Waterford)

Situated in the southwest of Ireland, Munster covers the most area of any province. Its six counties are home to 1,033,045 people. Though this region has its share of lesser-known, out-of-the-way towns and villages, in general Munster is prime tourist territory. The West Coast in particular is very popular with tourists. There tends to be more rain here than average, and a lot more in mountainous areas.

County Clare

County Clare is bordered by water—Galway Bay to the north, the Shannon River to the south, Lough Derg to the east, and the Atlantic Ocean to the west. The Cliffs of Moher rise dramatically 198 meters (650 feet) above the Atlantic. Less dramatic but still beautiful are the smaller cliffs at Kilkee, a seaside resort popular with Irish families. Doolin, a popular tourist area, is known for its pubs and traditional music. In northern Clare the Burren, an unusual area of lunarlike layers of limestone, produces several varieties of flowers, including orchids, despite what appears to be a barren landscape.

With a population of nearly 18,000, Ennis is Clare's principal town. Designated an "Information Age Town," Ennis was selected to participate in a Telecom Eireann (now Eircom) program to integrate technology within schools, businesses, public services, and households. For about $400, one person per household could purchase a computer, take a training course, and connect to the Internet, and many took the plunge. Shannon International Airport is located in Clare. Other main towns are Killaloe and Lisdoonvarna, the setting for the annual Matchmaking Festival.

County Cork

Many Americans make this, Ireland's largest county, their home, among a population of 420,346. Cork's extensive coastline of harbors, inlets, and sandy beaches borders prosperous farmland, shimmering lakes, bustling market towns, and secluded villages. East Cork is known for its quiet beauty, West Cork for its wild, rocky countryside and remote Gaeltacht areas where Irish is the primary language. Originating in the seventh century, Cork City, with a population of 180,000, is the second-largest city in Ireland. Numerous quays along the River Lee lend Old World charm amidst the bustle of urban growth and renewal. This major port city is well served by appealing shops, excellent restaurants, quality health care services, University College, and good public transportation, including an international airport. Traffic can be a problem, however, with large lorries (trucks) rumbling around and through town.

Other main Cork towns include Bantry, a fishing port and market town on Bantry Bay, where the influence of the Gulf Stream provides a climate supportive of palm trees; Clonakilty, a busy market town with sandy beaches; the ancient market town of Macroom; Mallow, a fishing center; handsome market towns, Fermoy and Mitchelstown; Skibbereen, a fishing port and market town; and Youghal (pronounced "yawl"), an ancient walled port and popular seaside resort. Kinsale, known for gourmet restaurants, is a popular, upscale seaside resort. Cobh (pronounced "Cove"), a picturesque seaside town in Cork harbor, has steep banks of colorful Victorian townhouses. A major emigration port, Cobh was the last stop made by the *Titanic* before its ill-fated 1912 journey across the Atlantic.

County Kerry

Exceedingly popular with tourists, this southwestern county extends from rugged, mountainous peninsulas along the south coast north to where the Shannon joins the sea. Renowned for their wild, rugged beauty, the Beara, Iveragh, and Dingle Peninsulas feature numerous antiquities among their surging mountains, shimmering lakes, lush woodlands, and sandy beaches. The Gulf Stream delivers a moist, warm climate favorable to tropical trees and fuchsia shrubs, which line the roads of Dingle and south Kerry.

A fair number of Americans, many smitten while vacationing, have settled in Kerry. Except for the area in and around Killarney, home prices are generally lower than the national average. Flights from Kerry's regional airport in Farranfore, between Killarney and Tralee, provide service to Dublin, the United Kingdom, and several continental European destinations.

There are six main towns in this county of nearly 126,000: Kenmare, which links the Ring of Kerry with the Ring of Beara; Killarney, renowned for its lakes and proximity to MacGillycuddy's Reeks and Carrantouhill, at 1,040 meters (3,414 feet) the highest mountain in Ireland; Cahersiveen, on the breathtakingly beautiful and heavily traveled Ring of Kerry road; Dingle, on the southern shore of the peninsula of the same name; Tralee, a tourist destination known for Siamsa Tire, a National Folk Theater featuring traditional music, dance, and costumes and the international Rose of Tralee festival; and Listowel, a pretty inland town near the mouth of the Shannon.

County Limerick

Limerick is a county of low, rolling pastures bordered to the north by the Shannon River, which flows through its chief city, also called Limerick. County residents number 165,017. Limerick City, Ireland's third-largest city, with a population of 79,000, celebrated 800 years of history in 1997. Commerce is evident here. In years past people, some considered Limerick a drab, industrialized city that tourists should pass through quickly on their way to more scenic vistas. (In those pre-boom days, areas of Dublin, now trendy, were similarly disparaged.)

Today, however, prosperity is transforming previously shabby areas of Limerick to create a more inviting environment. Traffic is a problem, but not on the scale of Dublin or Cork. Services are good, from lively pubs, colorful shops, and appealing parks to a host of hospital services and clinics. Just north of town, the University of Limerick enrolls 9,000 part- and full-time students. Many attractive small towns and villages dot the countryside, including Tidy Towns winner Adare, with its thatched-roof cottages and picturesque ruins. Main towns other than Limerick are Rathkeale and the medieval town of Kilmallock.

County Tipperary

The River Shannon and Lough Derg form the northwest border of the largest inland county, Tipperary. The Galty, Knockmealdown, and Comeragh Mountains range across its southern border, and the River

Suir bisects it from north to south. Tipperary is primarily agricultural, with rolling plains dotted by farms, castles, and abbeys. Away from areas popular with tourists, like the Rock of Cashel, housing costs are less expensive than in higher-profile counties. Approximately 133,300 people live in the county, and its main towns are Thurles, Nenagh, Clonmel, Tipperary, and Caher.

County Waterford

Home to 94,597 residents and the famous Waterford Crystal, this is a county of mild climate, sheltered caves and beaches along the coast, and beautiful mountains, valleys, and rivers. County Waterford hosts numerous festivals and draws legions of people who love to golf and fish. The port city of Waterford, with a population of 44,000, features a long quay and a variety of amenities. The refurbished Theatre Royal annually hosts an International Festival of Light Opera. The Waterford Institute of Technology enrolls 8,500 part- and full-time students. Public transportation is good, and Waterford's regional airport has a daily flight to London. Dungarvan, a market town and seaport, is the other main town.

Ulster, Republic (Counties Cavan, Donegal, Monaghan)

There are nine counties in Ulster. Three form part of the Republic, with a population of 233,604. The other six make up Northern Ireland, a separate country of 1.7 million people that is part of the United Kingdom.

County Cavan

Like other counties that often do not register on the radar screen of many tourists, Cavan falls into the "undiscovered" category. Near the Northern Ireland border, this primarily rural county is home for nearly 53,000 people. In prefamine times, as many as 250,000 lived in this landlocked county of gentle hills and rugged mountains. Efforts to promote tourism focus on world-class fishing afforded by Cavan's 365 lakes. Ireland's two mighty rivers, the Erne and Shannon, begin here. In 1994 work was completed to reopen an old canal to join these two major inland waterways. Cuilcagh Mountain, its highest point, at more than 1,820 meters (2,000 feet), straddles the Fermanagh border. Cavan Crystal, the second-oldest crystal factory in Ireland, offers tours and demonstrations of the craft of glass blowing. Cavan town also has a great bookstore, Crannog.

County Donegal

Ireland's fourth-largest and most northern county, Donegal is considered by many to be the most scenic. Its dramatic coastline features the greatest number of beaches in Ireland and, at Slieve League, the highest sea cliffs in Europe. A number of summer festivals, good fishing, and Glenveagh national park draw many visitors, though Donegal's size and remote location prevent it from being overrun by tourists most of the year.

Famous for its tweed fabrics, the county has a population of nearly 130,000 people, 2,000 of whom dwell in the bustling county town of Donegal. Other main towns are Ballyshannon, Letterkenny, and the seaside resort Bundoran. There are a host of charming fishing villages, including Killlybegs, one of Ireland's premier fishing ports.

County Monaghan

Bordering Northern Ireland, County Monaghan is a quiet place of gentle hills, farmhouses, and market towns. It is part of the drumlin belt, a sweeping band of steep hills shaped by thawing Ice Age glaciers. Tourists are less common here, but fishing enthusiasts praise the bounty of its pretty lakes. The county's population numbers just over 51,000. Monaghan, Castleblaney, Clones, and Carrickmacross are its main towns.

Ulster, Northern Ireland (Counties Antrim, Armagh, Derry, Down, Fermanagh, and Tyrone)

Northern Ireland offers superior health services, well-maintained roads, two progressive cities, bustling market towns, rich farmlands, pristine waterways, and a wealth of antiquities. Despite headlines that draw worldwide attention to tragic terrorist incidents and create a warzone impression, crime is generally not a problem; rates are among the lowest in all Europe. As in the South of the island, the winter climate is mild and wet, and summer is drier and warmer but rarely hot. Areas along the eastern coast are warmer and drier than those in the west. There are close ties with people in the neighboring counties of the Republic as well as with the United Kingdom and the United States. The families of eleven U.S. presidents have roots in Northern Ireland.

Although most of the once thriving linen mills are no longer active, the development of new industry in the North has grown in recent years,

boosted by foreign companies like DuPont, Emerson, and South Carolina–based B/E Aerospace. Tourism is a key industry and focuses on the North's spectacular coastlines, grand mountains, lush forests, and bountiful lakes. The Ulster Way, an 800-kilometer (500-mile) walking path, makes a full circuit of Northern Ireland, passing the bare Sperrin Mountains, the lakes and hills of Fermanagh, the Cuilcagh and Mourne Mountains, and the dramatic North Coast.

Many of the North's 1.7 million people reside in one of its two major cities: Belfast, on the East Coast; and Derry, in the northwest. Beyond these metropolitan areas, the country is rural, with many small to medium-size market towns. Most of it has been untouched by the long-standing political conflict that has produced alarming headlines year after year.

Should it be achieved, lasting peace is expected to encourage further economic growth and opportunity in Northern Ireland. The rate of investment by noncitizens in rental property and businesses in the North has increased steadily in recent years. The success of concerted efforts to achieve peace is encouraging the widely shared hope that age-old conflicts may now be put to rest. There is always the potential, however, for tensions to be rekindled and for incidents to arise that would discourage settling here. In the past, such tensions have created an air of uneasiness and mistrust in some of the border towns in the Republic. Depending on how events unfold, there may be risk in settling in or near the North. There may also, however, be opportunity.

County Antrim

Located in the northeast of Ireland, County Antrim's population numbers well over half a million people. A drive up the coast from Larne's busy ferry port through the fabled Glens of Antrim reveals the splendor of dramatic seaside vistas and green valleys lush with wild flowers and birdsong. The best-known valley is Glenariff, site of a state-owned Forest Park and the village of Waterfoot, known for traditional music. The square (more often called the "diamond") in the market town of Ballycastle is the setting for the annual Ould Lammas Fair, the oldest traditional festival in Ireland. From Ballycastle boats travel to Rathlin Island, known for its cliffs and caves as well as a bird sanctuary. Giant's Causeway, on the northwest coast, is Northern Ireland's most popular tourist destination, where cooling volcanic lava formed millions of years ago to create thousands of unusually geometric basalt columns. Of more recent origins, the Bushmills Whiskey Distillery is located on the banks of the River Bush. Established in 1608, it is the world's oldest distillery. Nearly one-third of Northern Ireland's population—approximately 500,000 people—reside in and around the capital city, Belfast, traditionally a center of linen manufacturing and shipbuilding. Still active today, the Harland and Wolfe Shipyards on Queen's Island built the opulent *Titanic* in 1912, doomed despite assurances of its invulnerability. The domed City Hall, an imposing castle above the city, the lavishly restored Grand Opera House, and the Tudor-Gothic splendor of Queen's University are examples of Belfast's many architectural treasures. Performance arts are well supported overall. The three-week Belfast Festival, including music by internationally esteemed artists, draws big crowds each autumn. Daily flights connect Belfast with key British cities, including London, Edinburgh, and Cardiff. Ferry service is also comprehensive.

Carrickfergus, a coastal town of 35,000 and once an important center of commerce but now one of recreation, features an impressive castle, built initially in the late 1180s. Just east of town is the Andrew Jackson Centre and the re-creation of the eighteenth-century thatched cottage that was the Jackson ancestral home. Near the northern shore of Lough Neagh is Antrim Town, with its well-preserved, 1,000-year-old round tower. Lough Neagh, the largest lake in the British Isles, is known for the extensive eel fishing it supports. Five miles west of Antrim is the sixteenth-century Shane's Castle, also a nature reserve and bird sanctuary.

Ballymena, a busy market town, is located in the center of County Antrim. Northwest of Ballymena is Culleybackey, ancestral home of Chester A. Arthur, the twenty-first president of the United States. A few miles northeast of Ballymena is Slemish Mountain, where St. Patrick is said to have been forced to tend sheep after his capture as a youth from Britain in the fifth century.

County Armagh

The Rivers Blackwater and Bann and Lough Neagh border Armagh, an inland county of nearly 145,000. The Blackwater River is one of Ireland's best fishing rivers and is famous for its big bream. Armagh's rolling landscape is typical of the drumlin belt, common to this area, where glacier activity formed many small oval hills, creating an effect described as a basket of eggs. Called the Orchard County, Armagh is known for the apples grown here for more than 3,000 years. It is also known for the game of road bowls, played exclusively on the quiet lanes of this county and Cork. Players hurl a small, heavy ball along a course of several kilometers (miles). Curves in the road provide great challenge and encourage lively wagering.

With a population of approximately 14,000, Armagh is the county's largest town. It features many fine Georgian buildings as well as Ireland's sole planetarium. An old jail stands at the southern end of Armagh's tree-lined Georgian mall, and at the northern end, a stately courthouse. Two cathedrals dominate Armagh, one Catholic, the other Protestant, and both named St. Patrick's. Nearby Navan Fort was the home of Ulster's pagan kings from 700 B.C.

Near Armagh and Portadown, a prosperous market town noted for fishing in River Bann, is the village of Loughgall. Situated in the center of apple orchard country, Loughgall was honored in 1998 with the overall title of Ireland's Best Kept Village and Best Kept Town.

County Derry

A county of hilly terrain, Derry, or Londonderry, is bordered to the east by County Antrim, to the west by County Donegal, and to the north by the Atlantic Ocean. On the coast Portstewart Strand features a beautiful sandy beach and highly regarded golf course. Nearby Magilligan Strand is Ireland's longest beach. To the south the low Sperrin Mountains are a main region for sheep farming.

The city of Derry lies on the River Foyle and is an important industrial center, and a port from which many Irish sailed for America. It was founded when St. Columba, also known as Columcille, built the first of many monasteries here in A.D. 546. Derry is called the Maiden City because, despite repeated assaults over many centuries, the fortress of its walls was never violated. Rebuilt in 1618, the 5-meters-thick (18-feet) and 1.6-kilometers-long (1-mile) circle of town walls is the best preserved in all Europe. The four original gateways still stand. Today Derry is a city of elegant Georgian houses, hilly streets, and a thriving arts community, with a population of nearly 100,000.

North of Derry, in Ballyarnet, is the Earhart Centre, commemorating Amelia Earhart's 1932 landing here, which distinguished her as the first woman to fly across the Atlantic. Limavady, a Georgian town of Elizabethan times, was home to Jane Ross, who wrote down a song from a passing fiddler, the "Londonderry Air," later transformed into "Danny Boy." Formerly the town was a leading producer of linen. The old mills and Ulster's first hydroelectric plant have been restored and are displayed in Roe Valley Country Park.

County Down

Located on the northeast coast and bordered on three sides by water, County Down features 320 kilometers (200 miles) of dramatic shoreline, ancient castles, and abundant wildlife. The county's interior unveils rolling fields of drumlins and the majesty of the Mourne Mountains, which range across the south. To the north is Strangford Lough, a large sea inlet and natural marine reserve. Its plankton-rich waters support an astonishing variety of marine life, including seals, pilot whales, and porpoises. The presence of a wide range and number of species makes this a Mecca for birdwatchers. Yachting, fishing, and boating are also popular here.

County Down is associated with St. Patrick, whose first church is said to have been a barn in Saul, a gift of the local chieftain in A.D. 432. *Sabhal*, the Irish word for "barn," is the origin of the name of this town just outside Downpatrick, where St. Patrick is buried. A walking route, St. Patrick's Way, marks his path to Saul from the mouth of the River Slaney.

The town of Banbridge is the county's center of commerce and industry. Hillsborough, Ireland's 1997 Best Kept Small Town, is known for the antiques and craft shops that line its steep main street. Down's resort areas include Bangor, with elegant Victorian houses, golf courses, and yacht clubs, and Holywood on Belfast Lough, location of the Ulster Folk and Transport Museum. Portaferry, with its aquarium and handsome square of Georgian structures, is one of many highly regarded fishing centers. Newcastle, a popular resort with a world-famous golf course, a harbor full of sailing vessels, and a Victorian seaside promenade, lies near Northern Ireland's highest peak, the 852-meter (2,796-foot) Slieve Donard. Nestled in the northern foothills of the Mourne Mountains, Castlewellan's National Arboretum showcases indigenous and exotic plants. Nearby, Tollymore Forest Park features wooded walks along the River Shimna.

County Fermanagh

A quiet, inland county, Fermanagh's length is spanned by the Erne River and its unique system of lakes, now joined to the Shannon via the Shannon-Erne Waterway. Fishing and boating on the uncrowded waterways draw visitors from near and far. Many also visit Belleek to view the Old World expertise that fashions its delicate and intricate pottery. Ancient archaeological figures abound in Fermanagh, especially on the hundreds of islands that dot this county's fish-filled lakes. East of Belleek on Lower Lough Erne is Castle Caldwell Forest, a nature reserve and bird sanctuary and one of Ireland's oldest state forests. White Island features early Christian figures and Devinish Island, a well-preserved, round tower. On Boa Island, accessible by bridge, a prehistoric, two-faced Janus statue guards an ancient cemetery.

Enniskillen is Fermanagh's largest town, a boating and fishing center and a former recipient of the Best Kept Large Town award. Enniskillen provides a wealth of historic sites, including a medieval castle, once the seat of the Maguire chieftains and now a museum highlighting the region's natural and military history. Nearby are two elegant eighteenth-century mansions, Castle Coole and Florence Court. Near the town are the Marble Arch caves, where a boat trip on a subterranean lake reveals the splendor of underwater caves.

County Tyrone

Tyrone, another quiet inland county, is the North's largest. It is dominated by the Sperrin Mountains. Numerous ancient burial chambers and monuments are found here, as well as early Christian remains and High Crosses. Near Cookstown the alignment of the Beaghmore stone circles is said to correlate with the movements of sun, moon, and stars.

Tyrone's largest town, Omagh, was the scene of a tragic bombing in 1998 that killed 29 people and enraged conflict-weary citizens on both sides of the border. Several rivers meet near the center of town, crossed by unique bridges like the narrow seventeenth-century King James Bridge and the early nineteenth-century five-arched Bell's Bridge. Jimmy Kennedy, who composed "Red Sails at Sunset" and "The Teddy Bear's Picnic" among other songs, was born in Omagh in 1902.

Formerly a thriving linen center, Cookstown is now distinguished by a lively Saturday market of livestock and street vendors. A busy town of the textiles industry, Dungannon is the site of the Ulysses S. Grant ancestral home. Close by, the Tyrone Crystal Factory conducts tours. Linen is still fashioned in Strabane, a busy town on the banks of the River Mourne. Nearby, in Dergalt, is the site of Woodrow Wilson's ancestral home, still occupied by family members.

Ulster American Folk Park, reminiscent of Williamsburg Village in Virginia, brings visitors to Camphill, outside of Omagh. Authentically restored dwellings portray the humble beginnings of the Mellon family, of American steel and banking fame. An annual Fourth of July celebration commemorates U.S. Independence Day.

GETTING AROUND IRELAND

Public Transportation

Ireland is well served by air, water, rail, and road transportation. Aer Lingus, the Irish international airline, flies to and from Europe and numerous transatlantic airports, including Boston, New York, Chicago, and Los Angeles. Delta offers regular flights from Dublin to Atlanta, Georgia. A number of other airlines have flights into Ireland's major airports, in Dublin, Cork, and Shannon; as well as to regional airports in Galway, Kerry, Sligo, Donegal, and Waterford.

Ferry services regularly carry passengers to ports in Scotland, England, Wales, and France. Rail services connect Dublin with most major cities and towns, and buses link many smaller communities. Taxi service in major cities and towns is good; drivers are courteous and helpful, and fares are reasonable.

CIE, the Irish transport system, manages several bus and rail services, known for being convenient, inexpensive—and occasionally overcrowded. Bus Éireann (Irish Bus) operates rural and long-distance services throughout Ireland and city services in Cork, Limerick, Galway, Waterford, Dundalk, and Drogheda. Bus Áthá Cliath (Dublin Bus) operates all city services in Dublin City and County, and some commuter routes into Counties Wicklow and Kildare. Iarnrod Eireann (Irish Rail) transports passengers around Ireland and into Northern Ireland. Dublin Area Rapid Transit (DART) is a light-rail service to and from coastal areas and Dublin City. Scheduled for completion within the next four to five years, LUAS will be a major new light-rail system; it is planned to serve key locations in Dublin City and County.

Those ages sixty-six and over qualify for free travel on public transport, and on some private bus and ferry services during nonpeak hours. An accompanying spouse travels free as well. People under age sixty-six with certain disabilities qualify, too. The Pension Services Office in Sligo will provide applications and a list of private services that honor travel passes. There are also various discount programs for touring by bus and/or rail. (The Resource Guide provides contact information.)

Hitchhiking

In the past hitchhiking was a common method for making both short and long journeys in Ireland. Many people, residents and tourists alike, relied on hitching to see the sights, run an errand, or return home from the pub. Today, while it is still relatively safe to hitchhike, fewer people do. Many women claim that they will no longer assume this risk, however minor. Thus they will neither hitch nor (unless they happen to recognize the hitchhiker) offer a lift.

Cycling

Many people in Ireland use a bicycle to travel to and from work or to run local errands. When the weather is good, cycling is a great way to get around and to explore the countryside. Roads can be hilly and bumpy, however, and the usual recommended safety approaches are warranted, especially on narrow roads in scenic areas.

Weather-protected storage for bicycles is advised. Alternatively, bike rentals are widely available at reasonable cost.

Driving

In Ireland, as in the United Kingdom, people drive on the left side of the road. Those of us who have spent many years doing it the other way may require a period of adjustment to reverse the right-side habit. We need to adapt, not just as drivers, but also as passengers and pedestrians.

Until your central nervous system makes the shift, take extra care. It takes time to rewire instinctive reactions, which may mislead you to enter the car on the wrong side, pull off the road onto the right shoulder, and look first to the left when you prepare to cross a road. (In cities, LOOK RIGHT signs painted curbside will remind you to reverse your instincts.) Intersections and roundabouts at first can seem a bit daunting. Conscientious practice, however, will soon prevail. Initially, test your left-side driving skills on less-traveled roads, away from busy city streets. Until you are fully comfortable and competent, forego long trips, nighttime driving, and unnecessary distractions like loud music.

Unless otherwise indicated, speed limits are 70 miles per hour on motorways, 60 miles per hour on main roads, and 30 miles per hour in cities and towns. Cars with trailers in tow are usually restricted to travel at 40 miles per hour.

"M" routes are motorways—divided highways with four or more lanes and an emergency lane in either direction. Other designations include "N," for national primary and secondary routes; and "R," for regional roads. Distances are usually posted in both kilometers and miles. The main roadways in Ireland have improved considerably over recent years. Many rural routes, however, are still narrow, curvy, and bumpy. Drive at a safe speed and remember that animals often enter the roadway. Be prepared to stop for flocks of sheep, the ultimate Irish traffic jam!

Avoid creating one hazard that residents of scenic areas claim is all too common. Puttering along on a country road, you round a bend and a gorgeous landscape, quaint cottage, or dramatic seascape leaps into view. Resist the urge to stop abruptly to gawk. Drivers behind you may be on their way to work and will not appreciate your disregard for their progress, however thrilling the tableau. Instead, continue on until you find a safe place to pull over (to the left!).

Traffic has been increasing steadily in many areas of Ireland. Rush-hour gridlock plagues Dublin, and traffic snarls have begun to emerge in other cities and some mid-size towns as well. Roadway construction often causes delays. Still, traffic in Ireland seldom approaches the terrible mess that people endure daily in many parts of other countries.

Road safety is of great concern in Ireland. Seat belts are mandatory for the driver and all passengers. In 1994, 404 people died in Ireland as a result of auto accidents. By 1997, this figure had jumped to 472 and then fell to 461 in 1998. Most fatal accidents occur in the early hours of the morning. One third of all road deaths are attributed to alcohol use, a few more to excessive speed.

Careless attitudes toward speeding, lack of compliance with the seat-belt requirement, and irregular enforcement have been suggested as significant contributors to the annual death rate. Gardai have set a target of reducing annual fatalities by 20 percent by 2002. Some see this goal as insufficient. If safety advocates have their way, additional strategies to combat speeding and driving under the influence of alcohol and stricter licensing procedures will be implemented.

To improve road safety as well as to reduce air pollution and noise, the government is launching a new program to inspect vehicles at testing centers around the country. Vehicles older than four years will be tested every other year to evaluate their brakes, steering, suspension, windshield, lights, axles, bodywork, safety belts, speedometer, noise, and emissions. A windshield sticker will indicate that a car has been deemed roadworthy. Because some cars in Ireland, especially in outlying areas, appear to be in less than top shape, the testing program will likely bring a fair amount of new business to automobile-repair shops.

Despite the need for extra care and patience, traveling by car is a fine way to explore the country. Many regions afford considerable driving pleasure, and even busy cities are quite manageable during nonpeak times.

Ireland is a small country, and it is fairly easy to get from here to there by car. Still, what looks like a short distance on a map may take longer than you think, because roads rarely bypass towns and can be narrow, slippery from rain, or periodically blocked by farm machinery and animals. Drive times for major routes from Dublin, assuming normal road conditions, will generally be as follows:

Driving time from Dublin to:

Galway: 3 hours	Tralee: 4–4½ hours
Cork: 4 hours	Dingle Town: 4½–5 hours
Limerick: 2½ hours	Kilkenny City: 2 hours
Shannon Airport: 3 hours	Tipperary Town: 2–2½ hours
Belfast: 2 hours	Wicklow: 1 hour
Sligo Town: 3–3½ hours	Wexford: 2 hours
Donegal Town: 4–4½ hours	Waterford City: 3 hours

Drivers' Licenses

A current U.S. or Canadian license will allow you to drive in Ireland for one year. After that you must apply for a provisional license and pass a multiple-choice test to ensure that you understand the basic rules of the road. You may subsequently register to take a road test, required to qualify for a permanent license. It is best to register early, since there is often a backlog of people wanting to be tested.

If you pass the driving test, you're eligible for a permanent license. If you fail, you can reapply for a provisional license and rejoin the 24 percent of drivers in Ireland who hold a provisional license only (often for many years). Drivers with a provisional license are supposed to have a fully licensed driver accompany them, but this rule is rarely enforced. Safety advocates cite this lapse in enforcement as a direct contributor to danger on the road. They also criticize the practice of rewarding those who fail a driving test with yet another provisional license.

While campaigns launched to discourage drunk driving have met with success, too many drivers continue to disregard speed limits. These factors plus a rising accident rate may soon lead to major reforms of the licensing system and even tougher measures to discourage speeding.

Owning a Car

Your need for a car in Ireland will depend on the locale in which you settle. You may want a car, especially if you choose a remote community where public transportation is more limited. Living in a city or mid-size town, you might choose to do without. Public transportation could provide what you need. A bicycle might serve for some destinations, though damp weather and hills can be challenging. More likely, you'll want the freedom to go where and when you want with ease. Owning and operating a car in Ireland, however, is quite costly. You'll need to allocate a larger portion of your budget for this expenditure.

Importing Your Vehicle

It is possible to bring your car into Ireland. To qualify for exemption from a number of import fees, the vehicle must be your personal property. (Establishing the vehicle as personal property will exempt you from paying vehicle registration tax, customs duty, and VAT.) This means that you have owned and operated it for at least six months before importing it and will not use it for commercial purposes. You will need to produce documents that support your home-country residence, intention to reside in Ireland, and ownership of the vehicle. These include your registration, proof of insurance, sales receipt, shipping ticket, and maintenance/repair records. The forms to complete are available from vehicle registration offices and customs stations.

You must bring your vehicle into Ireland within a year of your move. You may not sell the car within a year of registering it in Ireland, or you will then owe the taxes from which you have been exempted.

The high cost to purchase a car once you have settled in Ireland may encourage you to consider importing your vehicle. For several reasons, however, this may not be a good idea. It is more difficult to drive a right-handed vehicle on the left side of the road, since the driver position is on the side rather than toward the center of the road, and it will be difficult to obtain insurance coverage in Ireland for a vehicle that is designed to drive on the right. Finally, there is the inconvenience to you and other drivers that arises whenever you enter a parking garage and need to get out of your car and walk around to the opposite side to retrieve the machine-released ticket.

Buying a Car

Until the recent era of prosperity, it was unusual to see many new cars in Ireland. Since 1994, however, sales of new cars have increased about 20 percent each year. Owning a new car is a way to enjoy recent gains in disposable income as well as to communicate your success to others. Still, many people are satisfied with the economical, reliable transportation afforded by used cars. Sales of these are also rising, and classified ads are a good source for finding them. (The Resource Guide lists Web sites with search engines to locate car dealers and vehicles, new and used.)

The cost of a new or used car is much higher in Ireland than in continental Europe or North America. One strategy employed by many expatriates is to establish a relationship with a reputable mechanic in the community and ask this person to scout for a reliable used car. Car loans are readily available at low interest rates, with payment plans that permit skipping a payment once or twice a year. Automatic transmissions are available but not common. The following are examples of prices in recent advertisements:

New (1999) cars
BMW 316I, 4-door, 1,600 cc. $33,450
Chrysler Neon, 4-door, 1,800 cc. $21,712
Ford Fiesta LX hatchback, 1,250 cc. $16,425
Ford Ka, 1,300 cc. $13,365
Ford Mondeo Aspen, 4-door, 1,600 cc. $25,050
Ford Puma, 1,400 cc. $23,812
Honda Civic hatchback, 1,400 cc. $18,840
Jeep Cherokee, 2,500 cc. $44,148
Kia Mentor hatchback, 1,500 cc. $17,752

Land Rover Freelander, 1,800 cc. $29,362
Mercedes Benz E220D, 4-door, 2,200 cc. $46,552
Nissan Almera GX, 4-door, 1,400 cc. $20,392
Toyota Corolla Linea Terra, 4-door, 1,300 cc. $21,645
Toyota RAV 4, 3-door, 2,000 cc. $31,455
Toyota Starlet hatchback, 1,300 cc. $16,305
Volvo V40 station wagon, 1,800 cc. $28,537
Volkswagen Polo 1.0 hatchback, 1,000 cc. $15,300

Used cars

'98 Toyota Camry, 2,200 cc, 5,000 miles. $39,750
'98 VW Golf hatchback, 1,400 cc, 56,000 miles. $13,125
'97 Honda Prelude, 2,200 cc, 5,000 miles. $32,992
'97 Jeep Cherokee, four-wheel drive, 2,500 cc, 22,500 miles. $25,800
'97 Toyota Camry, 2,200 cc, 11,000 miles. $25,800
'95 Ford Escort, 1,400 cc, 35,000 miles. $10,875
'95 Ford Fiesta hatchback, 1,100 cc, 42,000 miles. $9,600
'95 Volvo station wagon, 2,000 cc, 53,000 miles. $17,775
'94 Isuzu Trooper, four-wheel drive, 3,100 cc, 29,000 miles. $31,425
'93 Honda Civic, 1,300 cc, 45,000 miles. $11,925
'93 Saab, 2,000 cc, 60,000 miles. $13,500
'92 Volvo 440, 1,600 cc, 71,000 miles. $6,750
'91 Honda Civic, 1,500 cc, 65,000 miles. $8,175
'91 Nissan Micra hatchback, 1,000 cc, 55,000 miles. $6,375
'90 Ford Fiesta hatchback, 1,200 cc, 70,000 miles. $4,800
'89 Volvo 240 GL, 2,000 cc, 160,000 miles. $4,275

Other Automobile-Related Costs

Once you have recovered from sticker shock at car prices, you will need to consider additional car-related costs that you will incur.

Vehicle Registration Tax

You must pay a one-time vehicle registration tax (VRT) upon registering any vehicle in Ireland, unless you import your car as part of a move and file for an exemption. The Vehicle Registration Office calculates this tax as a percentage of the expected retail price or open market selling price (OMSP). You must pay this tax within a day of taking delivery of the vehicle. You will receive a receipt and registration number.

Within several days you will receive a registration certificate in the mail. Unregistered vehicles may be confiscated.

Motor Tax

You are liable for annual motor (also called car or road) tax the first time you use your car in a public place. Motor tax is assessed based on engine size. For smaller cars that are easier to maneuver on narrow Irish roads, tax is less. For engines up to 1,000 cc, the road tax is $142; for engines between 1,200 and 1,800 cc, road tax ranges from $232 to $445. For the 2,200 cc engine of a Toyota Camry, the annual tax is about $630.

Insurance

Irish law requires that you insure your automobile. Basic coverage runs from approximately $450 to $1,100 per year, depending on a number of variables. Rates are higher for younger males and city dwellers. People driving on a full rather than a provisional license qualify for discounted rates. Discounts also apply when a car is garaged and/or has an alarm system. A driver with a clean record earns a no-claims discount from some insurers. Combining car insurance with homeowner's coverage will also reduce insurance costs. The insurance industry is fairly competitive, so utilizing the services of an insurance broker may help you to secure the best rates.

Petrol and Maintenance

Routine maintenance for most cars runs between $300 and $450 per year. A car's fuel economy is important in Ireland, where petrol (gasoline) is very expensive by North American standards. Sold by the liter, petrol rates have recently been around $0.83. That translates into a per-gallon rate of approximately $3.14. Smaller, efficient engines deliver better mileage than do those of high performance cars.

License fees

There is a $45 fee to take the driving test. Signing up for a driving lesson is an excellent way to prepare. A fee of $18 is charged for a provisional license. For a full license, you may pay either $18 for three years or $30 once every ten years.

Traveling for Pleasure

A wonderful part of the process of settling in Ireland is to hit the road and see the country. Ireland's small size and diversity make it a convenient and stimulating place for getaways. Many hotels offer off-season and midweek specials, and B&Bs are plentiful, comfortable, and reasonably priced. Exploring regions at a leisurely pace, guided by the growing sensibility of a resident as opposed to a tourist, is a delightful way to gain a fresh perspective on Ireland and its many charms. If possible, avoid traveling on bank holiday weekends and other major holidays, when people taking a much-deserved break from work crowd the roadways.

PRACTICAL MATTERS

For most of us, an international move constitutes a life change of major magnitude. Such a change may reawaken an adventurous spirit that has been to some degree stymied by years of fulfilling responsibilities to family and career. Many people find that adapting to a new way of life is a stimulating process of external and internal discovery. There may be times, though, when unfamiliarity makes us homesick or uncomfortable.

Leaving the familiar context of our former home, we challenge ourselves within the dynamics of a new environment. As we learn the ways of our new community, we begin to establish our place within it. Adapting to change may bring a sense of personal accomplishment that arises from making our way in a new world. A spirit of discovery serves us well. And as we'll see in Chapter 12, which explores further this process of transition, the absence of a language barrier does not mean that there are no real adjustments to be made. Cultivating an open mind and embracing the challenge that change invariably creates will enhance the potential for a rewarding transition experience.

On a more practical level, how well we cope with changes in our day-to-day routines and homespun habits will determine our level of satisfaction and comfort in a new land. In our increasingly globalized society, some aspects of Irish life will not be much different, and we may be surprised to discover a number of similarities. But there are differences, and the tens of thousands of North Americans living in Ireland today appear to have adapted to them with considerable success. Gathering information about matters of daily life in preparation for a move supports a smoother transition. This chapter will guide you through various practical matters that may arise in the process of settling in Ireland. To begin, let's consider how you should approach the issue of deciding what to bring with you to Ireland.

What to Bring

Deciding what to bring—and what to leave behind—will require thought and some degree of discipline. To reduce moving costs, which are based on weight and distance, try to practice a less-is-more approach. Considering that living and storage space is generally more limited in Ireland, it is usually a good idea to leave behind large items.

Oversized sofas, chairs, and tables may crowd an Irish "reception" (living or sitting) room, and bedrooms may not comfortably accommodate a queen- or king-size bed. Most rentals come fully furnished, but should you decide that you will need one or several pieces of furniture, buying them in Ireland ensures they will be consistent with styles there. If you are having difficulty deciding whether or not to classify a specific item as a "leave behind," note when you last used it. If this was longer than a year ago, think about leaving rather than taking it. If placing things in storage is an option you might consider, remember that over time, what you pay for storage rental might be a sum that could instead be allocated to purchase new items.

Organize all important documents related to your health, finances, and insurance, and carry them with you in a secure binder or pouch. Bring a few small items of sentimental value if leaving them will distress you, but try not to go overboard. Bring items that you are likely to put to good use in Ireland—your camera, binoculars, golf clubs, needlework, and fishing gear. Bring tools that may be hard to find or expensive to replace.

Acceptable dress in Ireland is generally casual. While people might dress up for an important business meeting, an evening at the opera, or a holiday party or other special event, comfortable clothes are suitable for most other situations. Especially in the countryside, clothing is chosen with outdoor elements and activities in mind. Good walking shoes for traversing country lanes and hills are a must. Fabrics that keep you warm and dry and protect you from wind are ideal. The right kind of rain gear will get lots of use. Remember that rainfall tends to be "soft"; heavy downpours, while they do occur in brief bursts, are not that common, except at higher levels in the mountains. A water-resistant coat that you can wear comfortably in light, misty rain, layered over a warm jumper (sweater) may be preferable to a bulky overcoat. Because it doesn't rain every day and there are usually a few days that are hot and sunny, bring a few items of clothing that are appropriate for warmer weather.

Many of us have a strong affection for numerous gadgets and appliances, which crowd the shelves of our kitchens, bathrooms, and garages. Small, battery-operated appliances, essential to our comfort in Ireland, may deserve to make the trip. Many of those that depend on electricity, however, may not, as the following section advises.

Electrical Current

In the United States and Canada, electrical current is delivered at 110 volts. In Ireland, the standard voltage is 220, and electrical plugs have three large pins. You can buy plug adapters, but using them will not deliver the current most of your U.S.–bought appliances need to operate properly. To avoid damaging a 110-volt appliance, you'll need a transformer that reduces Ireland's 220 volts to 110. Transformers cost about $35 each, and you'll likely need more than one. Even with a transformer, it is still possible that some appliances, especially television and video equipment, will not work properly. Thus, it may be easier to buy new appliances in Ireland rather than import your 110-volt appliances and a number of bulky, expensive transformers.

Unless you are planning to buy a new one anyway, one appliance that you may wish to bring to Ireland is your computer. Most desktop computers have a voltage-selector switch on the back that can be changed to run on a 220 system. With some laptops, the mechanism resets automatically. Consult your computer manufacturer for guidance. To minimize the risk of losing your data, be sure to back up all essential files before you switch to the 220-volt current.

Time

Ireland operates on Greenwich Mean Time (GMT), five hours ahead of Eastern Standard Time. Use of the twenty-four-hour clock, such as "1800 hours" to indicate 6:00 P.M., is not unusual. From late March until October, Ireland observes Daylight Savings Time. While winter days are short, in the summer, it stays light until 10:00 to 10:30 P.M., nearly 11:00 P.M. in the west.

The Irish approach to matters of time is such that business appointments and meetings will generally begin close to the appointed hour. Within Europe, the Irish have a reputation for being a bit lax about this; thus, if a meeting scheduled for 9:00 A.M. does not really get under way until 9:30, it will not be considered too unusual. For social gatherings the Irish are generally even more relaxed about schedule. Folks often arrive later than the indicated time and can stay late as well. Service people called to your home for repairs may not always arrive when scheduled, but they will usually phone to warn you of a delay.

Average Temperatures and Rainfall for Selected Locations (° Fahrenheit/inches)

Belfast, Northern Ireland

Avg.	Jan.	Feb.	Mar.	Apr.	May	Jun.	Jul.	Aug.	Sept.	Oct.	Nov.	Dec.	Annual
High	43	45	48	54	59	64	64	64	61	55	48	45	54
Low	36	36	37	39	43	48	52	52	48	45	39	37	43
Rain	3.2	2.1	2.0	1.9	2.1	2.7	3.8	3.1	3.2	3.3	2.9	3.6	33.9

Claremorris, County Mayo

Avg.	Jan.	Feb.	Mar.	Apr.	May	Jun.	Jul.	Aug.	Sept.	Oct.	Nov.	Dec.	Annual
High	45	46	49	53	58	63	65	65	61	56	49	46	55
Low	35	34	36	38	42	47	50	50	46	43	37	36	41
Rain	4.7	3.2	3.5	2.5	2.9	3.0	2.9	3.9	4.5	4.9	4.2	5.0	45.2

Cork City, County Cork

Avg.	Jan.	Feb.	Mar.	Apr.	May	Jun.	Jul.	Aug.	Sept.	Oct.	Nov.	Dec.	Annual
High	48	48	52	55	61	66	68	68	64	57	52	48	57
Low	36	37	39	41	45	50	54	54	50	45	39	37	45
Rain	4.8	3.2	3.8	2.3	2.8	2.3	2.8	2.8	3.8	4.0	4.6	4.9	42

Dublin Airport, County Dublin

Avg.	Jan.	Feb.	Mar.	Apr.	May	Jun.	Jul.	Aug.	Sept.	Oct.	Nov.	Dec.	Annual
High	46	46	49	52	57	63	66	65	62	57	50	47	55
Low	37	37	38	40	44	49	52	52	49	46	40	38	43
Rain	2.5	2.0	2.0	1.9	2.2	2.2	2.6	3.0	2.5	2.9	2.7	2.7	29.2

Kilkenny City, County Kilkenny

Avg.	Jan.	Feb.	Mar.	Apr.	May	Jun.	Jul.	Aug.	Sept.	Oct.	Nov.	Dec.	Annual
High	46	46	50	54	59	64	68	67	63	57	50	47	56
Low	35	35	36	38	42	47	51	50	46	43	37	36	41
Rain	3.5	2.6	2.6	2.2	2.2	2.1	2.2	2.7	3.0	3.3	3.0	3.3	32.7

Average Temperatures and Rainfall for Selected Locations (° *Fahrenheit/inches*)

Malin Head, County Donegal

Avg.	Jan.	Feb.	Mar.	Apr.	May	Jun.	Jul.	Aug.	Sept.	Oct.	Nov.	Dec.	Annual
High	46	45	48	50	55	59	61	62	59	55	50	57	53
Low	38	37	39	41	45	49	52	53	50	47	41	40	44
Rain	4.5	3.1	3.2	2.2	2.3	2.7	3.0	3.5	4.0	4.5	4.3	4.3	41.6

Mullingar, County Westmeath

Avg.	Jan.	Feb.	Mar.	Apr.	May	Jun.	Jul.	Aug.	Sept.	Oct.	Nov.	Dec.	Annual
High	45	45	50	55	61	64	66	66	63	55	50	46	55
Low	34	34	37	39	43	48	52	50	48	43	39	36	41
Rain	3.5	2.5	2.4	2.2	2.4	3.0	3.6	3.5	4.0	3.8	3.4	4.4	38.7

Rosslare, County Wexfor

Avg.	Jan.	Feb.	Mar.	Apr.	May	Jun.	Jul.	Aug.	Sept.	Oct.	Nov.	Dec.	Annual
High	47	46	49	51	56	60	64	64	61	57	51	48	55
Low	39	39	40	42	46	51	54	54	51	48	42	41	46
Rain	3.8	2.4	2.7	2.5	2.1	2.2	1.9	2.6	3.0	3.6	4.0	3.8	34.6

Shannon Airport, County Clare

Avg.	Jan.	Feb.	Mar.	Apr.	May	Jun.	Jul.	Aug.	Sept.	Oct.	Nov.	Dec.	Annual
High	47	47	51	55	60	64	67	66	63	57	51	48	56
Low	37	37	39	41	45	50	54	53	50	46	40	39	44
Rain	3.9	2.9	2.7	2.3	2.4	2.6	2.9	3.5	3.3	3.8	3.8	4.2	38.3

Valentia Island, County Kerry

Avg.	Jan.	Feb.	Mar.	Apr.	May	Jun.	Jul.	Aug.	Sept.	Oct.	Nov.	Dec.	Annual
High	48	48	52	55	59	63	64	64	63	57	54	50	57
Low	41	39	41	43	46	52	54	55	52	48	45	43	46
Rain	6.6	4.3	4.1	3.0	3.4	3.2	4.3	3.8	4.9	5.6	6.0	6.7	55.9

Dates

In Ireland, as in other European countries, it is customary to write dates in a day, month, year sequence as opposed to the convention of month, day, year observed in the United States. Thus, "11/12/99" represents December 11, rather than November 12. It takes a while to alter the habit of reversing the month-day order, but it is a necessary adjustment.

Temperature: Celsius versus Fahrenheit

When someone in Ireland exclaims "It's going to be twenty-two degrees today!" you are supposed to get out your sunscreen and the pair of shorts you've been saving for a warm, sunny day rather than stoke the fire and reach for a woolen scarf. For those who are accustomed to using degrees Fahrenheit, it takes time to adapt to hearing weather temperatures in Celsius. There is a formula for converting from one to another [Fahrenheit = (Celsius x $\frac{9}{5}$) + 32], but it's not realistic for most of us to calculate conversions in our head. Soon, you'll grow accustomed to the relative significance. Here are a few conversions to get you used to the idea:

° Celsius (C)	° Fahrenheit (F)
1–4	34–39
5–9	41–48
10–14	50–57
15–19	59–66
20–24	68–75
25–30	77–86

Holidays

The Irish know how to mark an occasion and do so with great flourish. Many holidays are similar to those observed in North America, though the manner of celebration will naturally have a uniquely Irish touch. Some holiday rituals owe their existence to ancient traditions. The "holy day" aspect of holidays with religious significance will generally be more evident than in North American celebrations. The following summarizes how many people in Ireland celebrate several key holidays:

St. Patrick's Day

A lively five-day festival each year in Dublin commemorates St. Patrick's Day. Overall, however, in Ireland the holiday is more of a religious observance than the untamed revelry of green beer and carousing in many parts of the States and Canada. Locals and off-season tourists will attend the parades held in most Irish cities, but these do not approach the scale of those in many U.S. cities and towns. Still, March 17 is generally a fun day out for the family, and young children in particular will enjoy the parades.

Halloween

Mirroring an ancient Celtic tradition, Halloween also marks the eve ("All Hallows Eve") of All Saints Day. Jack o' lanterns, trick-or-treating, and costumes are very much in evidence in Ireland. Many communities will have a bonfire and fireworks, though both are officially illegal.

Barm brack, a cakelike bread made with currants, is an old recipe traditionally prepared at Halloween. Another is colcannon, a dish of mashed potatoes and boiled kale. To add to the fun, children search for money that has been wrapped and added to the ingredients.

Christmas

The Christmas holiday emphasizes family togetherness and religious observation, though it has its commercial aspects as well. Irish people will typically trim a tree and decorate the mantel and dining table. A lighted candle in the window signifies a welcome to the Holy Family. Religious services are customary on Christmas Eve and Christmas morning. On Christmas Day families gather to exchange gifts and enjoy the holiday feast, often spiced beef, turkey, or ham. Dessert might be trifle custard poured over layers of sponge cake and fruit and topped with whipped cream. Or it might be Christmas cake, made with raisins, nuts, and candied cherries, baked for as long as six hours and finally sprinkled with Irish whiskey.

St. Stephen's Day

St. Stephen, the first Christian martyr, was honored by having his feast day designated as the day after that honoring Jesus' birth. Thus, on December 26, morning mass attendance is customary. Later in the day a tradition called "The Wren Boys" takes place. Young boys in the neighborhood dress up in straw masks and hats. People in the community often follow them as they make their way around the neighborhood, dancing and playing traditional music. In old times they would kill a wren (this is now a symbolic rather than an actual practice). They would carry the wren from house to house, and in a bid for donations, would chant the following verse, which varied slightly depending on region:

The wren, the wren, the king of all birds,
On St. Stephen's Day was caught in the furze,*
Though his body is small, his family is great,
So rise up good woman and give us a treat.
Up with the kettle and down with the pan,
And give us a penny to bury the wran.**

* gorse, a shrub
** wren

Little Christmas

Christmas holiday decorations are not taken down until January 6, known as the Feast of Epiphany, or Little Christmas. In the Irish language the day is called Nollaig Na Mban, or "Women's Christmas." This is a day when women traditionally were able to relax after the holiday bustle.

Easter

Good Friday is not a state holiday, so some people may be at work that day. For many others, however, Easter provides an extended, Friday-to-Monday break. Alcohol is not sold anywhere in Ireland on Good Friday, and any supermarket that sells it must close for the day. Good Friday is the one and only day of the year when the pubs are closed. Many people, especially the older generation, attend church services on Good Friday.

Easter Sunday draws significant numbers to Catholic mass, and even those who rarely attend church services will make an appearance. Easter egg hunts are not an Irish custom, but gifts of Easter confectionery are routinely offered. Children welcome these gifts of candy, especially those who may have given up sweets for the period of Lent, which commenced weeks before, on Ash Wednesday. Adults of Catholic faith often surrender their cigarettes for Lent and try their best to refrain from taking them up again.

Bank Holidays

The bank holidays that fall on the first Mondays in May, June, and August and on the last Monday in October create a much-anticipated long weekend break. People tend to make special plans, and pubs become more crowded and lively. If the weather is good, many people take to the roads, and traffic can be heavy.

The following is a list of public holidays, during which most shops, banks, and offices are closed and public transportation operates on a reduced schedule.

Public Holidays

New Year's Day, January 1
St. Patrick's Day, March 17
Easter Monday, date varies
Christmas Day, December 25
St. Stephen's Day, December 26
Bank holidays, first Mondays in May, June, August; last Monday in October

Vacations

Many Irish people take their holidays within the country; seaside resorts like Bundoran, Tramore, Kilkee, and Newcastle draw many natives. Those who can afford it may seek the warm climate and sunny skies of Spain, Turkey, Greece, the south of France, or the Channel Islands. North America is also a popular destination. In recent years it has become more common to choose vacation spots that in Ireland are considered exotic, such as Mexico and the Caribbean.

Services

In many contexts the Irish are excellent at providing good service. From the accommodating demeanor of restaurant waitstaff and department-store clerks to public servants who handle inquiries, there is usually a con-certed effort to please. In the small shops that serve local communities, there may be a wait at the counter while the cashier exchanges pleasantries and news with customers ahead of you. This is merely another form of attentive service, though it may seem less so if you are in a hurry.

In some service sectors in Ireland, a customer orientation is a more recent phenomenon. Many feel that public transport agencies, for example, have not always emphasized customer needs sufficiently. A bank may sporadically make errors in calculating interest due to customers; consumer advocates encourage everyone to check statements carefully. People who have been contracted to provide services in the home may not always appear at the time agreed. Increasing competition within Ireland and across the European Union marketplace has encouraged a greater focus on quality standards, consumer advocacy, and customer service. As this trend continues, those areas known for less than brilliant service will likely improve.

Home Maintenance

With the construction industry now employing more people in Ireland than agriculture, anyone with the appropriate tools and skills is in high demand. Anticipate as far in advance any repair work that your home may require. In major cities and towns, consult the "golden" (yellow) pages and local paper for listings. Check with your neighbors for referrals. In smaller areas there are usually several local people, well known in the community, who do repairs and minor renovations.

Auto Repairs

The salty, misty air around Ireland's coastal areas can be tough on a car's body. Bumpy country roads exact a toll on shocks, wheel alignment, and tires. With Ireland's high petrol (gasoline) prices, fuel economy is paramount; it requires a well-tuned engine and properly inflated tires. Windshield wipers get lots of use and need to be replaced regularly.

You may choose to do a lot of your own maintenance. If you are not so inclined or able, the services of a good mechanic will be of considerable value. Start your search for a reliable mechanic before car problems arise. You may have limited choices in smaller communities, and parts inventories may be less replete, but you'll benefit from a tighter network from which to solicit referrals. Cities and towns have well-equipped repair garages, but it may take a while to secure an appointment and to have the work completed, especially if special parts are required.

Water and Refuse Collection

In most areas, including Dublin, domestic water service, sewage disposal, and garbage collection are free. In some areas these services are provided by the local authorities, by independent contractors, or via group water schemes; in these cases there is a modest charge of around $12 to $15 per month.

Tax relief can be claimed for payments that are made in full and on time within the previous calendar year. The maximum relief in any tax year is $225 at the standard rate. There is an expectation that water may soon become metered and charged under the influence of comparable systems within the European Union.

Post Office

Like other Irish institutions, An Post, the semi-state postal system, is in the throes of redefining itself in the face of competition. Approximately 8,000 people work for An Post, which handles 640 million items a year, mostly letters. In years past there were several mail deliveries each day except Sunday; if you posted a letter first thing in the morning, it would most likely arrive at its Ireland destination later the same day. Now there is one delivery per weekday and none on Saturday and Sunday. Despite the fact that zip codes, which speed mail sorting, are not used in Ireland, most letters within Ireland arrive within one day.

Postal rates went unchanged for some years, until 1998, when An Post consolidated several categories and *reduced* rates for most of them. To send a letter within Ireland, Britain, or Continental Europe currently costs 45 cents; to Canada, the United States, and the rest of the world, 68 cents.

More than just a place to buy stamps and mail letters, An Post provides savings and investment programs, issues social welfare and pension checks, accepts payments of phone and utility bills, and sells phone cards and television licenses. The agency also manages the National Lottery and has a Web site with a tracking service. Through its subsidiary PostGem, An Post owns the leading Internet service provider, Ireland Online (IOL).

Staff are congenial and willing to answer inquiries and provide literature. Many people establish deposit and special savings accounts. One complaint that frequently arises about An Post relates to its refusal, for security reasons, to give account information over the phone. You either have to appear in person or send a written request for information.

A European Union directive requiring liberalization (deregulation) over the next decade of European postal services means that An Post will see some portion of its service open to further competition within a few years. It already faces competition from a number of local and national courier services, including DHL, Federal Express, and UPS, which are well established in Ireland.

Many of An Post's 19,000 branches are rural, run by a postmaster or mistress, who receives a modest salary in exchange for running the service. In smaller areas, the post office provides another hub, in addition to local pubs and shops, to catch up on news of the community. Another indication of Irish cordiality, the delivery person driving the green An Post minivan is usually happy to give you a lift to the next town.

Telephone

Originally part of the postal service, the telecommunications industry was established as a separate entity in 1974. At that time the industry was in poor shape. Run as a monopoly by Telecom Eireann, customer service was dismal. It was not unusual to wait months for a new service connection. Great strides were achieved in the intervening years, however, bolstered by substantial investments in switching equipment. A degree of competition was introduced, which encouraged the creation of alternative infrastructures, data services, and mobile networks. These improvements created an environment favorable to the development of "call centers," phone-based customer service companies that now employ thousands in Ireland. Call center staff provide multilingual services, including technical support, reservations, and order processing for the worldwide customers of companies like Dell, Gateway, Coca-Cola, and Guinness. Within a relatively short time, call centers have become a leading generator of jobs and revenues.

Further deregulation of the telecommunications industry is under way. Consumers may choose an alternative to Telecom Eireann to carry long distance and international calls. A number of companies are entering the residential market. To improve its position as competition intensifies, Telecom Eireann is retooling its image to indicate a shift from the telephone company to a technology-driven communications firm. The former monopoly has reduced rates, pledged better service, and even changed its name: It will now be known as Eircom.

Service has already improved markedly. New connections are much more prompt, generally up and running within a week or two. Problems on a phone line are addressed promptly, and if a problem is not corrected within two working days, you are credited with one month's rental. Currently, the monthly cost for line rental is $15.

Equipment rental adds several more dollars. As more players enter the telecommunications market, all service providers are expected to decrease prices and launch new services.

The current system for telephone-call charges, which may be simplified by the process of deregulation, will initially seem complicated. Have patience and remember that a phone bill in North America may be equally complex.

Although competitors new to the market are promising to try to offer flat rates for local calls and for Internet service, local calls are not covered as they are in the United States and Canada by a single charge. Instead, the cost of a call is determined by the number of units used. Each unit buys a specified amount of calling time. The amount of time a unit buys depends on the time of day, the day of the week, and the destination of the call. The standard unit fee, including VAT at 21 percent, is now just over 17 cents. The standard rate applies from 8:00 A.M. to 6:00 P.M., Monday to Friday. Rates are reduced from 6:00 P.M. to 8:00 A.M. from Monday to Friday and all day Saturday, Sunday, and public holidays. From midnight Friday until midnight Sunday, all national calls are charged at local rates; reductions for other weekend services are also applied.

A unit for direct-dialed, local calls at the standard rate is three minutes. Thus, if you phone someone locally between 8:00 A.M. and 6:00 P.M. on a weekday and speak for thirty minutes, the call will cost approximately $1.75. If you wait until after 6:00 P.M., the same call costs only 35 cents. At current rates, therefore, don't expect to receive a large number of phone calls during a weekday!

A call to the United States and Canada costs approximately 48 cents per minute. Pay-phone, mobile-phone, and operator-assisted calls are more expensive than local calls from home. The use of phone cards, available for purchase at the post office and retail shops, is widespread in Ireland. Over 65 percent of the 8,000 public pay-phones in Ireland accept phone cards. Available in a range of unit denominations, they offer an economical alternative to high pay-phone and hotel-phone rates. Card-based mobile-phone service is also available. Fourteen percent of the Irish use mobile phones, and this area of the market is expected to see significant growth.

For Directory Service, dial 1190 for the Republic and Northern Ireland, 1197 for Great Britain, and 1198 for international excluding Great Britain. You may request three numbers on each call, and in each billing period, you are entitled to three free Directory Service calls. For emergency service dial 999 or 112 and specify the type of help you need, whether fire, police, ambulance, or special rescue services. Emergency calls are free.

When phoning within Ireland, use the area prefix unless you are calling within that same area. The prefixes are 01 for Dublin, 021 for Cork, 091 for Galway, 061 for Limerick, 0902 for Athlone, 049 for Cavan, 0903 for Roscommon, 073 for Donegal, 043 for Longford, 051 for Waterford, and 056 for Kilkenny. To phone Ireland from the United States or Canada, dial the international code (011), the country code (353), the city code without the 0, and the local number. Thus, if you want to phone Kennys Bookshop in Galway (091–562739) and you are calling from within the 09 area in and around Galway, you would dial 562739. From elsewhere in Ireland you would dial 091–562739. From the United States or Canada, you would dial 011–353–91–562739.

Internet

The number of people online in Ireland has increased rapidly, and that high growth is expected to continue. As in the early days of Internet service in North America, service glitches occasionally occur. Ireland Online (IOL), owned by An Post, claims the most subscribers at well over 40,000. IOL serves primarily as a gateway to the Internet and does not at this stage offer the degree of features and content found on America Online (AOL). There are about half a dozen other Internet service providers (ISPs), including Telecom Eireann/Eircom. Costs for the service itself are around $18 to $23 per month. Costs for daytime connection through the phone line are currently 2.4¢ per minute. Thus the phone cost for an hour on the Internet during peak weekday rates is $1.44.

Media

National, regional, and local newspapers are readily available in Ireland. (You can purchase many Irish newspapers at major newsstands and large bookstores in North America, but additional postage makes them expensive, and the distance delays their delivery time.) A number of these publications maintain active Web sites, enabling you to follow the news from your computer, assuming you have access to the Internet. *The Irish Times* has a superb, award-winning Web site with a searchable archive. *The Irish Independent, Belfast Telegraph,* and the *Sunday Business Post* are also on the Web, as are many smaller, local papers. *The Connaught Telegraph, Cork Examiner, Clare Champion, Galway Advertiser, Limerick Post, Longford Leader, Munster Express,* and *Sligo Weekender* are examples of the many regional and local papers that are available online. You can check the weather, browse classified advertising, follow property news, and gain insight into a community from stories of local issues, people, and events. (The Resource Guide provides a listing of the Web site addresses for many Irish newspapers.)

National radio and television services are administered by Radio Telefís Éireann (RTE), a public broadcasting company that transmits on two television and five radio channels. CanWest, the Canadian media company, is the largest shareholder in a consortium that in September 1998 launched TV3 Television Network, an alternative to the state-owned networks. Satellite channels, including CNN, and British programming are widely available. RTE broadcasts programming in the Irish language on a national radio station, Radio na Gaeltachta, and a national television station, Teilifís na Gaeilge.

There are numerous local radio stations around the country. Connemara West Radio, in Letterfrack, County Galway, is an example of community radio at its finest. Broadcasting several hours per day, it features lively interviews, traditional music, and news of local events. Programming reveals the cornucopia of life in a rural community. Announcers might comment on the level of play at yesterday's local football match, the enormous trout that John Price caught in a local stream, or the chaos that ensued when Mrs. Cashin's cow became stuck in a ditch. The radio host will often extend wishes to congratulate a recent graduate, celebrate a birthday or anniversary, or welcome someone home from a journey. In addition to such homespun delights, the station communicates news of important community issues and inspires its audience with the local talent of musicians who perform and writers who read from their work.

Television programming can be very good, offering documentaries, world news coverage, and quality films. There is plenty of lowbrow programming, too, though it isn't interrupted so often with commercials. The annual Eurovision song competition, which launched Riverdance and other successful acts, draws a huge audience. Chat shows are very popular, as are soap operas, especially Britain's *Coronation Street* and the Irish-produced soaps *Fair City* and *Glenroe*. Many American favorites, like *Friends, Ally McBeal,* and *ER* are available, airing a while after they are telecast in the United States. Older U.S. shows fill the airwaves, from *Dynasty* and *Cheers* to the *Golden Girls* and a very young Roger Moore as *The Saint.* Shows often have odd starting times, which takes some getting used to. While many start on the half-hour or hour, some start at times like 7:35, 2:45, or 11:05.

Television License

If you have a television, you must have a current TV license. The fee for a color set is $105, less for black and white. You can purchase your license, which must be renewed annually, at any post office. You may pay cash or regularly buy Television Savings Stamps to save for the cost of a license. You may also elect to have your payment debited from a bank or credit card account. Since nonpayment is often discovered, compliance is high. Sales of television licenses bring in approximately $1.5 million per year.

Shopping

The decrease in unemployment, rise in wages, and overall improvement in the Irish economy have encouraged a boom in shopping centers. You'll find them, with parking lots jammed, in and near major cities. The presence of small independent shops, which continue to thrive, offers a pleasant alternative. Shops tend to be open from 9:00 A.M. until 5:00 or 6:00 P.M., with one late-night closing, usually Thursday or Friday. Some of the larger supermarkets and department stores now open on Sunday.

Employees are routinely gracious. When you ask where to find an item in the grocery store, they'll escort you to its location.

Ireland's cities have become much more sophisticated in recent years, and shops offer a wide range of products, including electronics, home decorations, apparel, and sporting goods. Even small shops in rural areas carry a surprising variety of goods. While the inventory may seem limited to those used to more choices, when you need to buy something, it won't be difficult to find (unless, unfortunately, you're craving pretzels, which I have yet to discover, despite a thorough search).

Pets

For over a hundred years, strict quarantine laws have been in effect in Ireland, mirroring those in the United Kingdom. Currently, these regulations require you to place your pet in a government-approved kennel for six months when entering the country. Lissenhall Quarantine Kennels and Catteries, in Swords, County Dublin, is the only approved quarantine facility in Ireland. Reservations are required well in advance, and costs are high, as much as $1,500 for a cat and $2,250 for a dog.

People moving from the United Kingdom to Ireland do not have to quarantine their pets. If you hope to avoid quarantine by transporting your pets first to the United Kingdom, however, you will not succeed. You'll have to subject them to quarantine in the United Kingdom for a similar stretch.

Fortunately, long-term efforts to reform the quarantine process recently appear to have achieved results. Support groups in London, bolstered by veterinary science experts, have succeeded in pressuring the government to reexamine a policy deemed cruel and unnecessary. In March 1999, the Agriculture Minister announced plans for a major overhaul of Britain's quarantine laws. Commencing with the launch of a pilot vaccination-based program within a year, the goal is to have a new policy fully operational by 2001.

Under the new system, pets meeting certain criteria will be able to travel freely to and from Britain, the European Union, and other specified rabies-free countries. Pets will need to be vaccinated against rabies, microchipped, blood-tested at an approved lab, treated for parasites not present in the United Kingdom, and issued with a health certificate.

Tipping

*S*ervice charges of 10 to 15 percent are usually included in restaurant checks. It is not necessary to tip, but when service is exceptional, it is fine to recognize this by rounding up the bill. If no service charge is indicated on the bill, leave 10 percent. A 10 percent tip is appropriate also for taxi drivers. Most people do not tip the bartender in a pub but will leave a small gratuity for table service.

Ireland is likely to incorporate the changes made in the British policy. Currently, the British government's position regarding the inclusion of the United States and Canada within the new plan is under review. Good sources for updates as the new policy emerges are support groups like Passports for Pets and Quarantine Abolition Fighting Forum (QUAFF). Consult the Resource Guide for contact information.

For some people, quarantine requirements have represented a major obstacle in contemplating a move. The advice sometimes given, "Leave Fluffy at home," doesn't consider the close relationship many enjoy with their pets. People do occasionally attempt to smuggle pets into Ireland, and the results can be disastrous. If caught, the owner may be fined and must pay to ship the pet home or choose instead to euthanize it.

Within the current regulations, and until reforms are established, there is an alternative in Ireland to conventional public quarantine called "public/private quarantine." Subject to approval well in advance of importation, it may be possible to quarantine your pet at the Lissenhall facility for one month and then provide private quarantine at your home in Ireland for five months. To do this, you will need to construct or adapt an approved shelter on your premises; it must prevent escape by your pet and access by birds and other wildlife. The Department of Agriculture and Food requires details of your proposed location and facility at last three months before your pet arrives. An official from the Department will inspect your facility prior to and during its use.

If you are devoted to your pet, as many are, it is well worth exploring the public/private quarantine alternative. Should you decide that it is best for you and your pet(s) to part company, do the responsible thing and make every effort to find a good home in your current community.

Religion

Though a variety of faiths are represented, Catholicism is the dominant religion in Ireland. More than 90 percent of the population claims this affiliation. While the Roman Catholic Church historically exerted considerable cultural, social, and political influence in Ireland, its power has declined. Weekly attendance at mass has decreased steadily over the past twenty-five years. The numbers of those entering religious orders have shown a similar pattern. The credibility of the Catholic Church has suffered in recent years, as a number of scandals involving priests have garnered extensive media coverage. Many Irish people find the Church out of step and reject its positions on contraception, divorce, celibacy, and women entering the priesthood.

The Catholic faith, despite its diminishing authority in Ireland, continues to maintain a prominent presence. Members of the clergy are visible everywhere you go. Church tenets and rituals continue to weave the fabric of everyday life. From the shrines flanking many villages, to holy pilgrimages attended by thousands, to the bishop-led procession to bless the fishing fleet, the tradition of faith is a visible and key component of Irish communities.

One Catholic-derived ritual that occasionally draws fire is the angelus, a twice-daily public call to prayer. Not long ago it was the custom for many families to say the rosary together, twice a day. For many years the angelus has been broadcast nationally by RTE radio and television stations every day at noon and 6:00 P.M. This pause for the angelus, marked by ringing bells, has been a source of controversy. Opponents claim that it favors the Catholic religion over others and violates the constitutional provision that the state "guarantees not to endow any religion." Others, some Protestant clergy among them, are not troubled by it and interpret it as a call to any kind of prayer, not necessarily Catholic. A recent national survey on the angelus indicated both monumental support for its continuation and a sense that its religious significance is receding.

In general, the Irish are an exceedingly tolerant people. Anyone who practices a faith other than Catholicism should experience no discomfort. Protestant churches, particularly the Church of Ireland, the Methodist Church, and the Presbyterian Church, are well established. Other forms of Protestantism—Lutheran and Baptist, for example—are also represented. In smaller communities there may be only one Protestant church, which will welcome members from all Protestant faiths.

There is a vibrant Jewish community in Ireland, and members of the Church of Jesus Christ of Latter-Day Saints also have a solid presence. Other faiths are represented, too. In recent years there has been an increase in followers of Islam, Buddhism, the Society of Friends, and the Church of Scientology.

If you eschew organized religion, you'll have plenty of company in Ireland, where not everyone attends mass or observes religious rituals. In small, rural communities your absence at church may be noted but rarely judged. One disadvantage is often expressed by those in smaller communities who don't choose to attend services: They lament the missed opportunity to catch up on news announced during services and gossip exchanged as people congregate afterward. "I'm always the last to hear the news" is a common protest.

People with Disability

In recent years various groups representing the interests of those in Ireland with disabilities have grown more active in pressing for reforms, and all agree that much needs to be done to combat prejudice, improve accessibility, and ensure fair treatment in the workplace. Health boards and, to a greater degree, voluntary organizations and religious orders provide services for the disabled with funds they receive from the government. Historically, the clergy provided these services. People with disabilities are considered to be better served in Northern Ireland, where the state is directly responsible for addressing their needs. In both the North and South, however, the disabled qualify for means-tested income support, tax concessions, and job-search assistance.

The Disability Federation of Ireland (DFI) is a national umbrella organization representing nearly seventy organizations that provide services to people with disabilities. Services range from information and support, education, training, housing and other accommodations, respite care, and paramedical and other professional services. One of the most active DFI-member organizations is the Irish Wheelchair Association (IWA), which maintains a resource-laden Web site. Headquartered in Dublin, the IWA provides general information, home-care and personal-assistant programs, and activities through day centers located across the country.

Increasingly demonstrative activist groups continue to demand that the government address the needs of the disabled. The Irish Council for People with Disabilities maintains a network of county-based advocacy groups. The National Parents' Alliance focuses on mental health issues. (For additional information on services for people with disability, see the Resource Guide.)

In 1998 Ireland established a National Disability Authority (NDA) to advise on policy and to develop standards for services to people with disabilities and monitor their implementation. For decades the disability movement in Ireland has campaigned for reforms, and it is hoped that the NDA will add strength to the demands for increased funding for residential services, respite care, personal assistants, and improved accessibility.

Wheelchair-accessibility is especially key. Although new buses to be put into service in the next few years will be wheelchair-accessible, the aisles of double-decker buses used today in Ireland's cities are not able to accommodate wheelchairs. Only six single-decker buses in Dublin are accessible by wheelchair, and all of them serve one route only, between Sandymount and Whitehall in Dublin. DART, Dublin's suburban rail system, is accessible to most wheelchair users. A gap between the platform and train at some stations, however, could prove precarious without an assistant. Regular trains have aisles that are too narrow for a wheelchair, but those in wheelchairs may remain in the chair in the vestibule area of the car. There are some taxis in major cities that can accommodate wheelchairs. Dublin airport is wheelchair-accessible.

While existing building regulations address access, their wording does not enforce compliance ("buildings should be accessible where it is reasonable and practical to make them so"). Consequently, amidst booming construction, some new buildings will not be accessible. The government does provide a grant of up to $18,000 for the costs of adaptations to make a home accessible.

The international symbol of access for the disabled identifies accommodations suitable for unaccompanied wheelchair users or other disabled persons ♿. The "Assisted" symbol indicates that premises are suitable for all disabled persons, including those in wheelchairs, with the assistance of one helper ♿. Displaying a wheelchair sign on your car entitles you to park free at meters in Dublin. Most shopping centers and public buildings designate parking spaces reserved for disabled drivers.

Personal Safety and Crime

Already low by U.S. standards, the crime rate in Ireland has decreased each year since 1996. Contributing to the decrease are a tougher approach to law enforcement, longer jail sentences, and an increased use of closed-circuit television in supermarkets, gas stations, and retail shops.

Crime does, of course, occur in Ireland. News broadcasts and headlines daily recount details of criminal activity in all parts of the country.

The rate of violent crime is quite low, however. When a violent crime does occur in Ireland, it will receive comprehensive national media attention. Crime related to drug trafficking and money laundering also earns a lot of press.

But theft, especially pickpocketing and purse snatching, is the most prevalent crime in Ireland. Thus, sales of home security systems are up, and many cars are equipped with antitheft devices. Thieves often target tourists and their rental cars. They may target the elderly, too. Be sure to report the loss or theft of a passport immediately to the local police and to your native country's embassy.

An Garda Siochana (Gaelic for "Guardians of the Peace") is one of the few unarmed law enforcement services in the world. There are 700 garda (police) stations around the country, and just over 11,000 gardai (pronounced "gar dee") are assigned to them. Each garda division has a crime prevention officer, who advises on methods to prevent crime, supports urban Neighborhood Watch and rural Community Alert programs, and visits elderly people living alone in remote rural areas.

A variety of voluntary organizations offers support to victims of crime. The Irish Victim Support Association provides emotional and practical support and operates a twenty-four-hour "help line."

There are a variety of techniques to minimize your risk for being the victim of crime:

- Always lock your car when it is unattended, even for brief periods.
- In cities or large towns, park in well-lighted parking lots.
- Do not leave luggage, valuables, or a mobile phone exposed inside a parked car, or luggage attached to a roof rack.
- Never leave your car running when you're not in it.
- Do not leave vehicle registration and insurance documents in your car.
- Do not carry large amounts of cash with you.
- Carry a handbag that can be held securely. Be vigilant in crowded streets, shops, or when stopping for a meal or drink. Placing a handbag on the floor is not a good idea.
- Have strong locks on all your doors and windows and a chain on each entry door.
- Have a viewer installed in your front door.
- Don't answer the door late at night.
- Install good lighting around your home.

- Install an effective security alarm. Contact your local crime prevention officer to see if you qualify for a security-device grant.
- Do not keep more money at home than is needed for immediate use.
- Keep credit cards, checks, and cash in a safe place.
- Request identification from anyone claiming to represent charity or utility services. Call the service for verification.
- If you'll be away from home, arrange for a neighbor to pick up your mail and newspapers.
- Keep a list of neighbors' phone numbers near the telephone.
- Be careful about sharing personal information with strangers.
- Dial 999 or 112 for emergency services.

Irish Tolerance

Smoking

A higher percentage of people in Ireland smoke than in North America. The air of conviviality in many pubs is also often clogged with tabacco smoke. If you are a smoker, you will appreciate the greater degree of tolerance that exists in Ireland, though you'll pay a lot more to enjoy it, with cigarettes selling at close to $5.00 per pack.

The long-standing tolerance of smoking may not survive the emergence of a concerted effort to discourage the habit. Thus, if you are bothered by smoke, you will be pleased to see an increasing emphasis in Ireland on promoting awareness of smoking's harmful health effects. Public service announcements do their part to drive home the message. Many restaurants provide space for nonsmokers, and some are even smoke-free.

Drinking

The enjoyment of alcoholic beverages is another area where Irish tolerance reigns. There seems to be greater acceptance of drinking as part of the culture and of those who drink, even to excess, as just having a good time. When it becomes obvious that someone in the pub has had too much, the reaction is one of indulgence as long as the person doing the weaving is not interfering with the enjoyment of others. In North America, embarrassed disapproval and a rapid escort out the door might be a more typical reaction. In Ireland someone who is casually characterized as having "a problem with the drink" might be judged without sympathy in North America as a pathetically unstable boozer.

An ability to acknowledge the influence of Irish culture on drinking norms will help the expatriate to adapt to what may be a different outlook. Bernie Dignam, a well-traveled and wise Irishwoman, and my dear friend of many years, offered an interesting theory about the role of drink in Irish life. She recently shared her perspective from an appropriate post—a cozy booth in the local pub. Bernie theorized that the Irish, having endured centuries of colonization and oppression from outsiders as well as the strict control of the Church, are as a result often disposed toward shyness and thus may need alcohol to be able to relax and enjoy themselves. She suggested that people from the States, on the other hand, some of whom are direct, even forward, don't seem to need alcohol to bolster their confidence.

She also noted that alcohol takes a serious toll on Irish health, family harmony, and road safety. The many people in Ireland who do not drink or who have given up drinking would likely be among those who would agree with her. Alcoholics Anonymous holds many meetings across the country.

Some people who are new to Ireland express the concern that their lack of affinity for drink may set them apart. The tolerance of the Irish, however, extends to teetotalers as well. No one will much care, or even notice, when you order something nonalcoholic, as long as you don't make an issue of your choice. Actually, a significant percentage of Irish people are themselves teetotalers. "An indication," Bernie observed wryly, "of our schizophrenic nature."

Asylum-Seekers

There are situations that challenge the culture of open-mindedness, even in tolerant Ireland. The arrival of economic prosperity has reversed a long-standing tradition of emigration. In recent years people from various countries where resources are limited have come to Ireland seeking opportunity. Some have come to escape the trauma of armed conflict.

Those who have arrived without sufficient means do not always receive the warm Irish welcome touted in tourist brochures. When incidents of unfair treatment occur, the Irish media and humanitarian groups express concern and outrage that is shared by many citizens. Ireland's history as a people forced by poverty to leave home and seek a better life somewhere far away continues to generate Irish concern for suffering anywhere in the world.

The Traveling People

Some 4,500 families in Ireland make up the group of people known as "Travelers." Tracing their roots back to twelfth-century Ireland, theirs is a tradition of extended families that move from place to place. Before the mass production of plastic and enamelware, they earned a living by traveling by horse and cart or caravan from one farm to another to repair tin vessels and cookware and to sell new ones. They also earned a reputation for being knowledgeable about horses and engaged in horse trading. As the economy has shifted away from an agricultural base, Travelers have been driven into the cities.

They speak Cant or Gammon, their own language, and a majority are Catholic but practice rituals that differ from those of mainstream Irish Catholics. The target of bias, they have coexisted with Ireland's settled people in an environment that has often been tense. To discourage groups of Travelers from establishing camp, local authority councils sometimes place obstacles in areas designed for pulling off the roadway.

Social welfare programs attempt to address their higher infant mortality rate and shorter lifespan. Education programs designed to encourage attendance of Traveler children have met with some success, but widespread illiteracy continues to be a problem.

Communication Styles

The Irish are known everywhere for the lilt and melodic tones of their speech. Many are able to deliver innovative quips, wise words, and clever, colorful commentary with an ease that startles and reinforces their reputation as a people who possess the gift of artful conversation. Through centuries of oppression marked by concerted efforts to destroy key aspects of their culture, the Irish were compelled to conceal the practice of their faith and the use of their language. Perhaps this history of suppression, particularly as it concerns language, helps to explain an Irish tendency toward indirect expression, for it seems the Irish prefer not to utter the words "yes" or "no." For an expatriate who is more used to concrete, rapid-fire exchanges in absolute terms, this can prove a bit challenging. Let's say you're looking forward to a social event. Thinking that it might be nice to have company, you ask your pal, Kathryn, if she plans to go. "We might do," she replies cheerfully, leaving you to wonder at her intent.

Another aspect of Irish speech that can take people unawares is the common use of curse words in casual conversation. It's not that we haven't encountered these terms that may make hearing them unsettling, but the ease with which they spring from lips of young and old alike. It's not long, however, before the impact of routinely encountering certain colorful expressions begins to subside. Of course, every Irish person does not use curse words, many find them objectionable, and you'll rarely hear them in more formal conversation.

You will come across quite a few slang terms in Ireland as well as words that denote items for which you will be accustomed to using a different word. "Chips" to indicate French-fried potatoes or "jumper" for sweater are examples of the latter. An example of slang is the term "craic," which means good fun and lively conversation, as in "It's good craic," to refer to the atmosphere in a particular pub or social venue.

Some expressions characteristic of Irish speech are unique and full of character or history. "Thin on the ground" is a phrase lamenting the scarcity of something desired, as in "Computer-repair shops are thin on the ground." "Thick upon the ground" would indicate the opposite. To "chance your arm" is to stick your neck out and derives from a tale of

A Match Made in Lisdoonvarna

*I*f you are planning to come to Ireland on your own but are interested in establishing a long-term relationship and possibly marriage, you might consult a matchmaker. You will find them in Ireland, operating what is often a long-standing family business and advertising their services in newspapers and now even on the Web. Matchmakers arrange introductions for a fee ranging from $50 to $100. They encourage suitable, often shy people to meet one another and, if things work out, to marry.

An experienced matchmaker will usually have a host of tales to sup-port his or her skill in the art of bringing two people together. Not all introductions become matches, however, and a matchmaker will be forthright about the odds on success.

Each September in Lisdoonvarna, County Clare, the monthlong Matchmaking Festival draws thousands of people, in search of fun and good company or "craic," rather than a life partner. Still, a number of romantic tales recount connections forged at this festival or through the services of an able matchmaker. Festival followers are mostly Irish, the majority in their forties, fifties, and sixties.

risk taking in 1492. The Earl of Kildare cut a hole through the door of the Chapter House at Dublin's St. Patrick's Cathedral. As a reconciliatory gesture, he stretched his arm through it to grasp that of the Earl of Ormond, who had sought refuge there, and thus ended a long-standing feud between the two families. (The Resource Guide defines selected terms and phrases commonly encountered among the Irish.)

CREATURE COMFORTS: FOOD AND DRINK

Food and drink form the heart of every culture. Becoming familiar with Irish cuisine and learning to appreciate both its humble origins and its modern transformation are key to the process of feeling at home in Ireland.

Well regarded for its indigenous brewing industry, Ireland has not until recent years received much acclaim when it comes to cuisine. Rich pastures and unpolluted waters yield an abundance of fresh, first-rate ingredients, but what transpired on the way to the table used to leave something to be desired. The trend toward healthier eating and more innovative applications of classic food preparation techniques has encouraged dramatic change in Irish cuisine. This chapter explores Ireland's multitude of gifts to the epicure and to the "meat and potatoes" aficionado as well.

Beyond Boiled Potatoes: Cuisine in Ireland

Until the last decade or so, Ireland did not enjoy a reputation for good food. Bland and greasy would not have been an unfair characterization of many meals served, even in better restaurants. The unglamorous potato appeared in one form or another at every meal. A narrow selection of other vegetables was often overcooked to the point of tastelessness. Beyond standard items, grocery-store shelves offered little in the way of abundance or variety.

Well before the prosperity of recent years, a food renaissance emerged in Ireland in what is now called its gourmet capital. Centered first in Kinsale, County Cork, a new sensibility with regard to food preparation and presentation spread to many areas of the country. Improved economics have further elevated the expectation of and appreciation for good food. A more sophisticated palate has created demand for gourmet, international, health-conscious, and vegetarian styles of cooking. Modern Irish cuisine appears on trendier menus, using the freshest ingredients and contemporary preparation techniques to update and transform traditional recipes.

Although cities have seen the biggest improvement in restaurant quality and variety, even small-town restaurants serve well-prepared, fresh, and tasty dishes today. Irish seafood, baked goods, meats, fish, and dairy products of top quality grace many tables. Small cafes and exclusive dining rooms alike serve homemade soups that supply both good nutrition and sumptuous flavor.

Meat is still considered a basic part of the diet, but vegetarianism has moved beyond a passing fad and is gaining popularity, especially among younger people. There is more emphasis on eating with health in mind, and an annual "Healthy Eating Campaign" extols the virtues of reducing fat and increasing one's consumption of fruits, vegetables, and fish. Even low-fat potato chips have proved successful in the Irish market (but then, so has high-fat ice cream).

The availability of products in Ireland has also improved dramatically. Where once it was impossible to find chocolate-chip cookies, kiwi fruit, fresh chilies, pizza, Ben & Jerry's ice cream, or chunks of real parmesan as opposed to powdered, these products are now readily available, even in remote areas. Fresh fruits, vegetables, and herbs on offer locally are of great quality and good value. Chocolate lovers will relish exquisite handmade chocolates and will not be disappointed with the candy bar selection at any corner store.

For some reason, the Irish do not consume a lot of fish, as compared to people in other European countries. Nutritionists continue to urge them to incorporate more fish in their diet, and many varieties of fresh fish, including cod, haddock, halibut, trout, sea bass, mackerel, ray, whiting, and salmon are readily available. Seafood abounds and includes cockles, mussels, clams, scallops, oysters, crab, prawns, shrimp, and lobster.

Butterhead lettuce, cabbage, cauliflower, mushrooms, tomatoes, carrots, onions, and potatoes are in season year-round. In the summer fresh basil and coriander abound. Other herbs have a longer season. From May through November chives, dill, mint, parsley, sage, and thyme are easy to come by. Many other varieties of fruits and vegetables emerge in seasonal abundance, including asparagus, broccoli, cucumbers, endive, kale, peas, radishes, shallots, scallions, rhubarb, spinach, corn, and turnips. Summer brings berries in abundance—blackberries, blueberries, gooseberries, loganberries, raspberries, and strawberries.

Food is big business in Ireland, promoted as "the food island" by An

Bord Bia, its food board established in 1994. A multi-billion-dollar industry, there are nearly 650 food- and drink-manufacturing companies. Consisting of large concerns as well as many smaller specialty food companies, the industry exports almost half of what it produces. An Bord Glas, the horticultural development board, promotes the health benefits of fresh fruit and vegetables. The Irish Dairy Board is the marketing arm of the dairy industry. Through distribution companies located in the United States, United Kingdom, Belgium, the Netherlands, and Germany, it supplies industrial milk products and food ingredients to major food corporations.

Product Differences

Some foods look the same but taste different in Ireland, which can initially deliver a minor surprise to the North American palate. Some expatriates extol the flavor of Irish beef or pork, while others find it to be good but a bit stronger than what they're used to. Ketchup in Ireland has more vinegar and less sugar. (Some companies now market "American style" ketchup in Ireland, though you could add corn syrup for the same result, or perhaps try to overcome a dependence on sugar.) Dairy products in Ireland, especially the cheeses, are superior to U.S. products. Even the best American-made butter does not ring true to the Irish palate. Rashers have more meat than the fatty, stringy stuff Americans know as bacon. (The standard Irish rasher comes from "back" bacon, while what is available in the States is a cheaper cut that the Irish call "streaky" bacon.)

Packaging, names, and sizes are sometimes different, too. Milk, sold by the liter, has a slightly higher fat content. Potato chips are called "crisps," and "chips" refer to French fries. "Aubergine" is the term for eggplant, and zucchini may be called "courgette." "Castor sugar" is comparable to granulated sugar. Mars and Hershey bars are found everywhere, along with a wide range of Irish candy. Experimenting to determine your favorites among the new ones is part of the fun.

When you go to buy baking soda, you'll find a small plastic bag of something called "bread soda." Read the fine print, and the designation "sodium bicarbonate" will reassure you that it is the same product of multiple uses. You can use it to absorb refrigerator odors and also to soothe "nettle rashes." You will see more familiar packaging with names like Maxwell House, Kellogg's, Kraft, Hellmann's, and the ubiquitous Coke and Pepsi.

There is no need to be shy about asking for assistance, because people who work in the shops are very helpful. When you request the location of a product, they'll usually escort you to it.

Dining Out

People in Ireland are dining out more, and the choice of restaurants, especially in major cities, has expanded considerably. You'll find excellent Indian, Italian, Chinese, French, and "modern Irish" cuisine, and even gourmet pizza and Malaysian food, in and around metropolitan areas.

Dinner in a better restaurant can be an expensive meal, especially if you include wine. Though prices vary, the usual range is $20 to $40 per person, including service charge. Some restaurants offer early bird, tourist, and other specials. Eateries in outlying areas are generally less expensive.

Dinner is typically served in several courses. In less experimental restaurants, starters (hors d'oeuvres) could be smoked salmon, a seafood cocktail, soup (likely a chowder), or salad. Poached or grilled salmon is a characteristic entrée, as are leg of lamb, roast beef, chicken, pork, and grilled steak. The main dish is usually accompanied by a serving of carrots, green beans, and roasted, mashed, or boiled potatoes. Dessert could be lemon or treacly tart, profiteroles, or apple pie with ice cream.

Trendier restaurants will serve entrées like crispy duckling Gran Marnier, pan-seared scallops on a risotto of wild mushrooms, or grilled turbot fillet with red-pepper coulis. They may also offer the traditional Irish stew found in many pubs and more traditional eateries, but they may identify it as "terrine of Irish stew served with a confit of vegetables." It may taste about the same, but it will definitely cost much more in the trendier spot.

Away from the cities, restaurant variety is more limited. In most good-size towns, there are usually one or more upscale, elegant but pricey dining establishments, a number of reliable restaurants with more reasonable prices, and a few bargain spots. A typical example of a good bargain eatery, as long as you are not dieting, is Cafolla's Café in Westport, County Mayo. This is a typical sit-in chipper or chip shop. Far from elegant, but jammed with locals, this family favorite will pile your plate with a generous portion of cod and chips for $5.30.

Food is not prepared brilliantly everywhere in Ireland, and it is possible to have a disappointing meal. Although even good restaurants can occasionally have an off night or produce an entrée that is not what you hoped, restaurant reviews and guides, the Internet, and people in the community can help you to make informed choices and thus avoid disappointment. There are also restaurants and take-away (takeout) establishments that have not incorporated the trend toward lighter food and show no signs of closing up their doors. Chippers, popular with everyone but especially with people going home from the pub, do a brisk business in high-fat burgers, fish, chicken, chips (fries), and sausages, mushrooms, and onion rings dipped in batter and deep fried. (Traditionally, Friday was a meat fast day, so the chipper provided a handy option. Today even Chinese restaurants provide take-away chips.)

The traditional Irish breakfast usually provides good value (and lots of calories) for as little as $3.00, a bit more in fancier places. A large and filling meal, it generally consists of rashers, sausages, pudding, egg, tomato, and mushrooms with toast or bread and tea or coffee. B&Bs tend to add extras like cold or hot cereal, brown scones, and fancy jams.

Cafes serve tea, coffee, scones and other pastries, homemade soups, salads, and sandwiches. Most pubs serve soup, hot and cold sandwiches, and hot meals between noon and 3.00 P.M.; some serve hot meals in the evening. Here the gourmet approach will not be so much in evidence, but the food is generally quite good and reasonably priced. Entertainment may also be part of the experience if you go to a pub for a meal.

Busy lives succumb to fast-food convenience in Ireland as elsewhere in the world. Take-away is very popular, and ready-made meals now command more and more shelf space in shops. McDonald's has become a major presence in cities and small towns, with seventy-five restaurants planned by the year 2000. Nutritionists squawk as Irish people flock—but no one disputes the health of McDonald's sales figures in Ireland, especially for the signature French fries. Super Macs, an Irish-owned chain, offers a broader range of foods. In addition to filling the standard burger-and-fries order, it serves pizza, chicken, fries flavored with cheese or curry, and a number of ice cream flavors.

Home Cooking

In Ireland most meals are prepared and enjoyed in the comfort of home. Especially in smaller towns and rural areas, people do not go out to eat as often as they do in some parts of North America. Because mealtimes tend to be family oriented and houses tend to be small, it has not been that common for people to entertain at home over dinner, except for special occasions; but more people seem to be doing so. In any case, the pub fills the need for social gatherings, many of which are impromptu.

Because the storage capacity of kitchens in general and refrigerators in particular is limited, people tend to shop more frequently and purchase smaller quantities in Ireland. Most good-size towns have a shopping center where people buy their weekly groceries. They also often stop off at local markets, which are well stocked and generally do not overcharge. Larger supermarket chains, like Superquinn, SuperValu, Centra, Tesco Ireland and Dunnes Stores, however, are doing good business. Many are now open on Sunday. They often label goods as "Irish made" or "Produced in Ireland" to encourage people to buy home-developed products. Buying Irish, after all, means protecting jobs. The chain stores accept credit cards and sponsor discount programs with special member cards. Some of the stores stock large quantities of household, gardening, and hardware items. Some sell clothing, too. Many stores will accept orders over the phone or by fax, and some will even deliver free of charge. The opportunity to order groceries by Internet may be available in the near future.

Department stores are beginning to have kitchen-equipment departments, and cooking-utensil/supply stores are springing up here and there. You may not find exotic implements, but basic cooking gear and small appliances are well supplied. Darina Allen of the highly regarded Ballymaloe House cooking school and restaurant outside Cork hosts a popular television series, *Simply Delicious*, where the emphasis is on adding flair to classic recipes.

Cookers (stoves) tend to be smaller and are often electric, and you may need to turn on a power switch before each use. Particularly common in rural areas, aga cookers (ranges) use solid fuel, such as turf, coal, or wood; in addition to cooking food, they may heat the home. Cookers may also be fueled by natural gas. Recipe and package directions that tell you to "Use Gas Mark 5" refer to the dial that sets the cooking temperature.

The following chart shows the corresponding gas mark for degrees Celsius and Fahrenheit:

° Celsius	° Fahrenheit	Gas Mark
149°	300°	2
163°	325°	3
177°	350°	4
191°	375°	5
204°	400°	6
218°	425°	7
232°	450°	8
260°	500°	9

Elaborate breakfasts are not commonly prepared at home on weekdays in Ireland. People who have children and/or must get to work each day might reserve the full Irish breakfast for weekends and settle for a quick bowl of cereal, oatmeal, or an egg and toast during the week. Convenience foods that target the busy working adult are definitely increasing in popularity. On the other hand, open-air markets in many towns are crowded with folks buying locally supplied produce and other foods. These markets are gaining in popularity, and major cities sell an array of locally produced foods in colorful street stalls. None matches the variety and success of the English Market in Cork City, known for high-quality traditional and specialty foods as well as superb produce, meat, cheese, bread, and pastries.

Traditional Dishes

In his haunting memoir of childhood hardship, *Angela's Ashes*, Frank McCourt revealed that his Limerick family survived on tea and bread. That they managed to sustain themselves on so meager a diet is testimony not only to their courage and fortitude but also to the merits of Irish bread. It is undeniably superb, especially brown bread, with its crusty outer layer and chewy, grainy core. One or two slices smeared with butter and served with a cup of tea make a scrumptious snack. Brown-bread scones are sublime, and brown bread and a bowl of steaming soup make a heavenly, satisfying meal.

While cookies don't appear to have a place in Irish traditional cooking, cakes or tarts are an essential component. These are often made with apples or other fruits; some recipes include whiskey or ale. Barm brack, a traditional cakelike currant loaf, is delicious. Often served around

Halloween, there is a custom of placing a ring in the cake mixture and identifying the one who gets the slice with the ring as the next to marry. The Irish are well known for their stew of mutton, carrots, potatoes, and leeks. Mutton, the meat from a more mature sheep, is not always as easy to find as lamb, which comes from a younger animal.

A number of other traditional dishes are—surprise—potato-based. Boxty is a kind of bread made of raw and cooked potato mashed with butter, milk, and flour. Before baking you mark it with a cross on top so that it can be divided. Champ consists of potatoes boiled and then mashed with salt, pepper, butter, and spring onions that are first soaked in milk and boiled in water. Champ is graced with loads of melted butter swimming on top. Similar to champ, colcannon is a mixture of mashed potatoes and boiled kale, traditionally served around Halloween, when kale is in season. Money is wrapped and added to the mixture, and children relish the search as much as the food.

Dublin coddle is another favorite. It is a hearty dish, made with pork or beef sausages, rashers, potatoes, and seasoned with onion, garlic, sage, parsley, and sometimes apple slices or cider.

For North Americans, the term "pudding" conjures visions of a smooth, sweet dessert. In Ireland, however, the term more often indicates a type of sausage (though it refers also to a dessert form, especially Christmas pudding). Some North Americans acquire a taste for pudding quickly, while others never quite manage to enjoy it. Drisheen, or blood pudding, is made with sheep's blood combined with milk, chopped mutton suet, bread crumbs, and allspice. The mixture is poured into beef casings,

National Dish?

Corned beef and cabbage is considered as Irish as the hot dog is American, yet it is not by any means the authentic national dish many have come to associate with Ireland. While you'll find it here and there, it is not routinely prepared in restaurants or at home. Bacon and cabbage, with the bacon being closer to ham, is more com- monly eaten. Neither is Irish coffee a true traditional beverage. People will be happy to serve up this combination of black coffee, whiskey, and sugar in a tall stemmed glass, topped with whipped cream. It is, however, a request encountered more frequently in the States, though in Ireland it is sometimes served after a fancy meal.

boiled, and then cut into slices and fried with chopped onion or boiled in milk thickened with bread crumbs or cornstarch. Pig's blood and liver are the main ingredients for black pudding.

An edible seaweed, carigeen is used in many Irish kitchens as a spice, garnish, or a wrapping in which to bake fish. It is also boiled with milk, sugar, and spices to make a blanc mange–style dessert pudding. Health-food stores carry it, and it is supposed to be beneficial for stomach and respiratory complaints. Gathered from rocks along the ocean, it is left to bleach in the sun, then washed and dried.

Before we move on to the topic of drink, a few words are in order on the subject of Ireland's traditional, most popular, and nonalcoholic drink, namely tea. Irish tea is served hot and strong, usually with milk. If you prefer to drink your tea with lemon, you'll usually be able to, though lemon is not the standard fixing, and some cafes, restaurants, or homes may not have it on hand. At home people switch on the kettle and drink tea any time of day. They might enjoy a cup or two at breakfast, followed by tea with a snack before and/or after lunch. They might have another cup upon arriving home from work and another with or after the evening meal, and perhaps yet another cup before bed.

Tea bags are used more often than loose tea, and Lyons, Bewley's, and Barry's are popular brands, available in decaffeinated form. Although more Irish people are drinking coffee these days and cappuccino and café latte are available, tea still ranks far ahead.

Libation in Good Company

Inaccurate and unflattering stereotypes aside, the Irish are credited with having a certain fondness for drink. They certainly do crowd the pubs, and it is estimated that there is one pub for every 350 or so people in Ireland. Perhaps drinking alcohol is just more visible among the Irish because people tend not to enjoy a drink at home as often as they might in other countries.

The Irish pub is much more than a place to satisfy your thirst. Like a community magnet, the pub summons people to participate in local events, impromptu social gatherings, or a weekly game of cards. You might go in to enjoy a cup of tea, to sway in time to foot-tapping, traditional music, or to savor a hearty and inexpensive meal. The pub is the logical spot to meet up with friends before going off to a party or to gather after attending a business meeting, christening, funeral, or football (soccer) match.

The charm of many pubs arises from their retention of original decor and features. Occasionally, you'll come upon one with a "snug"—a small, enclosed room with a hatchway that opens directly onto the bar. In days gone by this is where women would go to be served without engaging in the unseemly behavior of mingling among the men. In cities individual pubs tend to draw a dedicated, homogeneous crowd. Large theme pubs in Dublin are a favorite of the younger set. Small-town and rural pubs tend to draw customers from various age and economic groups who mingle comfortably.

Some who have moved to Ireland claim that they ease right into the comfort of the pub's accepting, welcoming environment. Others say that they feel somewhat shy in the pub, especially in the evenings. Some expatriates express that they are also not comfortable with the ease that is generally associated with drinking. Others find it a symbol of freedom and wonder if North Americans are just more uptight than Irish and European cultures when it comes to drinking.

People take turns buying rounds, and it is polite to return the gesture. Teetotalers are not made to feel uncomfortable, and pubs serve plenty of alternatives to alcoholic beverages. It's not unusual for people to go out as late as 10:00 or 11:00 P.M., often arriving just before last drinks are served. Pub hours vary, closing earlier in winter than summer. In outlying areas some pubs will ignore the rules for closing hours. There is pressure to expand hours—but also concern that doing so may drive up the accident rate. Generally, pubs are able to serve drinks during the week from 10:00 A.M. to 11:00 P.M. in winter and until midnight in summer. Some city pubs have an extension that allows them to serve later. Once service stops people may remain for a half-hour to drink up. Pubs are supposed to close from 2:00 to 4:00 P.M. on Sundays, and they then serve until 11:00 P.M. The two-hour closing period is called "holy hours."

The beverages of choice are beer and whiskey. You'll find a wide range of beers from light ales to dark stout. Guinness, with its signature creamy head, has long dominated the Irish market. It is not unusual for people to critique how well the barman negotiates the meticulous, two-stage pulling of the pint or to remark on the quality of the Guinness, which they attest can vary significantly from region to region and pub to pub. Among the

Irish and now around the globe, there is real affection for the dark stout, which has been brewed in Dublin since 1759. In years long past Guinness was promoted as a health tonic, but the company now discourages any claims of medicinal benefits. Some used to assert that Guinness built strength and that pregnant women who drank a glass a day would make their babies stronger. Some years ago those who donated blood were given Guinness to hasten the reproduction of red corpuscles!

For those who find the Guinness too bitter, other stouts like Murphy's or Beamish are recommended. Microbreweries have begun to emerge in Ireland, crafting freshly brewed beers, including North American–style lagers, in places like the Porterhouse in Dublin, Tipperary Brewing in Thurles, and Biddy Early Brewery in Inagh, County Clare.

The Irish term for whiskey is *uisce beatha* (pronounced "ishka baha"), which means "water of life." Usually served neat or with water, Irish whiskey has a different smell and taste than the Scotch whiskey typically served in North America. Whereas most whiskey is distilled once or twice, Irish whiskey is distilled three times in large, copper stills. Power's, Jameson, and Bushmills are popular brands. A hot whiskey, considered to help clear a cold, is made with honey, lemon, and cloves. Poitin is a traditional, potent, and illegally distilled whiskey, a legal version of which has now been launched. Bulmers is a cider made from the fermented juice of crushed apples. Bailey's Irish Cream is a popular liqueur that blends whiskey and milk.

Ireland has one of the lowest rates of wine consumption in Europe. The French consume six times as much wine per capita, and the British twice as much. Considered less a luxury item in the prosperity of recent years, wine sales have grown in Ireland, particularly among women and young people. Wines from Germany, Chile, Australia, New Zealand, France, Greece, and South Africa are widely available. International wine fairs and local wine tastings encourage appreciation for variety. Excise duty and VAT make wine more expensive than other drinks, though you can find good value if you wait for specials. Wine can start as low as $6.00 a bottle and range far above that.

THE SPORTING LIFE

The Irish are an active people who find time amidst the demands of hard work to embrace a broad range of leisure activities with enthusiasm. For a small country, Ireland supports a remarkable variety of leisure pursuits, including many that take full advantage of the natural beauty of the outdoors. Spectator sports featured in local, regional, national, and international venues exhibit the skill and courage of participants and inspire the ardent crowds that cheer them on. This chapter explores a number of sporting pastimes that you may choose to experience in Ireland.

On the Pitch (Field)

As spectators or participants, the Irish are passionate about sports. Sporting events and the athletes who distinguish them command a great deal of media coverage and inspire lively conversation in the pub. Regulated by the Football Association of Ireland, the sport called "soccer" in the States and "football" everywhere else commands a loyal following. Known for its rugged play and potential for injury, rugby is also played in Ireland; it is especially popular in the Limerick area. American football games are occasionally shown on television, and there are even clubs that play the American version in Ireland.

Gaelic football and hurling are two avidly supported games of speed and skill played throughout the summer. A combination of rugby and soccer, Gaelic football is played with a smaller and heavier ball than the one used in soccer. A sport of ancient times when it was played in bloody matches that went on for days, hurling is distinctly Irish. Similar to hockey, players use a curved, wooden stick called a "hurley." The ball, or "sliothar," is similar in size to a hockey ball but has raised ridges to enable players to balance it on the hurley while sprinting down the pitch (field). Hurling is especially prominent in the Munster and Leinster Provinces, in County Galway, and in County Antrim in Northern Ireland. Emigrants have carried the sport to Irish communities abroad.

Established in 1884 to revive and preserve the heritage of traditional forms of Irish sport, the Gaelic Athletic Association (GAA) has been a powerful force in the organization and promotion of athletic events in

Ireland. The GAA regulates Gaelic football, hurling, handball, and camogie (women's hurling) and has clubs in the United Kingdom, Australia, Canada, and the United States. Because they are drawn from community organizations, teams inspire much local support, and matches display the spirited expression of community pride. Major GAA events as well as concerts are held in GAA's Croke Park, a stadium that holds about 68,000 people. In September the All-Ireland finals in Gaelic football and hurling draw capacity crowds.

A new national stadium is in the process of being constructed in West Dublin. To be called The Arena, it will seat 45,000 and allow Ireland to host major international as well as national athletic events. Plans include an athletic track and a retractable roof. If all goes as planned, it will host its first event in the fall of 2001. The stadium will provide a venue for rock concerts as well.

On the Track

For centuries the Irish have maintained a special relationship with the horse, their national animal. They have distinguished themselves as first-rate when it comes to breeding, raising, and training championship bloodstock. Some claim that the credit for the quality of Irish stables lies with the combination of limestone subsoil and a moist climate, yielding lush and mineral-rich pastures that ensure strong bones. However it happens, some of the world's top thoroughbreds can be traced to Irish stud farms.

Esteemed by horse lovers everywhere, this small country has produced some of the world's top thoroughbreds, draught, and sporting horses. Ireland's export of bloodstock is a vital and profitable industry that attracts deep-pocketed investors from around the globe. Hundreds of mares from the United States, United Kingdom, and France are brought to stud in Ireland every year.

In the mid-1940s The National Stud was established in County Kildare to promote improved bloodstock and to develop new methods of horse management. This famous stud farm provides stables for standing stallions, foaling, and boarding. The National Stud also maintains a horse museum and the world-famous Japanese Gardens, developed in the early 1900s. Another leading stud farm is the renowned Tipperary Coolmore Stud.

For the equine enthusiast, Ireland offers numerous activities, including trail riding, riding centers, show jumping, and horse racing. Close to thirty tracks host well over 200 race meetings per year. The Irish Horseracing Authority (IHA), established in 1994, owns and runs a number of racecourses and manages on-course and credit betting services. The minimum for most bets is $1.50. Established in 1790, the Turf Club is the agency responsible for administering racing rules in all thirty-two counties of Ireland. It also owns The Curragh in Naas, County Kildare. One of Ireland's most famous racecourses, The Curragh, has hosted the annual Irish Derby since 1866.

Racing festivals and horse shows take place all over Ireland. The most prominent of these is the Summer Festival Meeting at Galway Races. The Leopardstown Racecourse, just outside Dublin, holds an annual Christmas Festival—three days of race meetings just after Christmas. The International Rose of Tralee Festival features a six-day racing program in August; each September the Kerry Grand National draws crowds to Listowel Racecourse, who also come for the Harvest Festival. The Laytown races take place once a year on the beach at low tide along part of County Meath's short coastline. Punchestown, in County Kildare, is the venue for a spring jumping festival. For many the highlight of the year arrives in August with the Dublin Horse Show, which draws contestants and spectators from around the world.

Dog Racing

Greyhounds race in Dublin's Shelbourne Park as well as in other stadiums around the country. Wagering is a key element of an evening at the dog races. Meets normally consist of eight races over various distances. Race cards detail the previous performances of each dog. Greyhounds race from starting boxes in numbered positions, usually one to six. Bord na gCon, the Irish Greyhound Racing Board, regulates dog racing from its headquarters in Limerick. In recent years corporate sponsorship has extended the appeal of dog racing to a new generation. The breeding and training of greyhounds engenders the same level of passion of those involved with horses, though on a smaller scale.

On the Water

It is said that one is never farther than 120 kilometers (75 miles) from the sea in Ireland. Endless stretches of scenic, rugged coastline, mighty rivers, and sparkling streams and lakes support numerous water-related pastimes. The absence of big industry has averted the pollution that has spoiled the waterways of other lands, and those of Ireland are considered the purest in all of Europe. Surfing is popular, especially in the west, where the National Surfing Championships are held. Many are devoted to water skiing, jet skiing, and windsurfing. Enterprises like the Diving and Watersports Centre in Kilkee, County Clare, and Scubadive West on the Renvyle Peninsula in Connemara, County Galway, offer instruction and rent equipment.

Ireland's coastline provides many beautiful beaches. They are a popular destination during eagerly anticipated spells of warm, sunny weather. Quite a few are "blue flag" beaches, a European designation of safety and water quality and other environmental standards. Mayo often receives more blue flags than any other county. Marinas are also eligible for blue flag awards.

Communities do not apply for blue flag status for all beaches. Some are free of crowds but thus too remote to be staffed with lifeguards. Ocean turbulence on the west coast can be dangerous for swimmers, and drownings are reported after many a sunny day.

Expatriates may be surprised to encounter public service campaigns in Ireland designed to raise awareness about the dangers of sun exposure. Many Irish are fair skinned and often so appreciative of the appearance of sun that some tend to regard sunscreen as interfering with their solar delight. Thus many a burned face will appear after a weekend of sunshine. Though the danger may seem mild to those familiar with the strength of the sun's rays in places like Arizona and Florida, applying sunscreen is a wise practice in Ireland, even on cloudy days.

Of all the water-related leisure activities Ireland affords, two that engage hordes of enthusiasts among locals and tourists alike are fishing and boating, profiled next.

Angling in Ireland

Regarded as the ultimate fishing destination among European countries, Ireland's clean waters and mild climate sustain a wealth of angling opportunities and an abundance of warm- and cold-water species. Local newspapers routinely carry photos and details of a particularly spectacular catch. Although people can and do fish nearly year-round, spring and summer abound with fishing festivals throughout Ireland. Some, like the sea angling festival at Culdaff, County Donegal; the Irish Open

Pike Pairs Championship, in County Longford; the Canal Angling Festival in Edenderry, County Offaly; and the Carrick-on-Shannon Fishing Festival, in County Leitrim, reward skill and results with trophies and cash prizes. Angling centers often offer instruction on fly casting and other fishing techniques.

It is advisable to seek clarification on local angling regulations, which can be somewhat confusing. Central and regional agencies maintain various requirements and restrictions. Many lands are privately owned, and access requires a fee. A permit and a license are two different things: the former is obtained from a private owner, and the latter is sold by State Fishery Boards.

The season for a given fish may vary from county to county and from one river to another. Detailed information and appropriate licenses and permits are available from local angling centers and tourist offices.

Coarse Fishing

Coarse fishing, allowed year-round, includes pike, bream, carp, perch, tench, roach, rudd, and eel. Famous for their size and fight, pike are now protected, due to their dwindling numbers. Fishing for pike with live bait is not allowed in Ireland, but dead bait or floats will prove just as successful.

Sea Angling

Popular year-round, deep-sea fishing and shore angling from rocks, beaches, and piers do not require a permit. Types of fish found in these waters include shark, pollack, hake, some species of cod, sea bream, gray mullet, and ray. Coastal areas along the west and south are considered by many to provide the best sea angling. Deep-sea fishing boats that will accommodate six to eight anglers can be chartered locally for between $200 and $400 per day. Daily rates for individuals range between $25 and $45.

Game Angling

Game angling for salmon, sea trout, and brown trout generally requires a license and, since most property is privately held, a permit as well. Fly rod, worming, and spin fishing are allowed for both salmon and sea trout. On many rivers and lakes, fly fishing is the only form of angling allowed for brown trout. Although spinning and worming are permitted on some rivers and lakes, it is essential to clarify the rules by consulting local authorities. Boats are widely available for hire and may be rented for approximately $30 to $60 per day, depending on size and whether or not they are motorized.

Boating

Ireland's abundance of pristine waterways provides easy access to lakes, rivers, sheltered bays, and open ocean for cruising, yachting, sailing, boating, canoeing, and kayaking. Coastal waters in the west tend to be rougher. Many lakes, including Lough Derg on the River Shannon, are renowned for boating, sailing, and cruising.

Sailing and canoeing instruction is offered at a number of facilities, including Outdoor Education Centers in the Burren area of County Clare and in Birr, County Offaly. Other centers offer dolphin-watching boat trips, canoeing and camping holidays, and pleasure cruises along the lakes and rivers.

Yachting, sailing, and rowing regattas are held throughout the summer. In the four-day Round Ireland Race, large and small vessels circle the island clockwise from Wicklow. The Royal Cork Yacht Club, the oldest in the world, sponsors a biennial week of racing at Crosshaven that draws thousands of participants and observers.

On the Road

Road Bowling

Road bowling, another sport that is uniquely Irish, is played on summer Sundays. As the name suggests, a segment of public road, usually a less-traveled, winding country lane, becomes the outdoor equivalent of a bowling alley. The winner is the bowler who manages to roll or toss a heavy ball to the finish line some 5 kilometers (3 miles) away using the fewest throws. Curves in the roadway challenge the bowlers, who may try to arc the ball around or toss it across the curve, but who will be penalized if the ball leaves the road. Road bowling, which inspires spirited betting, is played only in a couple of counties. It is especially popular in Cork.

Motor Sports

Road rallies are a popular weekend pastime in Ireland, and many towns will sponsor a local club. The Automobile Association (AA)

Circuit of Ireland Rally traverses both the North and South and includes a separate category for classic cars. Killarney, Donegal, and Galway host international road rallies. The Motor Cycle Union of Ireland organizes races and rallies around the country. Galway hosts a well-attended annual rally of vintage motorcycles. The International NorthWest 200 in Portrush, County Antrim, draws huge crowds every spring.

On the Fairway

The claim that Ireland is a paradise for golfers is not exaggerated. The quality, variety, challenge, and accessibility of more than 400 parkland and links courses justify a worldwide reputation as a premier golf venue. In 1999 Ireland received the Hertz International Travel Award for Golf Destination of the Year. Over the past decade, investment in upgrades and new courses has brought even greater acclaim to the sport. Membership has jumped in the Golfing Union of Ireland, established in 1891 and the oldest in the world.

A number of courses were designed by names well known internationally, including Jack Nicklaus, Arnold Palmer, and Trent Jones. Eddie Hackett earned the nickname "King of the Links" for his design of more than eighty-five Irish links courses. Hackett's designs have drawn fervent praise for their sensitivity to natural terrain.

A genuine golf devotee could play a different course in Ireland every day of the year, and no course would be farther than a day's drive. Each course has its own unique personality. If you love picturesque beauty, tranquillity, and challenge, you'll find a course that suits you from among a number of options. A preference for playing close to home also yields numerous choices from nearly any base in Ireland. Especially outside of tourist season, little advance planning is required to gain entry to many courses. Guided or self-drive golf tours are widely available, and the choice of accommodations, ranging from inexpensive B&Bs to exclusive resorts, is vast.

Ireland hosts a number of local, national, and international golf tournaments for men and women professionals, amateurs, seniors, and juniors. The annual Murphy's Irish Open is considered to be the largest sporting event in Ireland. In the year 2005 the K Club, in Straffan, County Kildare, will host the Ryder Cup.

Costs

Fees vary from one golf course to another and are usually higher on weekends than weekdays. You can pay anywhere from $19 to $105 per day, though most courses charge between $24 and $30. Club membership fees also range from bargain to exorbitant. In the Midlands and other less populated areas, club dues can be quite reasonable, offering full membership and greens fees for as low as $200 and $12 respectively. Joining one of 385 clubs affiliated with the Golfing Union of Ireland (GUI) will entitle you to GUI membership and a recognized handicap, thus allowing you to enter competitions all over Ireland. Some clubs, especially popular ones in the densely populated east, have stopped accepting members, but plenty of others continue to offer memberships.

Types of Courses

Whether you're an accomplished golfer or one who plays primarily for fun and relaxation, you'll enjoy the challenging play and surrounding scenery on Ireland's courses. Utilize the practice grounds and driving ranges to develop or polish your skills and then apply them on links, parkland, or pitch-and-putt courses.

Links

Developed along sandy, low-lying coastal areas, links courses incorporate elements of the natural environment, such as wetlands and sand dunes. Occasionally, a much-prized tree may grace the landscape. The roughs are truly daunting, consisting of thick heather and gorse. Forget searching for the stray ball. You are better off taking the drop and moving on to the next challenge. Greens are generally located in hollows of fine, short grasses of many hues. Fairways follow the natural terrain, where sandy hollows form bunkers and natural wetlands provide challenging water hazards.

Parklands

Found primarily in rich grasslands, parklands courses sport trees, shrubs, and water hazards with aquatic plants. Typically, there is very little rough along the fairways, though play can be equally challenging. Both nine- and eighteen-hole parklands courses tend to be less crowded than links courses.

Pitch and Putt

First played in the 1930s, pitch and putt, also known as short golf or par three golf, has grown in popularity in recent years. The Pitch and Putt Union of Ireland (PPUI) has affiliate clubs in more than twenty counties. In Pitch and Putt, each player is allowed to use only two clubs, one of which must be a putter. The game can be played on nine-, twelve-, or eighteen-hole courses. The maximum distance from the tee to the green is about 70 meters (76 yards), and an eighteen-hole course cannot be greater than 1,000 meters (1,094 yards).

Husband-and-wife teams or entire families will play this highly social and relatively easy game. Equipment is inexpensive and play moves quickly, with a typical game lasting about an hour. Club membership is reasonable, with annual fees ranging from $45 to $90 for individuals, with discounted family rates available. Joining PPUI entitles members to participate in county, provincial, open, and national championships.

Aspects of Play

The more rapid pace of play in Ireland may surprise you. An eighteen-hole round played in three hours is often the norm, even on the most challenging courses. You may want to hire a caddy, who will pack the burden of your clubs and provide invaluable tips on the course. Formerly forbidden, caddy cars (motorized carts) are now common, especially in larger clubs.

Mild weather and fewer tourists from late April to May and September to October make these the best months for golfing. Remember that Ireland's climate bears no resemblance to that of Palm Springs; even in summer, you should count on encountering cool temperatures and damp air. People do play year-round, and with adequate preparation you rarely will be unable to play because of weather. It is seldom too cold for golf, and the rare snowfall melts quickly. Brilliant sunshine and spectacular rainbows often follow the odd downpours.

Seasoned golfers will advise you to leave the umbrella behind. Quality rain gear provides superior protection, and a wool sweater adds warmth. Thermals are effective for comfort in colder weather. All-weather gloves are a good idea, too. Above all, you need golf shoes that are completely waterproof.

Since the most popular courses can attract large numbers of players, it is always advisable to reserve tee times by contacting the course directly. Some of the larger clubs require reservations. Although a host of players may be on the course when you arrive, most clubs manage players very well, and the course will seldom seem crowded. Should your first choice be booked, you should be able to find another course close by to accommodate you. During summer months you may avoid a crowd of locals and tourists if you schedule an early tee time, say 8:00 A.M. Or you may choose to play later in the day, since sunset will come as late as 10:30 P.M. and even later in the west.

Where to Play?

With so many choices, golfers who are new to Ireland often want to know where they should play.

The Resource Guide provides a brief profile of a variety of courses across Ireland, selected for the range they provide in course design, amenities, and fees.

Business Opportunities

Business on most every level is thriving in Ireland. The change from a decade ago, when Ireland ranked as one of Europe's porrest countries, to the emergence of a vibrant "Celtic Tiger" economy represents a significant transformation. A sense of what's happening in the world of Irish enterprise, informative in and of itself, also offers some insight into the changing social and cultural dynamics that are shaping life in Ireland. Employment opportunities have encouraged young people with ambition to stay instead of emigrating. Many who left the country in leaner times are now coaxed to return to fill vacancies in high-growth industries. As more women enter the workforce, and as business travel increases, the patterns of family life are changing. Prosperity has created a new class of affluent Irish entrepreneurs, whose success has inspired others to pursue new ventures. For managers who received share options, a wave of mergers has conferred soaring portfolios. However, the plight of those who have not benefited directly from economic prosperity, often the chronically unemployed, has become more visible alongside the rapid gains of others.

Beyond surveying the business climate to expand your understanding of Ireland, you may choose to participate on some level in Irish enterprise. Perhaps you have a unique expertise that may be needed in Ireland. You might want to explore the potential for full- or part-time employment, starting up a small business, or investing in Irish companies. This chapter highlights aspects of the economic environment in Ireland that may be relevant to new arrivals.

If you're currently retired or about to take that step, why is the subject of Irish commerce relevant? Isn't retirement a time to enjoy yourself and put away the stress of the working life? For many retirees, it is. They make the transition brilliantly, with no regrets. Even when the career they've left was one to which they were utterly devoted, after feeling a bit out of kilter for a week or two, they ease right into the next life stage, content to pursue new interests. Years later they claim that they have had no desire to return to any form of employment. They've closed the door on that part of life and are completely content in their new, surprisingly busy life. Often the things that occupy them represent a radical shift from the activities that for decades kept them immersed. A wealth of leisure activities in Ireland, from golf, fishing, bicycling, hiking, and sailing to gardening, crafts, spectator sports, travel, photography, painting, and writing guarantee a calendar brimming with rewarding pursuits.

Others, however, miss the social interaction and general bustle of the work environment. Their work ethic may be so ingrained that they feel more alive when they are actively engaged in some form of work. Often drawn to volunteer their time to a local service organization, they may evolve into a leadership role. Or they may start up a small business, franchise, or consulting firm, with the freedom of a flexible schedule. Opportunities abound in Ireland to indulge all of these interests.

Still others have a lifelong tendency to worry about money. This worry motivates them to be very strategic about managing their funds. Often they feel more secure if they can have some money, even a small amount, coming in. Generally, they don't insist on having the most glamorous job in town. They just feel more at ease when they are generating some kind of revenue stream, however small. The growth of part-time employment and labor shortages in service and other industries indicate continued potential for casual employment.

Business Is Booming

Rapid economic growth, low inflation, and falling unemployment have brought prosperity and a new confidence that Ireland has positioned itself well as a bridge to the vast European market. Between 1994 and 1998 Ireland's gross domestic product (GDP) grew an average of more than 8 percent per year, compared to a European Union average of less than 3 percent. A commitment to technological innovation has spurred development, and thousands of new jobs have been created by startups and existing businesses expanding their operations. Ireland's geographic location and EU membership provide direct access to a burgeoning European market of 400 million. With a young, skilled, and well-educated workforce, Ireland has become an ideal place in which to do business.

Ireland's Government Is Pro-Business

The government of Ireland appears to be steadfast in its commitment to continue its support of an environment favorable to business. Ireland provides a number of benefits to attract foreign business interests, including significant tax breaks. The government has vowed to reduce the corporate tax rate from the current standard of 28 percent (25 percent of the first $150,000 of income) to 12.5 percent by the year 2003. Companies that manufacture goods in Ireland will continue to enjoy a rate of 10 percent until 2010. "Manufactured goods" are defined broadly. In addition to typical products, these include such activities as fish farming and processing; mushroom cultivation; software development and data processing; film production for cinema, television, training, or documentary purposes; and repair and maintenance of aircraft. The Revenue Commissioners will give opinions in advance as to whether the nature of a proposed business qualifies for the reduced 10 percent rate.

The Irish government's commitment to maintaining a pro-business environment is supported by the activities of a number of organizations and associations. Main addresses, phone numbers, and so on are provided below. (The Resource Guide lists full data, including contact information for various offices or branches.)

Enterprise Ireland

Glasnevin, Dublin 9
tel: 01 808 2295
fax: 01 808 2040
E-mail: client.service@irish-trade.ie
Web site: www.irish-trade.ie
Enterprise Ireland seeks to strengthen Irish companies and promote strategic alliances. It runs a center in Dublin that provides information on Irish and other EU companies, products, and markets. Enterprise Ireland has offices worldwide, including one in New York City and two California locations, in Campbell and Palo Alto. Staff in these branches assist Irish companies moving to the United States and provide information about doing business in Ireland. Enterprise Ireland also helps companies to access funding for startups, R&D, and business expansion.

Trade between the United States and Ireland has seen marked growth in recent years. In 1995 a special program was launched to encourage partnership deals between Irish and U.S. businesses. In 1998 the U.S.

Small Business Association (SBA) signed an agreement with Enterprise Ireland to promote strategic alliances between small companies and entrepreneurs in Ireland and the United States.

IDA Ireland

Wilton Park House
Dublin 2
tel: 01 603 4000
E-mail: idaireland@ida.ie
Web site: www.idaireland.com

The Industrial Development Agency (IDA), which has an international network of offices, encourages investment from overseas, especially in manufacturing, health care and pharmaceuticals, engineering, and international and financial services. The success of IDA's efforts has contributed to the current number of overseas companies operating in Ireland—approximately 1,200 companies employing a total of 116,000 people. Five hundred of these companies are U.S. subsidiaries that, from their Ireland base, employ 70,000 people in the manufacture of electronics, computer products, medical supplies, and pharmaceuticals or the business of retailing, banking and finance, and other services.

The IDA's track record of generating successful inward investment is superb, but not without the occasional flaw. While a number of U.S. and Canadian companies are well established on spreading complexes in Ireland, not all firms manage to continue operating in Ireland, however generous the incentives. Some have abandoned the program, and jobs are lost as a result. After setting up and hiring on 1,100 full-time workers, Seagate abruptly closed its plant in Clonmel, County Tipperary, and had to repay its government grants. After a decade of manufacturing in Donegal, Fruit of the Loom scaled back its operation and moved certain jobs to Morocco to take advantage of cheaper labor costs. The company had to pay financial penalties, which the IDA agreed to reduce in order to retain a certain number of jobs for another year. Long-term prospects of keeping the plant in Donegal are considered doubtful. Especially in outlying areas, where alternatives are limited or nonexistent, job losses that result from company closure are devastating to workers and their community.

In many instances the hoped-for win-win results have been achieved. Drawn by generous grants and a rich pool of qualified new graduates, companies like Intel, Motorola, and Hewlett-Packard (HP) are well established in Ireland. HP has offices in Dublin, Belfast, Cork, and Limerick and manufactures printer cartridges at its facility in Leixslip, County Kildare. Intel has invested $2.5 billion in its Ireland operation and employs 3,400 fulltime and 800 contract workers at its sixty-acre Leixslip site, formerly a stud farm. Intel works closely with a number of Irish colleges, universities, and technical schools to sponsor scholarship, mentoring, and intern programs, and it has donated computer labs to local high schools.

FAS

27–33 Upper Baggot St.
Dublin 4
Tel: 01 607 0500
Fax: 01 607 0600
Web site: www.fas.ie

The Irish Training and Employment Authority, FAS, assists job seekers, community groups, and employers with training and employment services. Based in Dublin, FAS provides local assistance through a national network of employment services offices and training centers.

Shannon Development

Shannon, County Clare
Tel: 061 361555
Fax: 061 361903
Web site: www.commerce.ie/shannon-dev

Shannon Development (US)
Ireland House
345 Park Avenue, 17th Floor
New York, NY 10154
Tel: (212) 371–5550
Fax: (212) 308–1485

This organization's mission is to encourage and sustain economic growth in the Shannon region. Some of its programs include the promotion of tourism and rural development in the region, promoting air traffic at Shannon Airport, and managing the National Technical Park at Plassey in County Limerick.

Udaras na Gaeltachta

Na Forbacha
Galway
Tel: 091 592011
Fax: 091 592037
Web site: www.udaras.ie

Also known as the Gaeltacht Authority, this group promotes the economic, social, and cultural development of native Irish-speaking regions. It seeks to preserve and extend the Irish language, support community development, and promote job-creating industries and services.

IFSC

(Contact via IDA)

International Financial Services Center (IFSC), established in 1987 in Dublin, has become a leading location for international banking, investment, and insurance activities. Citibank, Merill Lynch, Bank of America, and Chase Manhattan are among the firms with offices in the IFSC. IFSC operations are entitled to special tax breaks and allowances. Ireland's Central Bank regulates IFSC activities.

SFA

Small Firms Association
84/86 Lower Baggot Street
Dublin 2
Tel: 01 660 1011
Fax: 01 661 2861
E-mail: sfa@iol.ie
Web site: http://ireland.iol.ie/sfa

Launched in 1972, the Small Firms Association (SFA) promotes the development of small companies, defined by the EU as those that employ fifty or fewer people, a criterion met by most businesses in Ireland. The SFA advises its membership of owner managers on a number of issues related to operating a business and provides debt-collection services and discounts on health and other forms of insurance. The SFA sponsors training programs, conferences, and exhibitions, and lobbies the government in support of small business. Its main office is in Dublin, and it has a number of regional offices around the country.

Enterprise Boards

City and county enterprise boards, located throughout Ireland, focus on businesses that employ fewer than ten people. These groups provide advice and financial support to start-up and existing businesses in manufacturing and services industries.

Key Irish Business Sectors

Agriculture

At one time agriculture was the dominant industry in Ireland, but electronics, software, and pharmaceuticals have now eclipsed it. On the 14 percent of land that is suitable for agriculture, farmers grow mostly grains. Barley is used by brewing and distilling companies and as feed for farm animals. Advanced production methods have boosted the quantity and value of overall production even as the number of people working on farms has decreased. As larger farms continue to absorb smaller ones, a greater reliance on farm machinery has reduced the use of horses and donkeys. Because winter temperatures are so mild, grazing cattle and sheep can remain outside most of the year.

Overall, agriculture still has a solid base and earns Ireland a reputation for producing high-quality livestock, meat and dairy products, food ingredients, and wheat, barley, potato, and sugar-beet crops. A subset of agriculture, equipment and supplies, has emerged as an important sector in the economy. Products such as feeding systems, plows, tractor hitches, and fertilizer spreaders are marketed in Ireland and in other countries around the world.

Drinks Industry

A $3 billion industry, the beverage sector's domestic revenues have been boosted by a buoyant economy, and exports have performed well, too. Guinness dominates this highly competitive industry. Other players include Murphy-Heineken and Beamish & Crawford.

The Irish market is more pub-oriented than it is in North America and continental Europe, and Irish off-license shops (package stores) represent a smaller market segment than in most countries. Thus, a product's presence at the bar counter of Ireland's 10,500 pubs is crucial, and companies spend millions in marketing and promotion. Bailey's Irish Cream, the number-one selling liqueur in the world, is popular in Ireland and throughout the world. Australian wines have made inroads, and microbreweries have arrived in Ireland. Local microbrewery creations like Black Biddy, Bees Endeavor, and even American-style lager microbeers provide an alternative to the standard pint of Guinness stout.

Electronics

Electronics is a high-growth sector, comprising a mix of multinational and Irish-owned electronics manufacturers. Companies like IBM, Hadco, Motorola, and Hewlett-Packard produce cables, connectors, circuit boards, and other electronic components. They also contract to assemble finished products. Clients include Apple, Compaq, and Philips.

Telecommunications

One of the fastest-growing industries in Ireland, this sector has produced rapid growth from product manufacture and services provided by multinational and domestic companies. The sector furnishes telecommunications equipment, services, and network management. AT&T, Esat, and Lucent Technologies are some of the well-known firms in this dynamic sector.

Textiles

The yarns and fabrics industry supplies mainly wool and linen to leading fashion houses. Subsectors include industrial fiber, upholstery for aircraft seating, and recycled fabrics for industrial use. Another subsector is apparel, which supplies department stores and mail-order houses around the globe.

Software

Ireland has become, after the United States, the second-largest exporter of software in the world. Many of the world's leading software companies have a presence in Ireland, including Microsoft, Oracle, and Sun Microsystems. There is also a vital core of indigenous firms. Software created in the United States must be revised, translated, and reprogrammed to adapt it to meet the needs of other countries. Ireland is a leader in this process, called localization, for the European market.

Packaging

This sector serves other rapidly growing industries by providing cartons, labels, caps and tubing. Clients include companies in pharmaceuticals, electronics, consumer goods, as well as familiar names in computers: IBM, Intel, Compaq, Dell, and Microsoft.

Health Care

Through the results of a number of multinational companies, Ireland has become a leading manufacturer of high-tech medical products. Many of the world's top medical-device companies have facilities here. Some companies, like American Home Products, Pfizer, Abbott Labs, and Boston Scientific, have more than one plant in Ireland.

In the pharmaceuticals arena domestic and multinational companies in Ireland engage in R&D, clinical-product trials, and manufacturing and marketing of human and veterinary medicines. Active U.S. players include Merck, Pfizer, Sandoz, Schering Plough, Smithkline Beecham, and Sterling.

Consumer Products

In addition to world-famous Waterford crystal, products include jewelry, pottery, china, cutlery, sporting goods, toys, gardening, furniture, and floor coverings. These are exported to clients around the globe, including Harrod's in London and QVC in the States.

Tourism

Tourism continues to be an important source of income for Ireland, generating nearly $4 billion annually and employing a significant percentage of the workforce. Heritage Parks, B&Bs, restaurants, golf courses, shops, pubs, and many other businesses depend a great deal on tourists. More people visit Ireland every year than reside there, and in the summer's high tourist season, the country's population swells to nearly twice its size.

The primary markets for Irish tourism are Germany, the United Kingdom, France, and the United States. In recent years, specialized walking, cycling, and golf tours have performed especially well. Poor summer weather or troubles up North may affect tourism. In 1998, however, a summer of little sun and headlines that reported conflicts did not prevent a healthy increase in tourism revenues. If lasting peace comes to the North, it is expected to draw more tourists to Ireland.

Financial Services

The growth of this sector owes much to the government's establishment of the International Financial Services Center in central Dublin. The IFSC's thirty-nine-acre office complex is home to hundreds of international institutions that operate directly from Dublin or post a satellite office there. Companies like Merrill Lynch, Bank America, and Chase Manhattan that participate in the IFSC program benefit from low corporate taxes and unrestricted currency movement, in addition to favorable double tax treaties.

Opportunities for Business and Service

Employment

The growth of technology-based industry has created a wealth of new opportunities for employment. Irish and foreign firms in this sector report increasing concern about a shortage of qualified workers. Anyone taking up residence in Ireland with technological skills should be able to find work, if the obstacle of obtaining a work permit can be overcome. As Chapter 2 explains, you cannot apply for a work permit on your own. Your prospective employer makes the application and must satisfy the requirement that a search for someone with similar skills in Ireland or a European Union country has proved fruitless.

There are a number of reciprocal exchange programs that permit U.S. and Canadian students to take short-term work in Ireland. One program, Work in Ireland, provides a four-month work permit and orientation to Ireland, after which participants locate lodging and a job on their own. Youth and Student Travel (USIT), the corresponding organization in Ireland, assists thousands of Irish students to visit the States every summer.

What if you're not a student or your skills are not so high-tech? Many businesses in the services sector are also experiencing labor shortages. Hotels and restaurants in particular have lost many prospective applicants to the high-tech industry. Part-time opportunities in tourism as well as across many sectors are expected to expand considerably. If labor shortages intensify, work-permit regulations may be relaxed, and candidates other than Irish and EU nationals may receive consideration. Recruitment agencies, newspaper classified advertising, and the Internet are excellent sources for information about jobs. As it is for addressing many needs, networking in the community is always a good vehicle.

Volunteerism

If it's activity you seek but not income, there is a plethora of opportunities to offer service. Volunteerism flourishes in Ireland, through local schools, scouts groups, churches, hospitals, animal shelters, and community centers. The Samaritans, a group of 2,500 volunteers, aid people in crisis, as do volunteers for the National Network of Women's Refuges. Charity shops like Cerebral Palsy Ireland and Women's Aid rely on volunteers to help collect, sort, and display donated goods. The Carmichael Center for Voluntary Groups in Dublin runs a Resource Center that will match people wishing to volunteer with the organizations that need their help. Global Volunteers coordinates volunteer teams for short-term assignments in Ireland and other countries around the world. Their projects focus on supporting peace and promoting understanding between people of diverse cultures. See the Resource Guide for contact information.

Small Business

Over the past decade the small business sector has been recognized as a key component in a healthy Irish economy. A new breed of Irish entrepreneurs has gained public respect and admiration. Bolstered by prosperity, the Irish seem to be more willing to take the risks associated with starting a new business. Small businesses are generally considered to be those that employ fifty or fewer people and have an annual turnover (sales) of less than $4.5 million. A mid-size company is one that employs between 50 and 250 people, and companies with more than 250 employees are considered large. Jefferson Smurfit and Marks and Spencer are among the large, well-known Irish companies that started small.

Small businesses employ over half the private-sector workforce in Ireland. Most employ fewer than ten people. Their role in helping to reduce chronic high unemployment has been considerable, but small businesses struggle with a shortage of skills in management and marketing. The Small Firms Association has supported skill building through seminars, conferences, and training programs.

Start-Up

For the enthusiastic, results-driven retiree, entrepreneurship may be an exciting pursuit. Anyone with an entrepreneurial orientation will see potential in the buoyant Irish economy. Those who desire a less active pace, however, should consider carefully the energy, long hours, financial resources, and record keeping required to start and maintain a business.

A person who is neither a citizen of Ireland or of the European Union and who intends to establish a business in Ireland or be self-employed there must first apply to the Department of Justice to obtain business permission. The applicant must provide a comprehensive business plan describing the venture, produce evidence of adequate financing, and detail the number and nationality of staff to be employed. The business must meet requirements related to employing Irish or other EU nationals and the use of Irish rather than imported goods. Exceptions to some requirements may be considered if the applicant has been legally resident in Ireland for period of five or more years or is the spouse/dependent of an Irish or EU national. Banks, state agencies, credit unions, and venture capital firms may provide funds, often in exchange for part ownership.

Running a Pub

Some people dream of running a pub in Ireland. Life as a publican, however, has little to do with romantic notions and involves a lot more than pouring drinks and chatting up the locals. The hours are long, and the work can be strenuous. A flair for dealing with the public is an obvious requirement, but community support is also critical. A community's perception of the owner can make or break a pub. It is so Irish an institution that expatriates may be better off enjoying rather than attempting to manage a pub in Ireland. Forming a partnership with someone well regarded in the community and with direct experience might be a wiser strategy than sole proprietorship.

With more than 10,000 pubs in Ireland, even small villages will have several, and competition can be fierce. Successful pubs may fetch a steep price. In 1998 the Coast Inn in Skerries, County Dublin, was reputed to have achieved a price of around $3 million. The Wishing Well, a pub in Ferns, County Wexford, was sold for $450,000, and GF Handels on Baggot Street in Dublin sold for close to $3 million. Pubs in less busy areas will be more reasonably priced and still have good trading potential. Many include residential living space. The following are recent ads for pub sales:

- Bailieboro, County Cavan: "3 story residential/licensed premises with retail unit, currently bookmakers. A second lot includes eight one-bedroom self-contained flats. $450,000."
- Listowel, County Kerry: Refurbished public bar on ground floor. Lucrative and steady trade. First and second floors suitable for private residence or self-contained apartments. Offers over $300,000."
- Drumgole, County Monaghan: "2 story licensed premises with excellent residential accommodation and large shop. Lounge, bar toilets, 5 bedrooms, sitting room, kitchen, bath, office. Shop unit with 2 stores. $270,000."
- Cloghan, County Offaly: "Lovely old world residential/licensed premises. Easily managed, nicely decorated. Accommodation includes 4 bedrooms, 2 reception rooms, dual system central heat. Enclosed yard and landscaped garden. Located on main Limerick/Sligo route. Offers over $262,500."
- Ballinlough, County Roscommon: "Residential public house with 6 bedrooms. Bar with pool table, lounges. $225,000."
- The Hive, Ballydine, County Tipperary: "Well-established landmark premises. Huge function rooms, modern catering kitchen, public bars and lounge, several stores, car park, flower gardens. 5 bedrooms, sitting room, dining room, kitchen, and bath. Offers over $450,000."
- The Seanachi, Ballinalack, County Westmeath: "Roadhouse 10 miles from Mullingar, fully fitted bar and lounge, residential accommodation of 3 bedrooms, sitting room and bath. $225,000."

Tourist Accommodations

A venture that is less disruptive of daily life than running a pub is providing tourist accommodations. Many tourists in Ireland, especially those on a budget, prefer the inexpensive rates of private accommodations. Even those who can afford to stay in upscale hotels, however, will often choose the homey, informal atmosphere for which Irish B&Bs and guesthouses are known.

If a facility for tourist accommodation meets certain requirements, it may be listed with the Tourist Board. Such a listing requires periodic inspections and fees. Once approved, the accommodations will be listed in the annual guides that tourist boards distribute widely. You are entitled to display the official shamrock sign that indicates approval, and local tourist offices will refer walk-ins to your establishment.

In the Irish republic, Board Failte licenses a number of approving agencies, depending on the type of accommodation. The Town & Country Homes Association, Quality Approved Bed & Breakfast Association, and the Irish Farmhouse Holidays Association are examples of these. In Northern Ireland the Northern Ireland Tourist Board (NITB) administers certification of accommodation and also operates through groups like the Town & Seaside House Association and the Farm and Country Holidays Association. Not everyone chooses to be listed, since some tourists, often referred by word of mouth, will phone directly or even come to the door to request a rental. Though official agencies discourage these unregistered operations, they do exist. Typical rates for accommodation range from $15 to $30 per person in B&Bs, higher for guesthomes and other facilities.

Opening a B&B involves more than posting a sign and having a few extra towels on hand. Providing proper amenities may require a substantial financial investment; and before you can apply to be certified by the tourist board, you must obtain planning, fire, and environmental health authorizations, insurance coverage, and VAT registration. A friendly, outgoing personality is a must, as is the ability to coordinate a variety of household activities to deliver good service. Being ready at a moment's notice to welcome guests requires flexibility. Laundering linens calls for time and plenty of hot water. Rising well in advance of guests to prepare a full breakfast might be difficult for a night owl.

Specific requirements for agency approval vary depending on the type of accommodations, whether bed and breakfast, country home, townhome, self-catering holiday home, guesthome, farmhouse holiday home, or hotel. Generally, the facility must have:
- clean and well-maintained exterior and interior areas, of durable construction and structurally safe throughout.
- attractive signs that can be read from a distance.
- adequate parking that does not disrupt the flow of traffic and won't require guests to carry luggage too far a distance.
- a well-appointed entrance area, where coffee and tea are offered upon arrival.

- a display of charges for accommodations and other services.
- a guestbook to record each visitor's nationality and date of departure.
- a display of brochures, maps, and leaflets that inform guests about local attractions.
- first-aid equipment.
- a well-appointed and ventilated kitchen of adequate size.
- a refrigerator with suitable capacity to meet the needs of family and guests.
- a separate dining room with sturdy table and chairs.
- a high chair for young children.
- one or more sitting rooms or lounges for guests to use, which may be shared with the host family and should be large enough to accommodate everyone likely to use them at any one time.
- bedrooms of sufficient size, each with separate access, lock and key, proper lighting and heating, a supply of clean linens, window coverings, and storage for clothing.
- a bathroom with adequate hot water, fresh soap, clean towels, and high-quality fixtures.
- a clothes washer and dryer installed in a separate utility room.
- storage areas for cleaning materials, and bed linens.
- sufficient staff to maintain a good standard of service at all times.
- separate sleeping accommodations for owners and family.

Providing additional services at an extra charge can enhance marketability. Ensuite (private bath) rooms are in high demand. Bedroom television sets; evening meals; direct dial phones; bicycle, boat, golf club, or fishing tackle rental; guided tours, facilities for children, access for people with disabilities, and participation in farmwork are examples of additional amenities that draw guests and may encourage them to stay longer.

Many accommodation facilities operate seasonally, generally from March or April through October. Some are open year-round. Provision of smoke-free accommodations is becoming more common, though still not the rule. Places that do permit smoking usually restrict it to the lounge area.

It is possible to start small, with just one or two bedrooms for guests. Often people who enter the B&B business have no direct hospitality experience, but they learn the ropes quickly. Those who are able household managers, competent cooks, and good-natured and flexible enjoy running this kind of business. Providing extras like freshly baked bread and hanging baskets of flowers help promote your establishment as a home away from home. Engaging in conversation with your guests, who are often eager to learn about Ireland and the immediate locality, is good for business. Ensuring the satisfaction and enjoyment of guests can significantly boost trade through repeat business and word-of-mouth referrals.

You can either buy a property suitable for providing tourist accommodations or adapt an existing structure. Tourist Board approval is not transferable with ownership; a new proprietor must apply to the relevant approving agency and comply with the current minimum standards. The following are recent examples of relevant property listings.

- Killarney, County Kerry: "I.T.B. registered, 12-bedroom detached home. Excellent trading location on banks of River Flesk. 12 ensuite bedrooms, residents' lounge, dining room, private apartment. $675,000."
- Aran Islands, County Galway: "B&B bungalow near Kilronan Harbor. $270,000."
- Mountshannon, County Clare: "Attractive bed and breakfast in picturesque village on shores of Lough Derg. Views of lake from downstairs lounge, kitchen, two of three bedrooms, and large upstairs lounge with balcony. Dining room, 1½ baths. Garden to lake with own harbor. Offers over $225,000."
- Letterkenny, County Donegal: "Detached residence on .5 acre site just off main road. Excellent condition. Entrance, sun porch, 2 reception rooms, study, 4 bedrooms, 2 ensuite and separate bath. Double garage, landscaped garden. Good potential for bed and breakfast. $180,000."
- Dublin City, County Dublin: "Eight bedrooms, five ensuite, new roof, wiring, damp proofing, central heat, double-glazed windows. Original doors and fireplaces. Two large reception areas with adjoining sunroom, family room, walled rear garden with patio areas. Views of Wicklow Mountains. For auction at guide price $675,000."
- Ardagh, County Clare: "Detached, 4-bedroom home with hall, sitting room, bedrooms ensuite and main bath. Double glazing, central heat, garage/workshop, 1 acre. $127,500."

- Galway City, County Galway: "Detached two-story residence in excellent central location within a short walk of City Center and close to University College Galway Hospital and University. Presently operating as successful B&B establishment, fully registered and approved by Bord Failte and listed with Town and Country Homes. $435,000."

- Lower Salthill, County Galway: "Seven bedroom B&B, fifteen-minute walk to Galway City, short walk to Salthill Promenade and beach. Hall, sitting room, dining room, inner hall with pine stairs, kitchen, utility, back hall. $412,500."

- Monasterevin, County Kildare: "Large 4-bedroom bungalow on ¼ acre of landscaped gardens. Ample car parking, walking distance to all amenities. Commute to Dublin in 35 minutes. Possible B&B potential. $210,000."

- Carrigallen, County Leitrim: "Spacious, 279-square meter (3,000-sq.-ft.) family residence has ideal potential for a bed and breakfast as it incorporates seven bedrooms with ample car parking to front and rear. Three bathrooms. Oil-fired central heat, PVC double glazing throughout, aluminum guttering 1.24 acres of mature elevated grounds. Two driveway entrances. Detached double-door garage. 4.8 kilometers (3 miles) from Killeshandra. Offers over $210,000."

- Knock, County Mayo: "Thriving B&B business, 8-bedroooom, large kitchen and prep area, utility room, large tree-lined site. $375,000."

  "Detached dwelling 183 meters (200 yds.) from Apparition Shrine. Ideal for B&B or conversion to restaurant. Porch, luxury lounge, kitchen, utility, storage. Three spacious bedrooms with built in wardrobes and modern bath. Large back yard and side entrance. $157,500."

- Trim, County Meath: "Former maternity hospital, now trading as successful B&B on elevated site with good views of Trim Castle and River Boyne. Family wing with two ensuite bedrooms, sitting room, dining room and laundry room. Nine ensuite guest bedrooms. Well-appointed kitchen. Planning permission granted for restaurant. Landscaped gardens and ample parking. For auction, guide price $750,00."

- Ballaghdereen, County Roscommon: "Two-story home with entrance hall, sitting room, bath with electric shower, large storeroom. Also 3 bedroom residence and workshop, ideal for use as guesthouse. $105,000."
- Castletowngeoghegan, County Westmeath: "Well appointed Lake District, 7 bedroom, 2 story residence, suitable for B&B. Excellent structural and decorative condition. $225,000."
- Gorey, County Wexford: "Extensive 12 bedroom bed and breakfast business in scenic, rural area. Magnificent views on 2.5 acres, near beach. Large entrance hall, utility room, lounge, private water. Graveled car park. Offers over $300,000."
- Arklow, County Wicklow: "Spacious bungalow on 1 acre with mature gardens. Currently a comfortable family home. Could easily be adapted for B&B. Set well back from road, in elevated position, with lounge, dining room, kitchen, family room, and 5 bedrooms. $337,500."

Franchising

A familiar and successful business model in the United States, franchising is relatively new to Ireland. Except for McDonald's, which arrived in Ireland more than twenty years ago and now has forty restaurants, only in recent years has franchising begun to take hold. The appeal of reduced risk, accelerated entry, brand recognition, and the training and marketing resources that franchising provides is encouraging their emergence in the North and the Republic. Franchising is expected to expand considerably in the years ahead.

More than one hundred franchising systems have a presence in Ireland. A dozen or so of these are Irish companies, and over a third are U.S. based, but most franchises originate in the United Kingdom. Bewley's, Ireland's well-known coffee, tea, and catering company, has expanded considerably over the past decade by locating company-owned and franchised outlets across Ireland and around the world. Supermacs, a fast-food family restaurant, and O'Brien's Sandwiches are two other Irish companies that have expanded through franchising. U.S. franchises in Ireland include Subway, Mailboxes, Etc., and Weight Watchers.

Franchise Direct, a service of McGarry Consulting, hosts a Web site with guidelines on basic aspects of franchising and a directory of franchisors. Each entry profiles the business, presents start-up investments, franchise fees, and indicates the locations targeted for expansion, often in Ireland. These include NIC Hygiene Specialists, a British commercial contract cleaning company; Celtic Milled Beauty Products, a County Kildare company that produces skin care and face and body treatments; A&W restaurants, the U.S. company that began in the root-beer business; Donato Group from Canada, with Mrs. Vanelli's Italian food and Made in Japan Teriyaki; and Signs Express, a British company specializing in computerized signage. McGarry Consulting also offers guidance for developing strategies for business start-up and helps identify overseas partnership opportunities between the United States and Ireland. (See the Resource Guide for contact details.)

Transferring Your Business

If you have had an established business that you now want to base in Ireland, the government permits you to bring in certain kinds of equipment and vehicles without paying customs duty, provided that you are able to produce evidence that you've owned them for longer than a year and meet a number of other restrictions. Irish embassy and consular offices can provide detailed information and various forms you must complete. Transfers from EU countries are less complicated than those from North America.

Taxes

Taxation can be a complicated matter, and annual budget provisions and finance bills often alter policy and rates. It is beyond the scope of this book to provide detailed tax guidance. Advice from a tax professional experienced in overseas relocation is recommended to guide strategy. You may also obtain information, detailed leaflets, and assistance with completing forms from the Central Revenue Office in Dublin or from a local tax office.

The following is a summary of current tax issues relevant to operating a business in Ireland.

Self-Assessment

You must notify the tax office when you start a business by completing Form TR1 for sole traders or TR2 for companies. You then receive a Revenue and Social Insurance (RSI) number or continue with the one assigned to you if you previously were a pay as you earn (PAYE) participant. Because those who are self-employed do not participate in the PAYE withholding process, they report income and pay taxes through the "Self-Assessment" system. While you are permitted to determine an accounting period that suits your business, the following schedule is typical: Under Self-Assessment, you pay preliminary tax on or before November 1 for the tax year that will end the following April 5. For example, the 1999/2000 tax year runs from April 6, 1999, to April 5, 2000; thus, preliminary tax is due by November 1, 1999. You then file a tax return any time between April 6, 2000 and January 31, 2001. Within a couple of months, the tax inspector reviews your return and issues a Notice of Assessment. If you've overpaid tax, you receive a refund with interest. If you owe a balance, you must pay it within one month or by April 30, 2001, whichever is later. There are no extensions, and late returns incur surcharges on balances due. Small, unincorporated businesses are entitled to file a tax return on Form BP1, a simplified version of the standard return.

Preliminary tax is your estimate of how much tax you'll owe for the year. It includes Pay Related Social Insurance (PRSI) and a 2 percent health levy. If your estimate is off, you may be subject to interest charges. You do not have to pay preliminary tax in the first year that your business is in operation. You can arrange to pay preliminary tax by direct debit, spread throughout the year.

You are expected to keep clear and accurate records of business transactions that reflect all payments and sources of income. Your records must show cash withdrawals; payments for rents, utilities, repairs, and motor expenses; and purchases you make for equipment and supplies and for services rendered to your business. An accountant can advise you on the most appropriate form of record keeping for your business. You should retain check stubs, receipts, invoices, and bank statements for at least six years.

Sole Trader versus Company

You can elect to be regarded as a sole trader, in which case individual income and PRSI tax rates (outlined in Chapter 4) will apply. If you choose to set up a company, an accountant or lawyer can assist you in the process of registering with the Companies Registration office in Dublin. You become the director and must set up PAYE/PRSI taxation on your salary.

If you establish your business as a company, then the following corporate tax rates are relevant. For 1999 business profits are taxed at 25 percent, up to $150,000. Above $150,000, the standard 1999 rate is 28 percent. By the year 2003 a single rate of 12.5 percent will take effect, phased in as follows: 24 percent in 2000, 20 percent in 2001, and 16 percent in 2002. Currently, businesses engaged in a broadly defined process of manufacturing are taxed at a special rate of 10 percent, which will continue for certain activities until 2010.

Taxable Profits

You calculate your profits by deducting business expenses from your turnover, or amounts you earn from sale or goods or provision of services, within the April 6 to April 5 tax year. These deductions include purchase of goods for resale, running costs of and lease payments for business vehicles, accountant fees, interest on business loans, wages, rent, utilities, and so forth. Entertainment of business clients is not deductible in Ireland.

You can claim for wear and tear on office equipment, machinery, and vehicles under the separate category of capital allowances. If your unincorporated business shows a loss, you may use it to reduce other taxable income or carry it forward to offset future profits of your business. Corporations cannot use losses to offset personal income.

Those who are sole traders may make tax-deductible contributions up to 30 percent of net income per year to a self-administered pension plan. Though a pension trustee approved by the Revenue Commissioners will oversee your program, seeking the guidance of an independent financial advisor is recommended. You may elect to retire at any age between sixty and seventy.

Employee Taxes and Deductions

If you will employ others, you must register as an employer and operate a PAYE/PRSI system for your workers if you pay them above certain modest levels. Hiring someone who has been unemployed for twelve or more months or who is disabled may entitle you to claim additional deductions.

Value Added Tax

Valued Added Tax (VAT) is a consumer tax collected by VAT registered traders on sales and services supplied in the course of business.

You must register for VAT if your turnover is likely to exceed certain annual limits: $30,000 for services and $60,000 for goods. You incur VAT on goods and services you acquire for your business, and you charge VAT on those you provide. You pay the amount by which the VAT you charge exceeds the VAT you incur. You receive a refund if you incur more VAT than you charge. If you supply goods or services in Ireland but do not have your business based there, you must register for VAT regardless of turnover level. Your records must reflect your VAT position. VAT payments must be made every other month but can also be made monthly. A final return for the year is also required.

Most goods and services are taxable, though there are a number of exempt items, including food, certain books, children's clothing and footwear, exported goods, medical services, and passenger transport. The local tax office can clarify whether you are supplying taxable goods and/or services.

The standard rate of VAT is 21 percent. A reduced rate of 12.5 percent applies for real property, building services, newspapers and periodicals, hotel and holiday accommodations, short-term car and boat hire, tour-guide services, restaurants and hot take-away foods, hairdressing, and certain agricultural services.

Capital Gains Tax

Capital gains tax (CGT) is payable on gains made when you dispose of certain assets like land, houses, and shares. All taxpayers report gains via Self-Assessment and must make preliminary payment by November 1 in the year after the tax year in which a chargeable gain is made. (Chapter 4 presents CGT rates and exclusions.)

Tax Audits

Every year a number of taxpayers are selected for audit. An inspector of taxes examines the tax return and supporting records. You are subject to audit for a period of six years after the end of the tax year in which the return is filed.

The Revenue Office can impose fines and even imprisonment for anyone convicted of an offense. Offenses include claiming a deduction to which you are not entitled, and the failure to notify the tax office when you become taxable, file a return, include all income on a return, or keep adequate records.

Investing in the Irish Boom

Investing in the stock market is a fairly new phenomenon for most Irish citizens. They have historically chosen land or property over the higher risk of securities. In recent years an allocation in either low- or high-risk investment vehicles will have generated a bounteous return. Still, of those in Ireland who earn more than $35,000 per year, a mere 10 percent own stocks or mutual funds. (In the United States, the comparable percentage is 85.)

Property, ever the investment of choice in Ireland, lost some of its appeal when the government removed some of the tax advantages in 1998. Investors were no longer able to use mortgage interest to offset rental income. This helped make the housing market more accessible for first-time buyers, but it also served to discourage apartment development to ease an overburdened rental inventory.

A number of factors are encouraging the public to take more interest in other forms of investing. People have more money than they used to. Investment products have increased in number and expanded in type. Employees may receive shares as part of their benefits package. When building societies go public, their members receive free shares. A reduction in capital gains tax has encouraged more buying and selling of stock.

Low returns on savings deposits have driven people to consider other options. There is, therefore, an increasing interest in a range of investment vehicles. Investment clubs of members who pool resources to screen and purchase stocks, popular in North America and the United Kingdom, have begun to emerge in Ireland.

The Stock Market

Much of the trading on the Irish stock exchange, ISEQ, is institutional and thus deals in large volumes of shares. The ISEQ soared from 1994 to 1997, wobbled along with other world markets in mid-1998, and closed out the year with a gain of 23.2 percent.

Stockbrokers, represented by the Irish Brokers Association, charge either a flat-rate commission or a minimum cash fee per transaction. The shares of a number of Irish companies trade on U.S. stock exchanges, including Smurfit, Ryanair, Elan, CBT, Esat, Iona, and ICON. The likelihood that stock exchanges from EU countries may link to form a single European stock market that will list large blue-chip companies will draw interest from the investment community.

Though robust, Ireland's economy is small. Its modest size and dependence on exports make it vulnerable when economic calamity arises in other economies. Irish companies that derive the bulk of their revenues from a domestic base are less affected by a financial crisis somewhere else in the world.

Overall, Ireland's economic outlook appears healthy. Lower corporate tax and interest rates are expected to foster continued growth in the revenues and earnings of Irish companies, though the stratospheric levels of recent years will likely taper off. Financial services and technology sectors are projected to perform well. Mergers are expected to continue, as companies seek the power and security of larger size as they enter the broader and more competitive European Union arena.

Investing in Northern Ireland

The benefits of a more stable political environment extend well beyond the economic opportunity it will likely provide in Northern Ireland. There is a sincere desire for an end to "The Troubles" if not always a unified notion of how to bring it about. Once a stable peace can be reasonably assured, the North should receive economic aid to support new development, see increased revenues from tourism, and experience further growth of investment in business and property. If it succeeds, cross-border cooperation through bodies established under the Belfast Agreement of 1998 will encourage shared development and trade between the North and South, which will in turn boost employment. Property investors in the Irish Republic, where the market has provided less value in the price boom, have already moved to the North to seek higher returns.

A key player in Northern Ireland since 1960, the DuPont Company manufactures industrial textiles and employs more than 900 people at Maydown, County Derry. The Industrial Development Board (IDB) has supported further investment by DuPont in the Maydown facility and has attracted companies like Seagate, Ford, and Emerson to establish branches in the North. The IDB's mission to encourage other companies to invest in Northern Ireland will be boosted further by a stable environment.

Will You Be Happy in Ireland?

It is important not to underestimate the challenge of moving to any foreign country, Ireland included. The decision to do so should be made only after a great deal of careful thought, and plans should be carefully crafted and continually reviewed.

Thorough planning will mean less stress for you. You'll feel less pressure, too, if you are able to create backup plans that make a reversal possible at any stage in the process. Even if you've spent a fair amount of time in Ireland, your experience as a visitor will have provided only a glimpse of the world you now intend to make your home. Once you survive the upheaval of a major move of household, you will confront the process of settling in new surroundings where many things may be unfamiliar. Becoming a resident of another country requires a transition that may ask a lot of you, though it may offer much in return.

Moving to Ireland may alter more than the external aspects of your life. If you are adventurous enough to abandon the shelter of familiarity for the challenge of a new environment, you, like many other expatriates, may be transformed.

Retirement, too, requires its own adjustment period. It may prod us to reinvent ourselves. We are no longer "Lou in Receiving," "Wendy, the stockbroker," or "Ted, that guy who does graphic design." Now, we're *retired, separated from service, empty-nesters, an ex-cop, or a former teacher*—expressions that imply withdrawal and define us in terms of what we used to do. Our vocabulary fails to capture the reality of a phase in which many of us will spend at least one fourth of our lives. Words like recareering and redirecting may more appropriately characterize this time in our lives. Increased longevity and improved health have enhanced the quantity and quality of life and delivered us from many stereotypes of "old age." Today the experience of many older people indicates this is a phase full of vitality, promise, and discovery and not some wistful, gloomy, and drawn-out denouement.

However positive the phase, the process of adapting to the freedom of retirement rivals the magnitude of earlier life transitions. Add to this the challenge of moving to a foreign country, and our coping abilities may be tested as never before. Fortunately, we command a repertoire of life skills we did not possess in adolescence or early adulthood, and most of us have learned to deal effectively with all sorts of challenges. Those who have a high tolerance for change are likely to experience a smoother transition when making an international move. Those who struggle with change, even when it is positive, will need more time to adapt.

Culture Shock

"Culture shock" is generally defined as the confusion and anxiety that arise when someone is exposed to an alien culture or environment. People's responses to culture shock differ. It may, therefore, affect one family member more markedly than another. Unlike the flu, the onset is not sudden. Rather than wallop you all at once, culture shock accumulates over time. It emerges from a series of undramatic incidents that may not register initially in your consciousness as anything more than a fleeting sense of discomfort from a minor glitch or awkward moment.

Some people assume that a common language, which is unarguably an aid to communicating freely, precludes culture shock. Since we'll all speak English in Ireland, the assumption goes, we'll find our comfort zone readily. Such false expectations make people especially vulnerable to culture shock. Though when you move to Ireland you are spared the considerable stress of having to learn a new language, you will still confront other demands of adapting to a different culture. The mirror of another culture may alter how you see yourself and, should you return someday, how you perceive your former community and your place among its people.

It is important to be able to recognize the signs and effects of culture shock. These will manifest in a number of emotions and/or behaviors. In the milder versions that most people experience, these include impatience, irritability, anxiety, and withdrawal.

For some caught more tightly in its grip, there is a reluctance to participate in the new community, a withholding of self, and a preference for devoting a lot of time, energy, and money to sustaining ties with home. Quite a different indication of culture shock arises as a form of extreme infatuation—a newcomer falls madly in love with everything about Ireland. He or she overidentifies with all things Irish, begins to denigrate his or her former homeland, and exudes a sense of superiority over those in the now unglamorous community left behind. While neither of these scenarios is particularly common, both indicate a poor adjustment that does not bode well for long-term happiness.

There are a number of things you can do to help minimize culture shock and ensure a smoother transition. This chapter will explore various strategies to help you adapt to life among Irish people.

Keys to a Successful Transition

Think in Terms of Trade-Offs

Moving residence from one legal entity to another always carries trade-offs. Occasional surprises, both rude and pleasant, pop up.

Take the example of familiar products. After you move to another area, you search doggedly but may fail to find a decent bagel, cherished brand of soup, or preferred blend of coffee. After a time you'll either be so enthralled by the regional cuisine that you miss those standbys less and less, or you'll have cajoled some kind soul into shipping you those delicacies you crave. In one form or another, you adapt.

Such mini-shocks are likely to occur on more than one level in a move to Ireland, where many things will be different. It is natural for people to focus more on the perceived losses, the not-so-nice surprises. Discovering an unanticipated expense or the unavailability of a faithfully used product may elicit a momentary sense of betrayal—your new environment has let you down! (Perversely, people sometimes miss things they didn't enjoy when they did have access to them. As one person who resettled in Ireland confessed, "What I miss most is hot dogs—real hot dogs. And I'm a vegetarian!")

Remember to note and appreciate positive changes—the trade-offs you earn as you settle in. When you pay a few more cents for butter, remind yourself that it's the best you've ever tasted. If you feel a sudden craving for, say, a cheese Danish, celebrate your access to the local bakery's brown-bread scones. And sometimes, in a new environment, we discover that what we like has changed. Though coffee and even upscale cappuccino drinks are widely available in Ireland, many coffee lovers find that they begin to prefer tea, so surrounded are they by people swallowing gallons of the stuff.

Something interesting happens to those who've been in Ireland for a while when they return to visit the United States. Rather than feel compelled to overindulge in things they've missed, they are often overwhelmed by what they now perceive as a nearly obscene excess of goods. As one expatriate shared, "I was eager to go to the supermarket in my former town, but when I got there, the sight of all that food—all those products piled high on the shelves—it made my stomach hurt."

Such cravings are not restricted to edibles. You might miss, for example, the invigorating force of your morning shower, the postal carrier whom you greeted daily for years, or the vast expanse of North America and the cloak of anonymity that its size and numbers seem to afford. It may help to ease these longings if you note that you are breathing cleaner air, enjoying a gentler pace, being treated regularly to stunning landscapes, and living among people who are glad to meet you and actually remember your name.

Often you'll be struck by similarities, too. As one expatriate said, walking along the street is made more enjoyable by her delight at recognizing family features in the strangers she passes. There are gifts, both concrete and intangible, that accrue to those who take risks and seek change. The Irish way of life bestows many that help to offset the occasional downside.

Be Prepared

To prepare yourself for the life that you will lead in Ireland, immerse yourself in Irish history and culture. Well before your move, visit the library, bookstores, and the tourist board. Learn all that you can about your home-to-be. Consider taking a subscription to *Inside Ireland,* a quarterly publication that provides the inside skinny on living in Ireland. In addition to providing a wealth of practical information on relocating to and living in Ireland, this newsletter includes feature articles, discount vouchers, and special supplements on real estate, accommodations, and genealogy. *Inside Ireland* also provides an information service, included in the $40 subscription fee. (All letters receive a personal reply. Responses to routine inquiries are free, and requests for information that require research are charged at cost plus 10 percent. Founder and editor Brenda Weir will send a free sample copy on request. See the Resource Guide for further information and the end of this chapter for an excerpt from *Inside Ireland.*)

Surf the Internet, where you can read Irish newspapers, connect with a pen pal, and scan message boards frequented by locals. You can even sample a virtual Guinness when you visit one popular Web site, the Virtual Irish Pub.

Plan to visit Ireland as often as and/or for as long a time as you are able before you commit to move. While there, network with local people, test your tolerance for the weather, and gather pamphlets from estate agents and government offices. Organize a binder of useful information. Because the media can provide a great window on a culture, devote some time to reading daily papers, watching television, and listening to the radio.

As the time to move approaches, being prepared refers as well to putting your affairs in good order. Some of the things you'll need to do:

- Take inventory. Determine the items you'll take, leave behind, give away, sell outright, and/or put in storage.
- Contact moving vendors for estimates.
- Depending on your plans for your current residence, make appropriate arrangements to terminate or transfer utilities and other services.
- Make airline and lodging reservations.
- Plan a garage sale and/or donate items to charity.
- Schedule appointments for thorough physical, dental, and eye exams.
- Investigate your options with regard to health coverage.
- Gather and organize your official papers, including medical, legal, financial, and insurance documents.
- Update your will.
- Renew your passport and driver's license.
- Request copies of health records and prescriptions.
- Notify your post office and UPS or other delivery services of a change of address.
- Notify Social Security and Medicare.
- Make sure that family and friends know how to reach you.
- Execute a power of attorney and leave it with someone whom you trust to act in your behalf. Carry a copy with you.

Conscientious preparation will ensure a more orderly transition. Accept, however, that your best efforts to prepare will not protect you entirely from inevitable moments of frustration. Initially, you may be charmed or intrigued by differences, but as time goes by, you may begin to long for the familiar. It's normal to feel occasionally overwhelmed by all that is different. Expect this, try not to be unsettled by it, and give yourself time to become accustomed to new circumstances. Soon you'll grow used to things, but living in a smaller space, driving on the left, converting posted kilometers to miles, determining if a size 36 shoe will fit, and deciphering a different currency may occasionally test your fortitude.

Cultivate Particular Traits

Your tendency to think, feel, act, and react in certain ways is probably firmly established and has likely served you well through many life events. Still, it is possible to develop new attributes or hone (or, if necessary, temper) existing traits. If the following are well grounded in your repertoire of personal skills, it won't hurt to polish them a bit. If you haven't been praised recently for your command of some traits noted in the following summary, you might want to commit yourself to working to develop them.

Tolerance

Try to keep an open mind about everything—customs that may seem strange or policies that don't make sense (to you, anyway). Strive for tolerance, especially with people. Try not to assume either that people will be very like—or unlike—you; just be open to who they are. Demonstrate your respect for Irish culture. At the same time, appreciate individuality by not attributing every difference that you perceive as related to culture.

You don't have to like everything about Ireland or everyone who lives there. For example, whether it is a discarded candy wrapper on the sidewalk or a bag of garbage dumped in the countryside, litter is an unpleasant fact of life in Ireland. Vigorous media campaigns and community efforts do have some effect, but you'll likely encounter more litter in Ireland than you may be accustomed to seeing.

It would be wise to avoid sharing negative opinions with nearly everyone you encounter. Unless someone asks you directly, eschew frequent comparisons detailing how your adopted environment fails to match attributes of the one left behind. You'll have an easier time if you are able to carry a live-and-let-live attitude. It's human nature to find fault, and you will, occasionally. Try to balance those impressions with positives.

Strive to embrace the culture and accept it for what it is rather than what you might wish it to be.

Resilience

Some people thrive on change and become edgy when things stay the same for too long, but these seem to be a charming and tiny minority. Even when they choose it and perceive it as positive, many people do not initially respond well to change. While it may be difficult to alter your basic temperament, you may be able to boost your ability to tolerate change, with a bit of practice. In the comfort of your current environment, you could set up some small changes and then coach yourself through them. You might alter your wake/rest routine or switch to a different brand of beverage or cereal. You could resolve to sample an unusual dish, listen to music you'd ordinarily ignore, see a film with an actor who is not your favorite, or pick up the book that someone's been begging you to read for months. Becoming more used to change will help you deal better with those changes you can't control.

Some of our resistance to change arises from fear, usually without basis. Sometimes it's plain stubbornness. When you live among the Irish, try not to cling to old habits that might create confusion. For example, though it will feel odd at first to reverse the order of dates, don't dig your heels in—just go along with this custom.

Listening Skills

Even if you've always been complimented for being a great listener, and especially if you've rarely been told this, work to improve your listening skills. Be receptive to those around you. Avoid dominating conversations to share your particular worldview. Your attentiveness to what others have to say will show respect and indicate that you realize that you have much to learn from the Irish people.

Sense of Humor

Your ability to see the humorous side of things will help you through any number of new situations. It's especially helpful to give yourself permission to make the occasional blunder and then be able to view this in an amusing light.

What we perceive as humorous is individual, subjective, and in some ways linked to culture. The Irish appreciation for good craic is evident in social situations. Sometimes it focuses on tale telling or "slagging" (a term that means trying to get a rise out of others by ribbing them.) Such teasing is generally good-natured but also can have an edge. You could seize the challenge, and perhaps you may be able to hold your own. It might be wiser, however, to simply observe for a while. You may occasionally miss the significance of a punch line or feel awkward when everyone else is chuckling and you're not sure why. You may not always be able to follow or keep up with rapid exchanges. Just remember that it's all in good fun, and in most cases no one is trying to make you feel out of place. You'll soon grow more accustomed to speech cadence and repartee.

Patience

Allow yourself plenty of time to adapt. Go with the flow. As time passes, you will feel more at ease. Don't try too hard to fit in. Adjust expectations you might have that you'll make friends easily and quickly. While Irish people are likely to be very friendly, on some level you will remain an outsider. Don't pout about it. Friendships take time to develop.

Try to be patient as well with minor inconveniences. Immersion heaters, for example, often have to be switched on in advance of washing dishes or taking a shower. This is a more efficient use of energy, but it does mean that a spontaneous shower will be a cold one.

Determination

Resolve to make things work. Hold positive thoughts even in the face of criticism. If well-intentioned friends or family members are less than supportive of your plans, don't allow their comments to weaken your resolve. Recognize that a remark like "You won't be happy there" is often a way to express the real message—"I envy your courage" or "I'm going to miss you."

The situation is different, of course, when the less than enthusiastic response to your dream of relocating issues from your mate. It is easier to make things work when partners share a similar degree of commitment to the move. One partner's reluctance may place an added burden on the other and contribute to tension when things go awry. Sometimes, however, initial reluctance may disappear, as exemplified by the situation of one couple who did not at first share the same opinion of a move to Ireland. As the wife recounted, "My husband did not want to go to any foreign country, but after a year in Ireland, you couldn't drag him away."

Challenge Stereotypes

We live in an era of heightened concern about what to say and how to say it so as not to offend anyone. There are people who say that they are weary of all the attention we feel we must pay to proper forms of expression. They proclaim that the pressure to be "politically correct" is cramping our style and reducing our enjoyment of everyday conversations by injecting them with an unnecessary layer of stress. Perhaps their claim has some validity. On the other hand, one could take the view that paying more attention to our manner of speaking serves to prevent a degree of unaware, insensitive, and potentially hurtful expression. However great a burden some might perceive it to be, taking care to express ourselves with sensitivity may be one way to show respect. The following is not meant to be prescriptive, to bash North Americans, or to glorify the Irish but to raise awareness and offer pointers for avoiding tension.

Like the members of most culturally identifiable groups, the Irish are subjected to stereotyping and can be appropriately sensitive to its manifestations. If you bear notions bred in Hollywood and are fond of uttering "stage Irish," you may be promptly stereotyped yourself as someone foolish. Romantic films like *Ryan's Daughter* and *The Quiet Man* are no more an accurate, complete representation of Ireland than are *Gone with the Wind* and *Lethal Weapon I* (and II, III, to infinity) a true picture of the United States. Though we hope they are a tiny minority, there are North Americans who communicate, directly or indirectly, a condescending attitude that Ireland exists as their personal "theme park" of quaint dwellings and adorable, backward people. Such a perspective will tend to obstruct a genuine connection with Irish people, to say the least.

While the veteran actor Barry Fitzgerald may have recited it often while in character, you won't hear Irish people say "Faith and begora" or "Top of the mornin' to ye," examples of stage Irish. You will encounter colorful language, words used in ways you're not used to, and a rich lexicon of slang. (The Resource Guide presents a list of common slang terms and their meanings.) Resist any temptation to memorize and immediately integrate these into your manner of speech. Allow yourself to adopt uniquely Irish forms of the language naturally, over time. Use an Irish expression when it will enhance communication rather than to demonstrate your prowess with vocabulary.

Do the Irish hold stereotypes about North Americans? Of course they do. Are they unfair? Sometimes, but not always. You will do yourself and other North Americans a favor if you try to avoid reinforcing them. Some of the stereotypes characterize people from the United States as overly materialistic, direct to the point of rudeness, and bossy, conveying the belief that they are entitled to be in charge of everything. Others include being blinded by national pride to flaws in U.S. foreign policy, naïve about world events, and ignorant about the Irish and other cultures. You can effect a form of stereotype damage control by cultivating tolerance, showing respect, and being sensitive and attentive to others.

There are also certain behaviors you should try to avoid and attitudes best kept in check.

Don't rush to offer suggestions on a better way to do something. It is true that outsiders often bring a fresh perspective, but it is also true that imposing it on others inspires neither trust nor admiration but more often resistance and resentment. Rather than being perceived as helpful, you may come off looking like a know-it-all. As one expatriate explained, "Americans are often driven to fix things, to make them right. When they say to the Irish, 'This is how you ought to do such and such,' you can sense the hackles rising. They won't say a word in return, but their behavior toward you changes." Another expatriate offered this advice: "If you find yourself thinking, 'Why don't they do it this way?' try to realize that 'this way' may not be best for them."

Another issue that arises for some, but not all, Irish people relates to the distinction between nationality and heritage and the semantics we use to characterize each. Millions of North Americans claim to have Irish ancestors. Many people in Ireland have family and friends in North America and symbolic ties to the country. They will often inquire about someone's connections with Ireland. If the well-meaning respondent exclaims, "Yep, I'm Irish. My grandmother was born in Ballycroy," she or he will most likely receive a warm smile and a nod. "I'm of Irish heritage," is a more appropriate description, or "I'm Irish American." The distinction may seem obvious, but that it is lost on some North Americans can annoy some Irish people. This is a delicate area, one in which some Irish and American people get annoyed with how annoyed some Irish people get about it!

One expatriate characterized Irish attitudes toward North Americans this way: "There are some Irish people who love to hang out with Americans and ask questions about the States. But there are others who, for whatever reason, don't like Americans and aren't afraid to say so. The latter are a minority, but they often talk louder than the rest!"

Again, you are not compelled to like everyone in Ireland. Generally, people will be friendly, polite, forgiving of minor blunders, willing to answer questions, and genuinely hospitable. Your ability to enter situations with an open mind and to be receptive to others will be appreciated and rewarded. The rewards may be abstract—respect for your values, genuine interest in getting to know more about you and where you come from, and your inclusion within the community. Rewards may also be tangible, like the soup sent over by a concerned neighbor when you are ill or the mechanic who drives half an hour to rescue you when your car breaks down on a lonely country road. A lot of things can go your way in Ireland when you have forged good connections from a foundation of mutual understanding and respect.

Get Involved

There is a multitude of activities to engage you as an active participant in Irish life. Unless solitude is your mode of choice, try not to isolate yourself. Make a concerted effort to become part of the community. Participating in local events and organizations will help you learn about Irish culture, develop your niche in the community, and accelerate a sense of belonging. The only caveat when you join a group: Try not to take over!

Allow Yourself to Be Homesick

Realize that you will at times experience that particular longing we call homesickness. Things that expatriates say they miss most include the convenience of having access to nearly anything they want and the comfort of familiarity. One expatriate explained, "I sometimes miss the ease with people that comes from not having to figure out what might really be going on." They miss a wider choice of items like linens, foods in general, and Mexican food in particular. They usually balance these yearnings against a list of things they don't miss, however. The following quotes provide some examples:

"I don't miss the pressure put on Americans to have bigger and better than their neighbors, whether they can afford it or not."

"The crime we had to deal with in our old neighborhood. We're still a little overprotective of our children after our training in New York City, but it sure is nice to let them play outside without having to worry all the time."

"I felt very alone in Chicago and in California. And I was always searching for the right clothes, the right house, but none of it ever felt right. I feel more a part of things in Ireland, and living here feels right."

"I don't miss freezing cold and tons of snow! People spend a lot of time talking about the weather here, and the word that pops up most of the time is 'depressing.' As far as I'm concerned, it's all in the mind. I've gotten used to the rain and the damp chill. We just don't walk around in shorts as much as we used to."

"I don't miss the difficulty of maintaining ties in the U.S., where everyone's so busy. I'd try to get a group of friends to agree to meet every Friday. They were all willing, but we could never manage to pull it off. Everyone in the States is so scheduled. Here in Ireland, the pace is more relaxed, and the pub is a wonderful source of fellowship and fun. If I want company, I just walk on over. Though I came here to focus on my painting, and I have, I wouldn't trade the time I've spent being social for anything."

Another expatriate addressed this issue a bit differently. She explained that what she missed least was a set of traits she'd left behind. "My mother noticed a major change in my personality. I was always a hyper, tense, and pressured person in America. Since moving to Ireland, I have calmed down dramatically. Last Christmas my sister wanted to get me bubble bath that was supposed to be calming. Our mother told her, "Don't bother. If your sister were any calmer these days, she'd be in a coma.""

Accept occasional pangs of longing as a natural part of the relocation process that will recede as you gain a stronger footing in your adopted community. The following are some strategies that may help to minimize homesickness:

- Bring small items of sentimental value. Displaying photos or other mementos around your living space may bring you cheer.
- Maintain family traditions, especially those that you follow during holidays. It can be fun to celebrate holidays unique to your home country. Invite your neighbors to join you.
- Sign on with an Internet service provider. E-mail is an inexpensive, convenient way to keep in touch with family and friends and also a way to form new alliances. You might even buy a scanner so that you can transfer photo files to share with those who might be missing you.
- Network with other expatriates. You may meet them casually or you may choose to actively seek them out through organizations (included in the Resource Guide) that exist to foster connections among those living far from home. There are people who believe

that having too much contact with other expatriates may delay your acculturation and make it easier to avoid taking the risk to extend yourself within your adopted community. Still, it is enjoyable to spend time with others of similar background with whom you'll often feel some sort of bond. Relaxing into the familiar rhythm of conversation and sharing impressions from relatively common ground may help to reduce a sense of isolation and ease your transition. Those who've preceded you along the transitional path may be able to share helpful pointers and general encouragement.

• Plan to visit your former home as appropriate. Spending a few weeks back where you came from can be a very effective cure for homesickness. Having returned to the place for which you long, you may be reminded as often about what you don't miss as what you do. A theme that emerges from many expatriates is how much they miss Ireland when they go away.

• Invite folks from home to visit. Hosting friends and family can sometimes put you more in touch with how you feel about a place. Playing tour guide can be as much fun for you as for your guests. Still, be careful not to become a revolving door for distant relatives or friends of friends who might like to camp out on your sofa year-round. Trying to keep up with people who are on holiday, eating as they do, and cramming your days full of activity may disrupt your efforts to create a normal life for yourself. Don't be afraid to say no, to limit visits, or to offer lodging but not necessarily your full-time services as tour guide.

One Expatriate's Experience

The following first-person account, reprinted with permission, originally appeared in the Spring 1998, twentieth-anniversary issue of *Inside Ireland*. It offers insight into some issues that expatriates confront in Ireland. The author, Anne Buell, resides with her husband, Wally, in the Connemara region in the west of Ireland in Claddaghduff, County Galway.

Life Here Is Manageable

We didn't actually set out to move to Ireland; it just happened to us. On a visit in 1985 a friend of mine revealed she had a site for sale: Two and a half acres right on the ocean. We bought and built and until 1991 spent our summers in Ireland and our winters in the Caribbean where we had retired to live on our 37-foot sailboat. However, paradise can be pretty one-dimensional and in 1991 we sold the boat and moved permanently to Ireland—or mostly permanently. We did build a little house in Vermont to use as a base when we visited our family who all live in New England.

Although we had spent almost six months a year in Ireland it wasn't until we actually were seen as spending the winters here that people took us seriously enough to include us in the community. For me, the Garden Club was the entree. It was, and still is, a wonderful group and fortunately for me they were ready for some American style enthusiasm which I learned to temper when one woman, in mock exasperation, threw up her hands and said "Oh you Americans! You think you can do anything." Lesson 1 in our different outlooks. But the gap in self-confidence is closing. The West of Ireland woman has definitely become a mover and a shaker albeit more quietly than her American sister.

Although he is not a joiner, the golf club became the focus of my husband's life; he is very content to play golf in anything under a force 8 gale,

and to read all the books in the library—so much so that the librarian advised him to discreetly initial the books he read so he wouldn't have so many repeats! He's very happy just going into the local town, having coffee in the pub and recognising and being recognised by more people than he ever knew when he was busy making a living in the States.

What keeps us here, besides the beauty of the landscape and the friendliness of the people, is the fact that life here is so manageable. In a small country like this it is possible to be in control of one's life. The pace slows down, priorities change, and there is time to wander around smelling the flowers.

If it wasn't for Value Added Tax (VAT), I wouldn't think it was expensive here but the 21% tax on clothes makes me swallow hard. As does the cost of automobiles (50% more), petrol (3 times as much as the US), and insurance. There is a $105 annual charge for a television license, though I've mellowed in recent years after getting a dose of American TV commercials on my visits there. Here we get at least 20 minutes of uninterrupted programming. What does ruffle my feathers a bit is the "wink and nod" system of government which seems to be alive and well when it comes to the rules of planning permissions for new houses and businesses, although I do think there is a tendency on the part of the public these days to demand more accountability.

On balance, for anyone moving here I would recommend letting go of the "American way of doing things." Enjoy the differences and remember why you wanted to be here in the first place. Expect to occasionally feel isolated, misunderstood, and frustrated. Resist the temptation to say "only in Ireland" when some inefficiency occurs. This makes you an observer instead of a participant. Immerse yourself in the daily life and customs of your community. You will still be an outsider, but your attending church, the local pub, relevant funerals, for example, will be noticed and appreciated.

We have lived here half time and full time for a total of twelve years now, and during that time Ireland has become at least as sophisticated as the United States. In all that time we have rarely come across anyone who didn't treat us with great courtesy and go out of their way to help us solve any problem, no matter how trivial.

We cherish the civility of this wonderful country, and so will you.

—*Reprinted with permission from* Inside Ireland: Information Service and Quarterly Review, *P.O. Box 1886, Dublin 16, Ireland. (Write for free sample copy.)*

RESOURCE GUIDE

Irish Language Terms

The following are some common Irish words or word parts. Many are found in place names.

Ard	a high place
Ath	ford
Baile, bally	settlement, town
Bawn	walled enclosure attached to a tower or castle
Ben	mountain, peak
Bia	food
Bodran	wooden-framed goatskin drum
Caher, cahir	stone fortress or castle
Cairn	heap of stones, often over a grave
Cashel	fort made of stone
Clochan	stone hut, beehive hut
Crannog	lake dwelling, artificial island
Currach	boat made of skin, grassy plain, or racecourse
Derry	oak-tree grove
Dolmen	Prehistoric megalithic structure of supporting stones and capstone
Dun	fortress
Failte	welcome
Inis, ennis	island
Kill	church
Knock	hill
Lis	area inside a fort or fence
Lough	lake, inlet
Mor	big
Ogham	early script with letters represented by lines
Rath	circular fort
Seisiun	informal music session
Slainte	cheers, to your health
Slan	goodbye
Sliabh, slieve	mountain
Strand	beach

Togher	road across a bog
Tra	strand, beach
Uilleann	bagpipes
Uisce beatha	whiskey

Slang

The following is a list of slang terms and expressions commonly encountered in Ireland and the corresponding American word or expression. Some are uniquely Irish, while others may have origins in Britain or other parts of the world.

Ages	long time
Agro	irritation, aggravation ("I don't need the agro")
Arse	backside
Aul fella	old man, father
Aul wan	old woman, mother
Babby	baby, little child
Banjaxed	broken, messed up
Bold	naughty, cheeky
Bollocks	derogatory term to indicate someone who is good for nothing
Boozer	pub
Boreen	narrow lane, country road
Bucketing	raining heavily
Chancer	one who takes risks
Chance your arm	stick your neck out
Chinwag	a chat
Chipper	fish and chips shop
Chips	French fries
Crisps	potato chips
Chiseller	child
Chuffed	pleased, satisfied
Cooker	stove
Cop on	get a clue
Craic	fun times and lively conversation
Culchie	used by city dweller to indicate a country person

Cute	sneaky, clever, scheming
Da	father
Dear	expensive
Dosser	layabout, slacker
Down to the ground	perfectly, to a tee ("That suits me down to the ground.")
Eejit	idiot
Fag	cigarette
Fair play	well done
Feck	substitute for the other "F word," a bit less offensive
Fella	guy
Flitters	tattered and torn
Fluthered	drunk
Foostering about	goofing off
Fry	breakfast of fried bacon, sausage, and eggs
Gas	funny
Giving out	scolding, chiding
Gob	mouth
Gobshite	idiot
Gobsmacked	astonished
Grand	nice
Guard	cop
Header	nut, head case
Heya	hi, hello
Holliers	holidays
Holy show	spectacle
Hot press	closet, linen cabinet with hot-water heater
Jackeen	used by a country person to indicate someone from Dublin
Jacks	toilet
Jam on your egg	wishful thinking
Jumper	sweater
Knackered	tired, beat
Lashing	raining hard
Local, the	nearest pub
Loo	bathroom, toilet

Lift, a	to be conveyed (note: to ask for a ride means to ask for sex)
Ma	mother
Manky	filthy; in bad taste, tacky
Messages	groceries, shopping
Midges	gnats, "no see-ums"
Pictures	movies
Pissed	drunk
Press	cupboard
Rashers	bacon
Ride	to have sex
Roundabout	traffic circle
Scratcher	bed
Slagging	making fun of someone
Snapper	child
Soft	misty rain, drizzle ("a soft day")
Sprogs	children
Stocious	drunk
Take-away	take-out
Thin/thick on the ground	scarce/in abundance
Wanker	jerk
Whinge/whingeing	whine
Yoke, yokey	thing, thingie
Your man/woman	this guy/woman ("So I told your man to deliver it tomorrow.")

Dialing Instructions

To dial the Republic of Ireland from the United States:
011 (international code) + 353 (country code) + city code
    (omit 0) + number
To dial Northern Ireland from the United States:
011 (international code) + 44 (country code) + city code + number

Books

Chambers, Anne. *Granuaile: The Life and Times of Grace O'Malley c. 1530–1603.* Dublin: Wolfhound Press, 1998.

Ferraro, Gary P. *The Cultural Dimension of International Business, third edition.* Englewood Cliffs, NJ: Prentice-Hall, 1998.

Fitzsimmons, Jack. *Bungalow Bliss.* Self-published, 1996.
Plans and advice on building a house. Available from Read Ireland and major bookstores.

Kinsella, Thomas (translated). *The Tain: From the Irish Epic Tain Bo Cuailnge.* Oxford: Oxford University Press, 1969.

Levy, Patricia. *Culture Shock Ireland: A Guide to Customs and Etiquette.* Portland, OR: Graphic Arts Center Publishing Co., 1996.

MacMahon, Bryan (translated). *Peig: The Autobiography of Peig Sayers of the Great Blasket Island.* Talbot Press, 1983.

McCourt, Frank. *Angela's Ashes.* New York: Scribner, 1996.

National Rehabilitation Board. *Respite Care Facilities for People with Disabilities.* Dublin: NRB Research Deparment, 1998.

O'Kane, Brian. *Starting a Business in Ireland.* Dublin: Oak Tree Press, 1998.

Phinney, Richard, and Scott Whitley. *Links of Heaven: A Complete Guide to Golf Journeys in Ireland.* Ogdensburg: Baltray Books, (year of publication unavailable).

Solnit, Rebecca. *A Book of Migrations: Some Passages in Ireland.* London: Verso, 1997.

Williams, Niall, and Christine Breen. *O Come Ye Back to Ireland: Our First Year in County Clare.* New York: Soho Press, 1987.

Williams, Niall, and Christine Breen. *When Summer's in the Meadow.* New York: Soho Press, 1989.

Automotive

Automobile Association (AA)
23 Rock Hill
Blackrock
County Dublin
Tel: 01 283 3555

AA Cork
9 Bridge Street
Cork
Tel: 021 505155

AA Galway
Headford Road
Galway
Tel: 091 64438

AA Limerick
Arthurs Quay
Limerick
Tel: 061 48241

Disabled Drivers Association
Ballindine
County Mayo
Tel: 094 64054
Fax: 094 64336
E-mail: ability@iol.ie

Driving Instructor Register
39–41 Glasnevin Hill
Glasnevin
Dublin 9
Tel: 01 836 8440
Fax: 01 857 0377
E-mail: dir@indigo.ie
Web site: http://indigo.ie/~dir

Bookstores

Cathach Books
10 Duke Street
Dublin 2
Tel: 01 671 8676
Fax: 01 671 5120
E-mail: cathach@rarebooks.ie
Web site: http://indigo.ie/;cathach

Fred Hannah's
27–29 Nassau Street
Dublin 2
Tel: 01 667 1255
Fax: 01 671 4330
E-mail: fred@hannas.ie
Web site: www.hannas.ie

Hodges Figgis
56–58 Dawson Street
Dublin 2
Tel: 01 677 4754
Fax: 01 679 3402
E-mail: books@hodgesfiggis.ie
Web site: www.hodgesfiggis.com

Kennys Bookshops & Art
Galleries
High Street
Galway
Tel: 091 562739
Fax: 091 568544
E-mail: kennys@iol.ie
Web site: www.kennys.ie

Read Ireland Bookstore
342 North Circular Road
Phibsboro, Dublin 7
Tel/Fax: 01 830 2997
E-mail: info@readireland.ie
Web site: www.readireland.ie

Business

Chambers of Commerce of
 Ireland
7 Clare Street
Dublin 2
Tel: 01 661 2888

Dublin Chamber of Commerce
7 Clare Street
Dublin 2
Tel: 01 661 4111
Fax: 01 676 6043
E-mail: info@dubchamber.ie
Web site: www.dubchamber.ie

Enterprise Ireland
Glasnevin
Dublin 9
Tel: 01 808 2295
Fax: 01 808 2040
E-mail: client.service@irish-trade.ie
Web site: www.irish-trade.ie

IDA Ireland
Wilton Park House
Dublin 2
Tel: 01 603 4000
E-mail: idaireland@ida.ie
Web site: www.idaireland.com

IDA Ireland (U.S.)
345 Park Avenue, 17th Floor
New York, NY 10154
Tel: (212) 750–4300

Ireland Chamber of Commerce
 in the United States
65 Broadway
New York, NY 10006
Tel: (212) 248–0008

Northern Ireland Chamber of
 Commerce and Industry
Chamber of Commerce House
Great Victoria Street
Belfast
County Antrim
Tel: 01232 244113

Shannon Development
Shannon County Clare
Tel: 061 361555
Fax: 061 361903
Web site: www.commerce.
ie/shannon-dev

Shannon Development (U.S.)
Ireland House
345 Park Avenue, 17th Floor
New York, NY 10154
Tel: (212) 371–5550
Fax: (212) 308–1485

Small Firms Association
84–86 Lower Baggot Street
Dublin 2
Tel: 01 660 1011
Fax: 01 661 2861
E-mail: sfa@iol.ie
Web site: http://ireland.iol.ie/sfa

Udaras na Gaeltachta
Na Forbacha
Galway
Tel: 091 592011
Fax: 091 592037
Web site: www.udaras.ie

U.S. Chamber of Commerce in
  Ireland
20 College Green
Dublin 2
Tel: 01 679 3733
Fax: 01 679 3402

Clubs, Associations, & Organizations

Alone (advocacy group for the
  elderly)
1 Willie Bermingham Place
Kilmainham Lane
Dublin 8
Tel: 01 679 1032

American Citizens Abroad
1051 N. George Mason Drive
Arlington, VA 22205
Fax: (703) 527–3260
E-mail: acage@aca.ch

American Women's Club of Dublin
P.O. Box 2545
Ballsbridge
Dublin 4
E-mail: webwoman@netlink.co.uk

Alcoholics Anonymous
109 S. Circular Road
Leonard's Corner
Dublin 8
Tel: 01 453 8998

Consumers' Association of Ireland
45 Upper Mount Street
Dublin 2
Tel: 01 661 2466

Environmental Info Service
  (ENFO)
17 St. Andrew Street
Dublin 2
Tel: 01 679 3144
Fax: 01 679 5204

Irish Energy Center
Glasnevin
Dublin 9
Tel: 01 836 9080
Fax: 01 837 2848

Rape Crisis Center
70 Lower Leeson Street
Dublin 2
Tel: 01 661 4911
Fax: 01 661 0873
E-mail: rcc@indigo.iol.ie

The Royal Institute of the
  Architects of Ireland
8 Merrion Square
Dublin 2
Tel: 01 676 1703
Fax: 01 661 0948
E-mail: info@riai.ie
Web site: www.riai.ie

Samaritans
112 Marlborough Street
Dublin 1
Tel: 01 872 7700

The Society of Chartered
Surveyors
5 Wilton Place
Dublin 2
Tel: 01 676 5500
Fax: 01 676 1412

Vegetarian Society of Ireland
P. O. Box 3010
Dublin 4
Tel: 01 872 1191

Education & Training

FAS—The Irish Training and
Employment Authority
27–33 Upper Baggot Street
Dublin 4
Tel: 01 607 0500
Fax: 01 607 0600
Web site: www.fas.ie

Colleges/Universities

Dublin City University
Dublin 9
Tel: 01 704 5566
Fax: 01 704 5504
E-mail: registrars.office@dcu.ie
Web site: www.dcu.ie

National College of Art & Design
100 Thomas Street
Dublin 8
Tel: 01 636 4200
Web site: www.ncad.ie

National University of Ireland,
Cork
Cork
Tel: 021 276871
E-mail: registrar@ucc.ie
Web site: www.ucc.ie

National University of Ireland,
Dublin
Dublin 4
Tel: 01 706 7777
E-mail: info@ucd.ie
Web site: www.ucd.ie

National University of Ireland,
Galway
University Road
Galway
Tel: 091 524411
Fax: 091 525700
E-mail: admissions@mis.
nuigalway.ie
Web site: www.ucg.ie

National University of Ireland,
Maynooth
County Kildare
Tel: 01 708 3822
Fax: 01 708 3935
E-mail: admissions@may.ie
Web site: www.may.ie

The Queen's University of Belfast
Belfast BT7 1NN
Northern Ireland
Tel: 01232 245133
Web site: www.qub.ac.uk

Royal College of Surgeons in
  Ireland
123 St. Stephen's Green
Dublin 2
Tel: 01 402 2100
E-mail: info@rcsi.ie
Web site: www.rcsi.ie

Trinity College
Dublin 2
Tel: 01 677 2941
E-mail: admissns@tcd.ie
Web site: www.tcd.ie

University of Limerick
Plassey, Limerick
Tel: 061 333644
Fax: 061 330316
E-mail: postmaster@ul.ie
Web site: www.ul.ie

University of Ulster at Belfast
York Street
Belfast
BT15 1ED
Tel: 01232 328515
Web site: www.ulst.ac.uk

Embassies

Embassy of Canada
Canada House
65 St. Stephen's Green
Dublin 2
Tel: 01 478 1988
Fax: 01 478 1285

Embassy of Ireland
130 Albert Street
Ottawa K1P 5G4

Ontario
Tel: (613) 233–6281
Fax: (613) 233–5835
Email: emb.ireland@sympatico.ca

Embassy of Ireland
2234 Massachusetts Avenue NW
Washington, DC 20008
Tel: (202) 462–3939
Fax: (202) 232–5993
E-mail: embirlus@aol.com

Irish Consular Offices

535 Boylston Street
Boston, MA 02116
Tel: (617) 267–9330

400 N. Michigan Avenue
Chicago, IL 60622
Tel: (312) 337–1868

345 Park Avenue, 17th Floor
New York, NY 10154
Tel: (212) 319–2555
Fax: (212) 980–9475

44 Montgomery Street, Suite 3830
San Francisco, CA 94104
Tel: (415) 392–4214
Fax: (415) 392–0885

United States Embassy
42 Elgin Road
Ballsbridge
Dublin 4
Tel: 01 668 7122
Fax: 01 668 9946
E-mail: aedublin@indigo.ie
Web site: www.indigo.
ie/usembassy-usis

Estate Agents (Realtors)

Hamilton Osborne King
32 Molesworth Street
Dublin 2
Tel: 01 676 0285
Fax: 01 676 7066
E-mail: info@hok.ie
Web site: www.hok.ie

Heaslip Auctioneers
27 Woodquay
Galway
Tel: 091 565261
Fax: 091 565863
E-mail: info@heaslip.com
Web site: www.heaslip.com

Institute of Professional
    Auctioneers and Valuers
39 Upper Fitzwilliam Street
Dublin 2
Tel: 01 678 5685
Fax: 01 676 2890
E-mail: lodonnell@ipav.ie
Web site: www.ipav.ie

Lisney
24 St. Stephens Green
Dublin 2
Tel: 01 668 2111
Fax: 01 676 6540
Web site: www.lisney.com

Philip Johnston and Company
350 Upper Newtownards Road
Belfast BT4 3EX
Tel: 01232 650146
Fax: 01232 471320
E-mail: enquiries@philipjohn-
ston.co.uk
Web site: www.philipjohnston.
co.uk

Sherry Fitzgerald
13 Hume Street
Dublin 2
Tel: 01 639 9300
Fax: 01 639 9399
E-mail: pwaller@dtz.ie
Web site: www.dtz.se/ireland

Festivals

For information about dates and locations, contact Bord Failte, the Irish Tourist Board.

Arts Festivals

Festivals highlighting traditional and other kinds of music, theater, and art are held throughout most of the year in numerous Irish towns and cities.

Visual arts are the main focus of the annual Eigse Festival in County Carlow, but there are concerts and music sessions, too. The popular Galway Arts Festival features music, theater, and a lively, colorful parade. The Boyle Gala Festival in County Roscommon entertains with classical music, visual arts, film, and dance. The annual Belfast Festival in Belfast City hosts a variety of theatrical, literary, film, comedy, jazz, and folk music events.

St. Patrick's Day Festival

Although it is primarily a religious holiday, St. Patrick's Day (March 17) celebrations take place in Dublin and throughout the country, and most cities will hold parades. In Dublin, a five-day festival of music, street theater, pageants, sports, and dance pays tribute to St. Patrick.

Fleadh Nua

Held annually in May in Ennis, County Clare, this is a jubilant festival of traditional music, song, and dance that features stage shows, competitions, and a parade.

Ballybunion Bachelor Festival

This summer County Kerry festival selects the Ballybunion Bachelor of the Year and features music, sporting events, and other competitions.

Cork International Choral Festival

Indoor and outdoor performances in Cork City feature choral groups from around the world at this annual spring event.

Comedy Festival, Kilkenny

This end of May Bank Holiday weekend festival features comedians from Ireland and elsewhere in the medieval city of Kilkenny.

Bloomsday

To commemorate the June 16 setting of James Joyce's masterwork, *Ulysses*, Dublin events include readings, performances, lectures, and street theater performed in period costume. The Joyce Tower in Sandycove, County Dublin, holds special performances and readings. Galway honors Bloomsday by opening the Nora Barnacle House in Bowling Green, the family home of Joyce's wife.

AIB Music Festival in Great Irish Houses

AIB Bank hosts musical performances in June in fabulous settings around the country, such as Irish heritage houses, the National Gallery, various castles, and exclusive private residences.

Wexford Strawberry Fair

The summer Strawberry Festival is a colorful, lively celebration in Enniscorthy, County Wexford, with free outdoor entertainment, exhibitions, music, and strawberries and cream.

Puck Fair

Dating from ancient times, this annual August bash in Killorglin, County Kerry, features horse and cattle sales, fireworks, music, storytelling, and the traditional crowning of the puck goat, who presides over the fair.

Rose of Tralee

Highlighted by the Rose Competition, a televised beauty and character pageant, this international festival entertains with parades, brass bands, and other forms of music each August in Tralee, County Kerry.

Lisdoonvarna Matchmaking Festival

This festival runs for an entire month each September in the County Clare town of Lisdoonvarna, once known for the health tonic of its spa waters. It tends to draw an over-forties crowd, mostly from Ireland, who enjoy music, parades, and an opportunity to engage a genuine matchmaker.

Galway International Oyster Festival

Galway City's annual homage to the oyster in September includes an oyster-opening competition with competitors from around the world, music and sing-alongs, and a gala banquet.

Blessing of the Boats

This September festival begins with a parade through Dingle's winding streets, ending at the small town harbor on County Kerry's Dingle Peninsula. All who attend are invited to climb aboard one of the many fishing boats that go out into Dingle Bay for the blessing of the fleet. The bay's resident dolphin, Fungi, usually adds to the festivities with a display of his leaping abilities.

Kinsale International Gourmet Festival

Early in October, the picturesque seaside town of Kinsale hosts this festival of cooking demonstrations, wine fair, cocktail parties and cabarets, and, of course, gourmet food.

Waterford International Festival of Light Opera

Waterford hosts this annual competition of amateur musical societies from around the world each May.

Franchising

International Franchise Association
1350 New York Avenue NW
Suite 900
Washington, DC 20005
Tel: (202) 628–8000
Fax: (202) 628–0812

McGarry Consulting/Irish Franchise Association
102 Pembroke Road
Ballsbridge
Dublin 4
Tel: 01 668 5444
Fax: 01 668 5541
E-mail: mcgarry@iol.ie
Web site: www.franchisedirect.com

Golf Courses

Dublin and the East Coast

St. Margaret's Golf & Country Club (parkland)

St. Margaret's, County Dublin
Tel: 01 864 0400
Fax: 01 864 0289
E-mail: stmarggc@indigo.ie
18 holes, par 73, 6,325 meters (6,917 yards)
$53 weekdays/$60 weekends
Close to Dublin City and the airport, this luxury golf development provides a challenging course, known for its American-style water hazards and contoured fairways. The three-story clubhouse is reminiscent of a nineteenth-century manor. The pro shop is well stocked with posh goods. other amenities include a bar, snack bar, and full-service restaurant, two practice greens, caddy hire, and clubs and caddy-car rentals. Visitors are welcome year-round. Club membership requires a stiff initiation fee of approximately $7,500. Note: Cell phones are not permitted on the course!

Deer Park Hotel & Golf Course (parkland)

Howth, County Dublin
Tel: 01 832 2624
Fax: 01 839 2405
E-mail: sales@deerpark.iol.ie
18 holes, par 72, 6,106 meters (6,678 yards)
$12 weekdays/$18 weekends
Ireland's largest golf complex covers 400 acres on the grounds of Howth Castle, about 12 kilometers (7 miles) north of Dublin City. There are five courses to choose from, ranging from one nine-hole and two challenging eighteen-hole courses to a twelve-hole short course and an eighteen-hole pitch and putt. The course and adjacent hotel share lovely views of Dublin Bay. Amenities include a restaurant and grill, lounge bar, indoor pool, sauna, and steam room. Greens fees are quite reasonable.

Hollystown Golf Club (parkland)
Hollystown, County Dublin
Tel: 01 820 7444
Fax: 01 820 7447
18 holes, par 72, 5,890 meters (6,441 yards)
$19 weekdays/$25 weekends
Twenty minutes from Dublin, the Hollystown course features mature trees and bubbling streams. A challenging course, with a tricky trio of par five's and a trying combination of par fours, makes the par seventy-two an elusive mark. Caddy cars are available for hire. Though amenities may be limited, the fees at this public club are most reasonable.

Luttrellstown Castle Golf & Country Club (parkland)
Clonsilla, County Dublin
Tel: 01 820 8210
Fax: 01 820 5218
18 holes, par 72, 6,447 meters (7,051 yards)
$52.50 weekdays/$60.00 weekends
Location of the 1997 Women's Irish Open, the castle grounds just outside Dublin City provide a peaceful setting on 560 acres of mature, rolling landscape. The Dublin Mountains provide a splendid background, and two lakes flow around holes nine through twelve. The third hole features a difficult water hazard. The Country Club has two restaurants and bars and a large practice ground and practice green. Clubs, caddy cars, and caddies are available for hire.

Southeast

Mount Juliet Golf Course (parkland)
Thomastown, County Kilkenny
Tel: 056 73000
Fax: 056 73019
E-mail: kmaccann@mountjuliet.ie
18 holes, par 72, 6,531 meters (7,142 yards)
$97.50 weekdays/$105 weekends
This Jack Nicklaus signature golf course is set on 1,500 walled acres of mature landscape and natural beauty of the former Mount Juliet estate. An extensive irrigation and drainage system provides year-round play on this championship course. Water comes into play on six holes,

and there are eight bunkers strategically placed throughout the course. Home of many International Opens, Mount Juliet challenges the professional and high-handicap golfer alike. Group and individual golf schools are regularly offered. The course features an extensive driving range, three-hole academy, and chipping greens. There are four bars and two restaurants, a pro shop, and clubs, caddy cars, and caddies available for hire. Metal spikes are prohibited.

West Waterford Golf Club (parkland)
Dungarvan, County Waterford
Tel: 058 43216
Fax: 058 44343
18 holes, par 72, 5,662 meters (6,192 yards)
$26 weekdays/$33 weekends
One hundred and fifty acres of rolling parkland along the banks of the Brickey River are the setting for this championship course. With a panoramic view of several mountain ranges, the first nine holes are laid out on a large plateau with a stream that comes into play at the third and fourth holes. The Brickey River crosses the southern boundary of the course, intensifying the challenge of the second, twelfth, fourteenth, fifteenth, and sixteenth holes. Catering, hire service, and a pro shop are available.

St. Helen's Bay Golf & Country Club (combination)
St. Helen's
Kilrane, County Wexford
Tel: 053 33234
Fax: 053 33803
18 holes, par 72, 5,570 meters (6,091 yards)
$27 weekdays/$30 weekends
Just about 1.5 kilometers (1 miles) from Rosslare Harbor, St. Helen's is considered to be Ireland's sunniest golf course. An unusual mixture of parkland and links course, early holes play uphill and provide panoramic views of the Wexford coast and countryside. These are restored famine walls at the first, ninth, and tenth, with water hazards on the eleventh and twelfth holes. The sea and beach flank the seventeenth and eighteenth holes to the end of the green. Full catering and pro shop on site, with clubs, caddy cars, and caddies available.

Midlands

Esker Hills Golf & Country Club (parkland)
Ballykilmurry
Tullamore, County Offaly
Tel: 0506 55999
Fax: 0506 55989
18 holes, par 71, 6,046 meters (6,612 yards)
$23 weekdays/$27 weekends
Set on 150 lush acres, this championship course was designed around the existing terrain of valleys, elevated plains, natural lakes, and woodlands. Panoramic views with the Slieve Bloom Mountains in the background create an ideal golfing landscape. Caddy carts, coffee shop, and pro shop available.

Glasson Golf & Country Club (parkland)
Glasson
Athlone, County Westmeath
Tel: 0902 85120
Fax: 0902 85444
E-mail: glasgolf@iol.ie
18 holes, par 72, 6,511 meters (7,120 yards)
$36 weekdays/$40 weekends
The beautiful Lough Ree on the River Shannon borders this championship course on three sides. The third hole takes concentration and an accurate drive. It's over 180 meters (200 yards) and has a very narrow green surrounded by four bunkers. The seventh has two lakes between the tee and the landing. Atop, a severe loop awaits a two-level green. The most famous hole is the par-three fifteenth, which is minus a fairway, as the entire hole is played over water, with the tee and green on different islands. Glasson offers three additional academy holes, practice ground and practice bunker, pitching greens, and putting greens. A full-service bar, restaurant, and pro shop are found at the clubhouse. Clubs, caddy cars, and caddies available with advance bookings.

Knockanally Golf & Country Club (parkland)
Donadea, County Kildare
Tel/Fax: 045 869322
18 holes, par 72, 6,414 meters (7,025 yards)
$27 weekdays/$33 weekends
Noted for panoramic views as well as a punishing opening hole, this championship course with large, mature trees gently meanders downhill to a stream. A pond fed by the stream swallows many a ball on the approach to the tenth, eleventh, and thirteenth greens. A full-service bar, restaurant, and pro shop are among the amenities offered at the clubhouse.

Southwest

Bantry Bay Golf Club (parkland)
Bantry, County Cork
Tel/Fax: 027 50579
E-mail: bpgcl@iol.ie
18 holes, par 71, 5,944 meters (6,500 yards)
$27 weekdays/$30 weekends
Designed jointly by Eddie Hackett and Christy O'Connor, Jr., this championship course is set on a sloping hillside and clifftop. With greens built to U.S. Golf Association (USGA) standards, the course also sports several daunting water hazards. The elegant clubhouse offers a full-service restaurant from mid-March to the end of October. Full bar facilities operate year-round. Clubs, caddies, and caddy cars available for hire.

Ballybunion Golf Course (links)
Ballybunion, County Kerry
Tel: 068 27146
Fax: 068 27387
old course: 18 holes, par 72, 5,982 meters (6,542 yards)
new course: 18 holes, par 70, 5,895 meters (6,447 yards)
$30 daily (one round)/$65 both courses (same day)
Ballybunion's championship courses are highly praised for their excellent condition and ability to challenge. The picturesque old course has winding fairways though enormous dunes, while the new course offers a succession of formidable par five's, large dunes, narrow

fairways, and small greens. The old links offers the ultimate challenge with an intricate sixth hole, a devilish eighth, and a very long fifteenth. This scenic area flanks the spectacular North Kerry coast. Practice bunkers, putting green, full-service clubhouse, club, and caddy hire available.

West

Ballina Golf Club (parkland)
Ballina, County Mayo
Tel: 096 21050
Fax: 096 21050
18 holes, par 71, 5,581 meters (6,103 yards)
$18 weekdays/$24 weekends

The course, part of a former estate and laid out in 1924, has retained an old stonework border and gateway. Designed by Eddie Hackett against a scenic backdrop of the Ox Mountains, this rolling course provides challenging play and panoramic views of gorse-covered hills.

Connemara Golf Club (links)
Ballyconneely
Clifden, County Galway
Tel: 095 23502
Fax: 095 23662
E-mail: links@iol.ie
18 holes, par 72, 6,610 meters (7,229 yards)
$37.50 daily/$24 off season

On the edge of the Atlantic Ocean, this championship golf links is uncommonly beautiful. Designed by Eddie Hackett and built by the local community, it is a magnificent example of a course dictated by nature. A most challenging course where par is rarely achieved, it twists and turns around great slabs of rock. The fourteenth and fifteenth greens are set high on the hillside with views of Ballyconneely Bay. The club offers full restaurant and bar facilities, a fully stocked pro shop, caddy cars, caddies, practice fairway, chipping and putting greens, and a driving net.

Lahinch Golf Club (links)
Lahinch, County Clare
Tel: 065 81003
Fax: 065 81592
18 holes, par 72, 5,599 meters (6,123 yards)
$60 daily
Considered the St. Andrew's of Ireland, this championship course
hosts the annual South of Ireland Amateur Open Championship.
Flanked by the seaside village of Lahinch, the course sports numerous
sand dunes. The blind shot of the sixth green, bordered by high dunes
on all sides, provides the ultimate challenge.

Enniscrone Golf Club (links)
Enniscrone, County Sligo
Tel: 096 36297
Fax: 096 36657
E-mail: enniscronegolf@tinet.ie
18 holes, par 72, 6,145 meters (6,720 yards)
$27 weekdays/$33 weekends
The sounds of the surf accompany your game on this course designed
by Eddie Hackett, playable year-round thanks to the fast-draining terrain
The tenth hole is a favorite. With a true hit from the elevated tee, you may
have a chance at a birdie. A family seaside resort since 1918, Enniscrone
opened the championship links in 1974. A deluxe clubhouse provides
full bar and catering facilities. The club shop will arrange caddy-car
rental. Caddies are available on weekends and school holidays.

Galway Bay Golf and Country Club (parkland)
Renville
Oranmore, County Galway
Tel: 091 790500
Fax: 091 790510
E-mail: gbaygolf@iol.ie
18 holes, par 72, 6,533 meters (7,144 yards)
$45 weekdays/$53 weekends
An outstanding championship course using the natural boundary of
the Galway coast, designed by Ryder Cup champion and World Cup
player Christy O'Connor, Jr., this parkland course incorporates many

water hazards. This is a full-service resort with hotel and conference facilities. There is a gourmet restaurant and grill bar. The pro shop is well stocked, and the club offers a putting green, chipping green, target practice area, and indoor practice facilities. Also available for hire, caddy car, clubs, caddy master, caddies, and bag carriers.

West

Westport Golf Club (parkland)
Corowholly
Westport, County Mayo
Tel: 098 28262
Fax: 098 27217
18 holes, par 73, 6,412 meters (7,012 yards)
$27 weekdays/$34 weekends

Situated on the outskirts of Westport and set on 260 acres of rolling parkland, this spectacular championship course offers breathtaking scenery and significant challenge. Before playing this course you might benefit from a lesson from the resident pro. The fifteenth hole features a drive over a sliver of Clew Bay. The hole can be gusty, requiring careful adjustment of clubs and attention to wind changes. The club has full-service catering with a bar, restaurant, and a pro shop. Practice and putting area available as well as caddy and caddy care hire.

Northwest

Ballyliffin Golf Course (links)
Clonmany, County Donegal
Tel: 077 76199
Fax: 077 76672
E-mail: ballyliffingolfclub@tinet.ie
old links: 18 holes, par 71, 6,046 meters (6,612 yards)
Glashedy links: 18 holes, par 72, 6,494 meters (7,102 yards)
$30 weekdays/$37.50 weekends

Ireland's most northerly links provides two contrasting courses: the old links, with traditional rolling fairways and natural terrain, and the new Glashedy links, set among dunes with notorious bunkers. The first three par fours are considered to be formidable. Ballyliffen offers panoramic view of surrounding countryside and coastline, bar and caddy service, pro shop, and a practice area.

Rosapenna Golf Club (links)
Downings, County Donegal
Tel: 074 55301
Fax: 074 55128
18 holes, par 70, 5,707 meters (6,241 yards)
$27 weekdays/$30 weekends
Secluded on beautiful Sheephaven Bay, Rosapenna is one of Ireland's greatest natural golf links. Designed in 1891 by Tom Morris of St. Andrew's, the first ten holes of this championship links follow the bay between the beach and a range of tall sand dunes. The last eight holes play inland and uphill in scenic meadows. Hotel bar and restaurant on site, pro shop, caddy cars and caddies available.

County Sligo Golf Course (links)
Rosses Point, County Sligo
Tel: 071 77134
Fax: 071 77460
E-mail: cosligo@iol.ie
18 holes, par 71, 6,043 meters (6,609 yards)
$33 weekdays/$45 weekends
Host of many of Ireland's major championships, this links course offers challenge and enjoyment to both expert and novice competitors. The wind from the sea is constant, but the views are splendid throughout. The third, fifth, tenth, and fourteenth holes are gratifying downhill drives. The clubhouse provides a bar, restaurant, and small pro shop. Caddy car and caddies (summer months) available for hire.

Northern Ireland

Ardglass Golf Course (links)
Ardglass, County Down
Tel: 01396 841219
Fax: 01396 841841
18 holes, par 70, 5,286 meters (5,781 yards)
$21 weekdays/$30 weekends
This seaside clifftop course provides breathtaking scenery and, on a clear day, a view of the Isle of Man. The course starts with exceptional opening holes on the edge of a cliff. Many humps, hollows, and deep bunkers on this links course challenge all skill levels. A charming clubhouse offers a bar, snack bar, and equipment rental.

Portstewart Golf Course (links)
117 Strand Road
Portstewart, County Londonderry
Tel: 01265 832015
Fax: 01265 834097
18 holes, par 73, 6,199 meters (6,784 yards)
$53 weekdays/$68 weekends
A natural seaside links built among the sand dunes and situated between a beautiful stretch of the Atlantic beach and the River Ban, the first hole ranks as among the best in the world. The sixth hole is particularly short, but good, with a tiny green surrounded by steep slopes. The seventh is a clever par-five hole that climbs to the green with a hill on the left and a drop-off on the right. Skilled players will enjoy the challenge. A recent addition of seven new holes has made this a truly first-class champion links. Compared to the greens fees at nearby Royal Portrush, Portstewart may be the best golf value in Northern Ireland. Prior booking is essential. Eating facilities available.

Spa Golf Course (parkland)
20 Grove Road
Ballynahinch, County Down
Tel: 01238 562365
Fax: 01238 564158
18 holes, par 7, 6,003 meters (6,565 yards)
$21 weekdays/$30 Sunday
A beautiful, wooded course with sensational views, the par-three fourth hole will demand a solid three-wood drive when the wind whips from the west. The par-three eighth hole is a skill tester, while the seventeenth tee has a brilliant panoramic view. The course is abundant with resident wildlife. The clubhouse offers a range of bar food and snacks, and a restaurant serves lunch and dinner meals. The course is closed to visitors on Saturday.

Health

Alzheimer Society of Ireland
Alzheimer House
40 Northumberland Avenue
Dun Laoghaire
County Dublin
Tel: 01 284 6616
E-mail: alzheim@iol.ie

Arthritis Foundation of Ireland
1 Clanwilliam Square
Grand Canal Quay
Dublin 2
Tel: 01 661 8188
Fax: 01 661 8261

Disability Federation of Ireland
2 Sandyford Office Park
Dublin 18
Tel: 01 295 9344
Fax: 01 295 9346
E-mail: dfi@iol.ie
Web site: http://ireland.iol.ie/~dfi/

Irish Cancer Society
5 Northumberland Road
Dublin 4
Tel: 01 668 1855
Tel: 800 200700 (toll free)

Irish Council of People with
    Disabilities
Con Colbert House
Inchicore Road
Dublin 8
Tel: 01 473 2554
Fax: 01 473 2262
E-mail: estgroup@iol.ie

Irish Deaf Society
30 Blessington Street
Dublin 7
Tel: 01 860 1878
Fax: 01 860 1960

Irish Guide Dogs Association
    Training Centre
Model Farm Road
Cork
Tel: 021 870929
Fax: 021 874152
E-mail: igda@iol.ie

Irish Wheelchair Association
Blackheath Drive
Clontarf
Dublin 3
Tel: 01 833 8241
Fax: 01 833 3873
E-mail: iwa@iol.ie
Web site: www.iol.ie/;iwa

National Association for the Deaf
35 North Frederick Street
Dublin 1
Tel: 01 872 3800
Fax: 01 872 3816
E-mail: nad@iol.ie

National Council for the Blind of
    Ireland
45 Whitworth Road
Drumcondra
Dublin 9
Tel: 01 830 7033
Fax: 01 830 7787
E-mail: ncbi@iol.ie

National Rehabilitation Board
(NRB)
24/25 Clyde Road
Dublin 4
Tel: 01 608 0400
Fax: 01 660 9935
E-mail: nrb@iol.ie
Web site: http://ireland.iol.ie/~nrb

RehabCare
Roslyn Park
Sandymount
Dublin 4
Tel: 01 205 7200
Fax: 01 205 7211
Web site: www.rehab.ie

Health Boards

Department of Health
Custom House
Dublin 2
Tel: 01 673 5777
Web site: www.doh.ie

Eastern Health Board
(Dublin city and county, Counties
Kildare and Wicklow)

Dr. Stevens Hospital
John's Road
Dublin 8
Tel: 01 679 0700
Tel: 800 520520 (toll free)

Midland Health Board
(Counties Laois, Longford,
Offaly, and Westmeath)
Arden Road

Tullamore
County Offaly
Tel: 050 621868

Mid-Western Health Board
(County Clare; Limerick city and
county; County Tipperary north)
31–33 Catherine Street
Limerick
Tel: 061 316655

North-Eastern Health Board
(Counties Cavan, Louth, Meath,
and Monaghan)
Navan Road
Kells
County Meath
Tel: 046 40341

North-Western Health Board
(Counties Donegal, Leitrim,
and Sligo)
Manorhamilton
County Leitrim
Tel: 072 55123

South-Eastern Health Board
(Counties Carlow, Kilkenny,
Tipperary south, Waterford, and
Wexford)
Lacken
Dublin Road
Kilkenny
Tel: 056 51702

Southern Health Board
(Cork city and county,
County Kerry)

Cork Farm Centre
Dennehy's Cross
Wilton Road
Cork
Tel: 021 545011

Western Health Board
(County Galway, County Mayo,
County Roscommon)
Merlin Park Regional Hospital
Galway
Tel: 091 751131

Health Insurance

BUPA
12 Fitzwilliam Square
Dublin
Tel: LoCall 1890 700 890
Web site: www.bupa.ie

The Voluntary Health Insurance
   Board
VHI House
20 Lr. Abbey Street
Dublin 1
Tel: 01 872 4499
Fax: 01 799 4091
E-mail: info@vhi.ie
Web site: www.vhi.ie

Housing
Rental Locators

Cork
Apartmentfinders:
Tel: 021 277718

Choices MIPAV
Tel: 021 272727
Fax: 021 272700

Dublin
Dublin Accommodation Finder
E-mail: briann@indigo.ie
Web site: www.daft.ie/ie4.html

Galway
Celtic Accommodation
Tel: 091 752 949
Home Locators
Tel: 091 679 5233

Sligo
Sligo Accommodation Agency
Tel: 071 68560

Insurance

American International
   Underwriters
505 Carr Road R23-7A
Wilmington, DE 19809
Toll Free: (800) 343–5761
Tel. (302) 761–3107
Fax: (302) 761–3302
E-mail: aiuna@ix.netcom.com
ASA, Inc.

International Insurance
  Consultants
P. O. Box 50659
Phoenix, AZ 85076-0659
Tel: (888) ASA–8288
Fax: (602) 753–1330
E-mail: asaincor@aol.com
Web site: www.asaincor.com

Other Government Agencies

Ireland

An Post
General Post Office
Dublin 1
Tel: 01 850 575859
Web site: www.anpost.ie

Central Statistics Office
St. Stephen's Green House
Earlsford Terrace
Dublin 2
Tel: 01 676 7531
Fax: 01 668 2221
E-mail: information@cso.ie
Web site: www.cso.ie

Department of Education
Marlborough Street
Dublin 1
Tel: 01 673 4700

Department of Justice
  Immigration and
  Citizenship Office
72–76 St. Stephen's Green
Dublin 2

Tel: 01 602 8202
Fax: 01 661 5461
E-mail:
immigrationinfo@justice.irlgov.ie
Web site: www.irlgov.ie

Department of Social,
  Community and Family Affairs
Store Street
Dublin 1
Tel.: 01 874 8444
Web site: www.irlgov.ie

Pension Services Office
College Road
Sligo
Tel: Sligo 071 69800
Tel: Dublin 01 704 3371

Canada

Citizenship and Immigration
  Call Centre
Montreal: (514) 496–1010
Toronto: (416) 973–4444
Vancouver: (604) 666–2171
Elsewhere in Canada: (888)
242–2100

Department of Foreign Affairs and
  International Trade
125 Sussex Drive
Ottawa, Ontario
K1A 0G2
Fax: (613) 996–9709
E-mail:
sxci.enqserv@extott09.x400.gc.ca

United States

U.S. Small Business Association
Office of International Trade
1441 L Street NW
Room 501-A
Washington, DC 20416
Tel: (202) 653–7794

U.S. Department of State
Ireland Desk Officer
Northern European Division
Washington, DC 20232
Tel: (202) 647–6071

Pets

Department of Agriculture and
Food (DAF)
Information Division
Agriculture House
Kildare Street
Dublin 2
E-mail: information@daff.irlgov.ie
Web site: www.irlgov.
ie/daff/import.htm

Greyhound Sanctuary
Woodford
Portumna
County Galway
Mount Shannon
County Clark

Irish Society for the Prevention
of Cruelty to Animals
300 Lower Rathmines Road
Dublin 6
Tel: 01 497 7874
Web site: www.ispca.ie

Lissenhall Quarantine Kennels
and Catteries
Lissenhall
Swords
County Dublin
Tel: 01 840 1776
Fax: 01 840 9338

Ministry of Agriculture, Fisheries,
and Food
Animal Health Division
Hook Rise South
Tolworth
Surbiton
Surrey KT6 7NF
United Kingdom
Tel: 0645 335577
E-mail: helpline@inf.maff.gov.uk
Web site: www.maff.gov.uk

Passports for Pets
20 Seymour Road
London SW18 5JA
Tel: 0181 870 5960
Fax: 0181 870 9223
E-mail: passports.
forpets@virgin.net
Web site: www.freespace.
virgin.net/passports.forpets

Quarantine Abolition Fighting
Fund (QUAFF)
P. O. Box 151 Chichester
West Sussex PO20 6LN
UK
Tel: 01243 264173
Fax: 01243 267599
E-mail: quaff@lagness.
prestel.co.uk
Web site: www.freespace.
virgin.net/simon.green/

Publications

InnSights (for owners of B&Bs
and small inns)
Virgo Publishing, Inc.
Box 40079
Phoenix, AZ 85067-0079
Tel: (602) 990-1101
Fax: (602) 990-0819
E-mail: karenh@vpiCountycom
Web site: www.innsights.com

Inside Ireland
Quarterly, $40 per year
Editor and Founder Brenda Weir
will send sample issue free upon
request made directly to her or
Inside Ireland's U.S. agent. (Please
mention *Choose Ireland*.)
P.O. Box 1886
Dublin 16, Ireland
Tel: 01 493 1906
Fax: 01 493 4538

U.S. Agent:
Inside Ireland
Publishers Mini Systems
1327 Alita Lane
Escondido, CA 92027
Fax: (760) 432-6560

Ireland of the Welcomes
Bimonthly, $21 per year
P.O. Box 54161
Boulder, CO 80328-4161
Tel: (800) 876-6336, (303)
678-0354
E-mail: iow@irishtouristboard.ie

Public Transportation

Bus

Bus Atha Cliath (Dublin Bus)
Main Office
59 Upper O'Connell Street
Dublin 1
Tel: 01 873 4222
Web site: www.bustravel.net/
ireland

Bus Eireann
Busaras Central Bus Station
Store Street
Dublin 1
Tel: 01 836 6111
E-mail: buse@cie.iol.ie
Web site: www.infopoint.ie/buse

Tralee Bus Office: 066 23566
Killarney Bus Office: 064 34777
Cork Bus Office: 021 506066
Galway Bus Office: 091 563555
Limerick Bus Office: 061 418855

Light Rail/Rail

Dublin Area Rapid Transport
(DART)
Tel: 01 836 3333

Iarnrod Eireann (Irish Rail)
Connolly Station
Dublin 1
Tel: 01 836 3333
Heuston Station
Dublin 8
Tel: 01 836 3333

Air

Aer Lingus
Dublin Airport
Tel: 01 837 0011

Relocation Services

International Relocation
Consultants
P.O. Box 1157
Greenwich, CT 06830
Tel: (203) 862–9450
Fax: (203) 629–8389
E-mail:
NUZ91A@mail.prodigy.com

MacDonald Price
8 The Heath, Cypress Downs
Templeogue, Dublin 6
Tel: 1 295 1478
Fax: 1 295 1478
E-mail: Relocation@MacDonald-
Price.ie
Web site: www.clubi.ie/
macdonald-price.ie

Settlers Ltd.
Hillside
Kilmacanogue
Bray
Tel: 01 286 2217
Web site: www.ireland.iol.ie/
bizpark/a/akc

Tax and Legal Information & Services

Deloitte Touche Tohmatsu
City Chambers
4 Lapps Quay
Cork
Tel: 021 277755

Earlsfort Terrace
Dublin 2
Tel: 01 475 4433

ICC House
Charlotte Quay
Limerick
Tel: 061 418577
Fax: 061 418310

Office of the Revenue
   Commissioners
Dublin Castle
Dublin 2
Tel: 01 679 2777
Web site: www.revenue.ie

In the United States:

Arthur Andersen
1666 K Street NW
Washington, DC 20006
Tel (202) 862–3100

Deloitte and Touche
10 Westport Road
Wilton, CT 06897
(203) 761–3000

Price Waterhouse
1251 Avenue of the Americas
New York, NY 10020
Tel (212) 489–8900

Travel & Tourism

Bord Failte—Irish Tourist Board
345 Park Avenue, 17th Floor
New York, NY 10154
Tel: (212) 418–0800
Fax: (212) 751–4758
Web site: www.ireland.travel.ie

Bord Failte Eireann
Baggot Street Bridge
Dublin 2
Tel: 01 602 4000

Northern Ireland Tourist Board
River House
48 High Street
Belfast BT1 2DS
Tel: 01232 246609
Fax: 01232 240960

Northern Ireland Tourist Board
   (United States)
276 Fifth Avenue, Suite 500
New York, NY 10001
Tel: (212) 922–0101

SWAP Ireland (Canada)
CFS Services
243 College Street

Toronto
Ontario M5T 2Y1
Tel: (416) 977–3703

Youth and Student Travel (USIT)
Aston Quay
O'Connell Bridge
Dublin 2
Tel: 01 677 8117

Work Abroad (United States)
Work Exchange Department
   Council
205 East 42nd Street
New York, NY 10017
Tel: (888) COUNCIL
E-mail: infor@ciee.org
Web site: www.ciee.
   org/work/ireland.htm

Volunteering

Cairde
25 Mary's Abbey
Off Capel Street
Dublin 7
Tel: 01 873 0800
Web site: www.cairde.ie

Carmichael Centre for Voluntary
   Groups
North Brunswick Street
Dublin 7
Tel: 01 873 5702
Fax: 01 873 5737
Web site:
http://homepage.tinet.ie/~juan/cc.
html

Concern Worldwide
Camden Street
Dublin 2
Tel: 01 475 4162

Co-Operation North
37 Upper Fitzwilliam Street
Dublin 2
Tel: 01 661 0588
Fax: 01 661 8456
E-mail: info@co-operation-north.ie
Web site:
   www.co-operation-north.ie

Global Volunteers Ireland
375 E. Little Canada Road
St. Paul, MN 55117-1627
Tel: 800 487 1074, 651 482 1074

Fax: 651 482 0915
E-mail:
   @globalvolunteers. org
Web site:
   www.globalvolunteers. org

Trocaire
169 Booterstown Avenue
Blackrock, County Dublin
Tel: 01 288 5385
Fax: 01 288 3577
E-mail: info@trocaire.ie
Web site: www.trocaire.org

Web sites

Agriculture

Farming in Ireland   www.farm.ie

Animal Welfare

Animal Rescue Ireland   www.esatclear.ie/~animalrescue/
Irish Animals on the Web   www.irishanimals.com
Birdwatch Ireland   http://homepage.tinet.ie/~birdwatch/
Dublic SPCA   www.dspca.ie

Architecture

www.archeire.com

Automotive

Motor Schools Association of Ireland
   http://ireland.iol.ie/~msainews/
MotorWeb   www.motorweb.ie
Used Car Network   www.carfind.ie
Vehicle Registration   www.revenue.ie/vrt.htm

Banks

AIB   www.24hour-online.ie
Bank of Ireland   www.bankofireland.ie

Books

Fred Hannah's   www.hannas.ie
Hodges Figgis   www.hodgesfiggis.com
Kennys Bookshop   www.kennys.ie
Read Ireland   www.readireland.ie

Business

Access IMI—Irish Management Institute Information Service
   for Small Business   www.access.imi.ie/
Business information service   www.finfacts.ie

Canadian Government

Government of Canada Primary Web Site   www.Canada.gc.ca

Chat

Virtual Irish Pub   www.vip.ie

Computer

Compaq   www.digital.ie
Dell   www.dell.com/ie

Counties

Fermanagh and Leitrim Community Online Network
   (FALCON)   www.falcon.ie
Kerry   www.kerryweb.ie
Local Ireland   www.local.ie
Out of Mayo   www.mayo-ireland.ie

Entertainment

2FM   www.2fm.ie
The Event Guide   www.dkm.ie/events/ireland/index.html
   www.entertainmentireland.ie
RTE   www.rte.ie

Food and Drink

Karwig's Wines, Ltd   www.karwig-wines.ie

Taste of Ireland Restaurant Guide   www.thecia.ie/
tasteofireland/restaurants
Wine Aficionados   www.mccabeswines.ie

Franchising

www.franchisedirect.com

Gay and Lesbian

Gay Switchboard Dublin   http://ireland.iol.ie/~gsd/
Foyle Friend   www.iol.ie/~nwgay/foylefriend.htm
Outhouse   http://indigo.ie/~outhouse/

Genealogy

www.familytreemaker.com
Irish Ancestors   www.irish-times.com/ancestor/index.html
Irish Genealogical Foundation   www.irishroots.com
National Archives of Ireland   www.nationalarchives.ie/genealogy.html

Health

Directory of Irish Hospitals   www.imd.ie/hosindx.htm
Support Groups   www.imd.ie/suppindx.htm

Internet Service Providers

Ireland Online (IOL)   www.iol.ie
Indigo   www.indigo.ie
Tinet (Telecom Eireann)   www.tinet.ie

Investment Services

NCB Stockbrokers   www.ncbdirect.com

Jobs

www.jobfinder.ie

Music

Irish Music Net   www.imn.ie

News/Publications

An Phoblacht Republican News   www.irlnet.com/aprn
Belfast Telegraph   www.belfasttelegraph.Countyuk
Clare Champion   www.clarechampion.ie
Connaught Telegraph   www.mayo-ireland.ie/ConnTel.htm

Donegal News   www.donegalnews.com
Examiner   www.examiner.ie
Galway Advertiser   www.galwayadvertiser.ie
The Independent   www.independent.ie
Ireland's Eye   www.irelandseye.com
Ireland Today   www.ireland-today.ie
Irish America   www.irishamerica.com
The Irish Emigrant   www.emigrant.ie
Irish Farmers Journal   www.farmersjournal.ie
The Irish News   www.irishnews.com
The Irish Post in London   www.irishpost.Countyuk
The Irish Times   www.irishtimes.com
The Irish Voice   www.irishvoice.com
The Kerryman
  www.kerryweb.ie/kerryman/default2.htm
Limerick Leader   www.limerick-leader.ie
Limerick Post   www.limerickpost.ie
Longford Leader   www.longford-leader.ie
Mayo News   www.mayonews.ie
Munster Express   www.munster-express.ie
The Nationalist and Leinster Times   www.lowwwe.com/nationalist
Skerries News   www.cognition.ie/skerries_news
Sunday Business Post   www.sbpost.ie
Sunday Tribune   www.tribune.ie
Western People   www.mayo-ireland.ie/Wpeople.htm
Westmeath Examiner   www.westmeath-examiner.ie
World of Hibernia   www.twoh.com

Northern Ireland

Infosite Ireland   www.infosites.net
Nidex—The Northern Ireland Index   www.nidex.com

Property/Real Estate

Century 21 Ireland   www.centruy21ire.com
Irish Auctioneers & Valuers Institute   www.iavi.ie
National Property Network   www.npn.ie
Real Estate Ireland   www.ibi.ie/property

Search/Directory of Irish Web sites

http://doras.tinet.ie/doras
www.niceone.com
www.searchireland.com

Shopping

www.celtic-gifts.com
www.celticlinks.com
www.irishop.com

Sports

www.failte-sport.com
www.gaa.ie
www.golfing-ireland.com
www.infowing.ie/fishing
www.irishgolf.com
www.where-to-fish.com

Tax Information

Internal Revenue Service   www.irs.ustreas.gov
Uncle Fed's Tax Board   www.unclefed.com

Travel/Tourism

The Irish Bus Site   www.bustravel.net/ireland/
Irish Tourist Board—Bord Failte   www.ireland.travel.ie

Vegetarianism

Vegetarian and Vegan Guide to Ireland   www.bealtine.ie/vegguide

Weddings

Ultimate Wedding Link Exchange   www.wedding-ireland.com

Index

About the Author

Patti Cleary is a freelance editor, writer, writing coach, and teacher with twenty years of experience in the field of publishing. Previously she worked for several publishing houses as an executive editor. She has traveled extensively in Ireland and is proud of her Irish ancestry. Currently a resident of San Francisco, California, she plans to relocate part-time to Ireland within a few years.